Cultural Universals and Particulars

African Systems of Thought

General Editors
Charles S. Bird
Ivan Karp

Contributing Editors
James W. Fernandez
Luc de Heusch
John Middleton
Roy Willis

Cultural Universals and Particulars

An African Perspective

Kwasi Wiredu

INDIANA UNIVERSITY PRESS
Bloomington and Indianapolis

MANUFACTURED IN THE UNITED STATES OF AMERICA

Library of Congress Cataloging–in–Publication Data

Wiredu, Kwasi
    Cultural universals and particulars : an African perspective /
Kwasi Wiredu.
        p.   cm. — (African systems of thought)
    Includes bibliographical references and index.
    ISBN 0–253–33209–5 (alk. paper). — ISBN 0–253–21080–1 (pbk. :
alk. paper)
    1. Philosophy, Akan. 2. Akan (African people)—Religion. 3. Akan
(African people)—Social conditions. 4. Philosophy, African.
5. Universalism. 6. Particularism (Theology). I. Title.
II. Series.
B5619.G4W57   1996
199'.6'089963385—dc20   96–14528

1   2   3   4   5   01   00   99   98   97   96

To William E. Abraham:
Pioneer in the field

Contents

Acknowledgments

With the exception of the introduction, the postscript and chapter 4, which was presented in a symposium at the Nineteenth World Congress of Philosophy in Moscow in August 1993, the chapters of this book appeared previously in the following publications: "A Philosophical Perspective on the Concept of Human Communication," *International Social Science Journal*, vol. 32, no. 2, 1980 (chapter 2); "Are There Cultural Universals?" *The Monist*, vol. 78, no. 1, January 1995 (chapter 3); "Universalism and Particularism in Religion from an African Perspective," *Journal of Humanism and Ethical Religion*, vol. 3, no. 1, 1990 (chapter 5); "Custom and Morality: A Comparative Analysis of Some African and Western Conceptions of Morals," in Albert G. Mosley, ed., *African Philosophy: Selected Readings* (Englewood Cliffs: Prentice Hall, 1995) (chapter 6); "Formulating Modern Thought in African Languages," in V. Y. Mudimbe, ed., *The Surreptitious Speech* (Chicago: University of Chicago Press, 1992) (chapter 7); "The Concept of Truth in the Akan Language," in P. O. Bodunrin, ed., *African Philosophy: Trends and Perspectives* (Ile-Ife, Nigeria: University of Ife Press, 1985) (chapter 8); "African Philosophical Tradition: A Case Study of the Akan," *The Philosophical Forum*, vol. 34, no. 1–3, fall-spring 1992–93 (chapter 9); "The Need for Conceptual Decolonization in African Philosophy," in Olusegun Oladipo, *Conceptual Decolonization in African Philosophy: Four Essays by Kwasi Wiredu* (Ibadan, Nigeria: Hope Publications, 1995) (chapter 10, by courtesy of Herta Nagl-Docekal of the University of Vienna); "Post-Colonial African Philosophy," ibid. (chapter 11); "An Akan Perspective on Human Rights," in Abdullahi Ahmed An-Na'im and Francis M. Deng, ed., *Human Rights: Cross-Cultural Perspectives* (Washington, D.C: The Brookings Institution, 1990) (chapter 12); "Philosophy and the Political Problem of Human Rights," in Ioanna Kucuradi, ed., *The Idea and Documents of Human Rights* (Ankara, Turkey: International Federation of Philosophical Societies and the Philosophical Society of Turkey, 1995) (chapter 13); "Democracy and Consensus: A Plea for a Non-Party Polity," *The Centennial Review*, vol. 39, no. 1, 1995. My thanks are due to the editors and publishers for permission to reprint them here.

I would like to thank Professors D. A. Masolo and Ivan Karp for reading the manuscript and offering helpful suggestions. I am grateful also to the staff of Indiana University Press for their efficiency and care. My wife has supported me in all my work and has aided me with insights into Akan thought. I express here my thanks to her, knowing that no words will be adequate.

Cultural Universals and Particulars

1

Introduction

The Universal and the Particular

General Considerations

This book confronts the issues of universalism and particularism in human culture. There is something paradoxical going on in discourse among cultures. While, on the one hand, there is an unprecedented intensification of informational interaction among the different cultures of the world, there is, on the other hand, increasing skepticism regarding the very foundation of such discourse; namely, the possibility of universal canons of thought and action. By a kind of (not necessarily explicit) self-critical recoiling from the earlier intellectual self-aggrandizement of the West, some very articulate movements of thought therein—notably, but not only, postmodernism—are displaying extreme abstemiousness with respect to claims of universality. At the same time, peoples previously marginalized (by reason of colonialism and related adversities) find the need, in seeking to redefine their self-identity, to insist on particulars—their own previously unrespected or neglected particularities—rather than universals. In so far as it might be thought, in view of all these, that there is a necessary incompatibility between the perspectives of universalism and particularism, the standpoint of these essays is that the impression is illusory.

General considerations are adduced in Part I to show the possibility and actual existence of cultural universals. This is important because without such universals intercultural communication must be impossible. The case is developed first by deploying considerations about the nature of meaning presupposed by the very possibility of human communication ("A Philosophical Perspective on the Concept of Human Communication"). Then, in "Are There Cultural Universals?" I continue the argument by specifying some cognitive and ethical universals. In both chapters there is an implicit biological orientation, the underlying idea being that the possibility of cultural universals is predicated on our common biological identity as a species of bipeds. This biological aspect of the matter is pursued in direct connection with what I take to be the three supreme laws of thought and conduct, namely, the principles of non-contradiction, induction, and the categorical imperative (roughly so called) in "The Biological Foundation of Universal Norms."

Religion and Morality

But if there are universals, there are also particulars. And in history some peoples have sought, sometimes somewhat successfully, to transpose or even impose their own fallible conceptions of universals, both cognitive and ethical, upon other peoples. More often than not, the alleged universals have been home-grown particulars. Not unnaturally, the practice has earned universals a bad name. But, rightly perceived, the culprits are the hasty purveyors of universals, not the idea of universals itself. Nor is there anything, in principle, amiss in peoples or individuals trying to convey "tidings" of universals or, for that matter, particulars to other peoples. The proviso, however, is that the thing must be done in the spirit of respectful dialogue. This is a rather minimal condition, requiring only that 'the other' be recognized as an equal participant in rational or, if that is what it actually is, irrational discourse. As is well known, this condition was frequently flouted (wittingly or unwittingly) in intercultural discourse in colonial times; and Africa, the source of my own existential engagement with this issue, has been a historic victim of this intellectual malpractice. The phenomenon has left traces in African life and thought about which something needs to be done in the interest of Africa's intellectual good health.

But the resultant issues are not of significance to Africa alone, for the following reason. The colonial and neo-colonial miscommunications have involved (as will emerge) not just degenerate intentions but also conceptual misapprehensions of a general philosophical interest. Thus, for example, the ethical stance of the missionary enterprise did in some aspects presuppose a conflation of morality with custom whose disentanglement calls for a philo-sophical clarification of the nature of morality. That is the objective of "Custom and Morality: A Comparative Analysis of Some African and Western Conceptions of Morals," the second chapter of Part II. Equally importantly, the missionary project involved questionable universalizations of Christian customs in a way which makes clarity about the concept of religion itself an urgent necessity. It turns out that the applicability of this concept to African life and thought is not at all unproblematic, and "Universalism and Particu-larism in Religion from an African Perspective," the first chapter of Part II, is devoted to sorting out the relevant conceptual issues with particular reference to a specific African culture, namely, the Akan.

Conceptual Contrasts

The conceptual issues arising from the interaction of cultures under study are, however, multifarious and go far beyond those touched upon in Part II. They span, in fact, the entire gamut of human thought. One reason for this is that the operative accounts of African life and thought have been formulated in foreign languages, originally by Europeans and now with the active participation of Africans trained in the implicit semantics of the foreign expository models. That in their expositions of African thought the foreign pioneers may have conceptualized the African thought-materials in categories embedded in their own vernaculars is not at all surprising, if one thinks about it for a moment. But there are three things in this connection that might need a little more reflection. First, those categories of thought may be inconsistent with the ones resident in the framework of the given African system of thought, such that formulations that appear to make sense in the foreign language may be quite radically incoherent in the African language concerned. Second, the cause or causes of such a situation may lie in defects in any one of the languages, foreign or indigenous. Third, it is possible, by a cross-cultural evaluation based on independent considerations, to get to the root of the matter.

What, then, are independent considerations? They are considerations that are not specific to the peculiarities of any given language and are, consequently, intelligible in all the languages concerned. They are possible at all because of the intrinsic self-reflexivity of natural languages (as distinguished from formalized languages), and the fact of their possibility is an irremovable impediment to all conceptual and cognitive relativisms. That relativism itself is a removable impediment to cogent thinking is part of the message of the second chapter in Part I, "Are There Cultural Universals?" In the present connection the point to be noted about independent considerations is that their very possibility can transform the untranslatability of a metropolitan formulation into an African vernacular from a curious fact about an "exotic" language into a source of fundamental conceptual insight for all; that is, irrespective of race, culture, and so forth. So that in confronting the conceptual problems arising out of the fact that African philosophy has been done, and will continue for quite some time to come to be done, in foreign languages, the African philosopher may be making contributions to general conceptual understanding. In other words, the universal may arise out of concern with the particular.

Sooner or later, moreover, African philosophy will have to be done in an African language or in African languages. The lack of a continental lingua franca is an obvious current disincentive to the use of the vernacular as the medium in academic work. It is obvious that the adoption of such a language policy would immediately make, for example, the philosophical excogitations of Kwame Gyekye of Ghana a closed book to Peter Bodunrin of Nigeria and vice versa. But this circumstance ought not to be a disincentive to the initiation of dialogue, in the vernacular, between the academic philosophers and those of their compatriots not literate in the relevant metropolitan languages. For this purpose it might be necessary for African philosophers, more frankly, for *us*, to propagate some of our results in our own vernaculars. (Actually, even now—that is, even before this mode of propagation is implemented—an African philosopher can, and in my opinion, ought to, experiment with vernacular formulations in his own philosophical introspections.) The exercise is likely to be extremely educative for us in the first instance, for we will be forced to face the conceptual challenges of the conflict of languages of which an African philosopher, working exclusively in some metropolitan language, might be serenely unaware. In "Post-Colonial African Philosophy" (Part III, chapter 11), I comment on certain aspects of the present language situation in African philosophy. But all the issues raised in this and the preceding two paragraphs are taken up at some length in "Formulating Modern Thought in African Languages" (Part III, chapter 7).

The foreign origins of the institutional education of contemporary African philosophers noted three paragraphs back makes earnest conceptual soul-searching obligatory for all of us. Philosophical nurture in a second language automatically converts it into a first language for the purposes of meditation. African philosophers, accordingly, think philosophically in English or French or German or Portuguese or some such language. Fundamental categories of thought in these languages begin to seem as natural to them as they do to native speakers. It might then seem to them, for example, that such conceptual contrasts as those between the physical and the spiritual, the material and the immaterial, being and nothingness, substance and attribute, and a whole host of others are universal necessities of human thought. Yet, it may well be—it is, in my opinion, the case—that if African philosophers try to think these contrasts through in their own language, they will find reasons, first of a vernacular-inspired kind, but ultimately of an *independent* character, to drastically reassess them. Such a reassessment must have wide-ranging reverberations in ontology and cosmology and other areas of philosophy besides. But suppose the African philosopher just continues, as many seem happy to do, to operate in the metropolitan language without a thought of the conceptual conflicts that reference to his or her own mother tongue might precipitate: Then since this mind-set is a by-product of an educational situation deriving historically from the accident of colonization, it may be justly characterized as a colonial mentality.

Now, I do not think that any contemporary African philosopher can claim total innocence of the colonial mentality. I, certainly, make no such claim. But we can and ought to try to liberate ourselves from it as far as is humanly possible. Unfortunately some, most assuredly, do not try, although they will fiercely brandish nationalistic phrases at the slightest touch. The first necessity is to realize that we have a problem. Truth to say, we have not yet accomplished even this. The next desideratum is to try to test philosophical formulations in a metropolitan language in our vernacular to see if they will survive independent analysis. To do this is to try to decolonize our thinking. Curiously, the need for conceptual decolonization seems to occur to African workers in literature more readily than in philosophy. More than a decade and a half after I first made a plea for conceptual decolonization in African philosophy (in a presentation at a UNESCO conference on African philosophy in Nairobi, Kenya, in June 1980) with as yet no widespread results, I return in "The Need for Conceptual Decolonization in African Philosophy" (Part III, chapter 10) to the same campaign, now with different illustrations of the need for it. The entire essay on "Formulating Modern Thought in Modern Languages" too can be read as an effort in the campaign.

A successful exercise in conceptual decolonization will usually be an unmasking of a spurious universal. But there is a subtle rider to be entered. A philosophical concept or problem, failing of universality through transcultural dissipation, need not be spurious on that account. It may be a matter of genuine philosophical interest in its own linguistic home. A philosophical topic of this sort I call tongue-dependent. Its status depends on the special characteristics of the vocabulary of a given language or even possibly on the peculiarities of its syntax. But it may still be an issue with which all who reason in that language about certain points must come to grips, whether they are native speakers or not. Of course, the importance of such an issue, though real, is local rather than universal. In "The Concept of Truth in the Akan Language" (Part III, chapter 8) I argue, among other things, that the question of the relation between truth and fact is one such topic. The point is that in the Akan language both truth and fact are rendered by the same phrases, and yet anything that can be said about the world by means of the concepts of fact and truth in English can also be expressed within the semantical economy of Akan. The problem of how the concept of truth is related to that of fact therefore does not arise in Akan. Nevertheless, it does not follow that the problem is not an important one for English-speaking philosophers. There is also a consequence for the future meditations of the Akan philosopher. If he or she has occasion to reflect on the problem of truth and fact in English, fully apprised of its vernacular non-existence, he or she will very predictably find certain theories on the matter quite unpersuasive. This will be particularly true of theories, for example, that accord an ontological status to facts distinct from that of truth. One can also foresee a particular perspective on the capabilities of certain common forms of the correspondence theory of truth as instruments of philosophic enlightenment.

For the avoidance of all misunderstandings, or as many of them as possible,

I would like to stress that my idea is not that, simply because there is not a separate word for some concept in Akan, it follows that the concept is empty or defective in some way—a suggestion that would be uncommonly absurd. The requirement for independent considerations that I have laid down guarantees that one must go beyond the simple fact, if fact it is, of word availability or unavailability. In the specific case of the relation between truth and fact the argument is not just that because Akan uses the same linguistic devices to express both concepts, the issue of their relationship is without a universal pertinence. A crucial premiss is that everything about the world that can be expressed in the language of truth and fact can be expressed in Akan terms too. Without this premiss the hypothesis would be left open that the sparseness of Akan in this regard is evidence of a semantical inadequacy rather than verbal economy. I view the general point here as so important that in "The Concept of Truth in the Akan Language" I have endeavored to elucidate it with an illustration drawn from logic.

Cross-cultural comparisons of concepts in philosophy are not always as directly or as straightforwardly based on verbal forms as in the foregoing illustration. The essay "African Philosophical Tradition: A Case Study of the Akan" (Part III, chapter 9) deals, among other things, with comparisons that are either more complex or more subtle. The concepts involved are those of God, Person, and Freedom. To illustrate only the last, which is discussed in the section entitled "Free Will as Responsibility," I argue that in Akan there is nothing corresponding to a problem of free will as distinct from the problem of responsibility. This claim is based not just on verbal usage but on the usages of normative interaction in Akan society, which, by the way, give a glimpse of the Akan ethos: A person either did something "with his own eyes" or not—a phrase which represents a non-complacent approximation to the relevant Akan concept in English. He is a free agent or a responsible one in the first alternative and only in that eventuation. In the second alternative, reaction is one not of moral reproach or the like but help—help in what is regarded as nothing short of the restoration of personhood. Personhood is lost to the *degree* to which an individual shows himself or herself not to be amenable to rational persuasion or moral correction. Within the Akan conceptual framework, that restoration would be a restoration of free will and, *ipso facto*, of responsibility.

Now, to put forward this equivalence of free will with responsibility as an interculturally valid thesis, one would, of course, have to advance "independent considerations." One would have, for example, to diffuse possible English-speaking reservations arising from the fact that in law, for example, there may be instances in which a person may not be held responsible for something he did out of his own free will. The matter revolves around the ambiguity of the concept of responsibility. A person may be the one who was responsible for a certain action; but it does not follow that he is to be *held* responsible for it. For example, he may, as Aristotle might point out, have acted out of crucial ignorance. Or he may have done it in sincere error. But furthermore, he may have done it in post-hypnotic supineness or straightforward mental derangement. Responsibility in the sense in which it is presupposed in moral culpability is responsibility uncompromised by such factors. This is the concept of responsibility that is pertinent to discussions of free will and determinism, for instance; and it is in that sense that Akan moral casuistry would lead one to equate free will with responsibility. This argument needs, of course, to be continued in the appropriate forum. But it serves here to illustrate a potentially fruitful interplay of conceptual universals with semantical particulars in intercultural discourse.

Democracy and Human Rights

All the issues noted above have practical consequences. The same is even more palpably true of those discussed in the chapters constituting Part IV. These are issues about democracy and human rights. It is hard to imagine more fertile grounds for breeding universals, both genuine and spurious, and particulars, both complementary and countervailing. To start with rights: that human rights are a universal concern probably needs no argument. The most fundamental of the declarations of the United Nations on the subject is actually a *universal* declaration. Even the hardest-boiled abusers of the human rights of others yield ground to none in their verbal championing of those same rights. Yet, lip service apart, declarations of human rights often sound hollow. This is because they are often framed in rather general terms. At certain levels of discourse this is perhaps inevitable. But, at all events, the level of discussion at which there is a concrete reference to the moral ideology of a specific culture is not one such level. Accordingly, I try in "An Akan Perspective on Human Rights" (Part IV, chapter 12) to articulate some Akan particularities in the matter of human rights. To dabble a little in theological imagery, these particulars are incarnations of the generalities which are so apt to sound well-meaning, but unfocused, in the abstract. The principal aim of that chapter is to outline precepts, not to evaluate their practice, though, lest it might seem too much like blowing one's cultural trumpet, I note some traditional deviations from the narrow path of human rights observance.

On the right occasion more might be said of the deviations. But there is one positive aspect of the traditional outlook on human rights of which too little is generally said. Yet, its relevance to the contemporary politics of Africa is of a life-and-death character—frequently, quite literally. I perceive in the traditional approach to governance in Akanland and in some other parts of Africa the principle that the citizen is entitled to representation by way not only of having a representative in the governing council but also of having some effect, through her representative, on the content of decisions. It might be thought that this is exactly what the electoral arrangements and decision procedures of majoritarian democracy are designed to achieve. But this is not so. Representation in the first sense is assured in some manner, but not in the second, not even theoretically. The reason is that it is possible for the will of small minorities to be of no effect on the content of decisions, at least to many intents and purposes. In the maturest democracies of the majoritarian kind constitutional palliatives exist for this situation. But they are just that—palliatives. They do not avail even to moderate the severities of the adversarial struggle for power or its retention, in which few holds are barred. In consequence, even at the best of times, majoritarian politics is, if not brutish, then nasty. Still, in spite of being thus morally unedifying, this mode of politics has not, in the West, blocked the avenue to economic development. On the other hand, in Africa, where minorities are usually ethnic groups, the struggles generated by majoritarian politics have led to radical disruptions that have devastated the prospects of economic development and other forms of progress. Hobbes called life in the imaginary state of nature "nasty, brutish and short." It is difficult to think that he would feel the need to cast about for an alternative phrasing were he to be invited (in spirit, of course) to characterize life under African politics in the last three decades.

With our sense of the universal validity of democratic values "tested and yet undismayed" by this sad situation, let us look again at the traditional approach to politics hinted at in the last paragraph. A little examination will discover that the duality of representation mentioned was pursued through the insistence on consensus in decision-making. Actually, consensus was an ideal pursued not only in political decision-making but also in other spheres of group interaction. But in politics my suggestion is (a) that it leads to a system of democracy conceptually different from majoritarian democracy, and (b) that Africa's political salvation, if it will ever come, will come through the former rather than the latter. These ideas are explored in the three chapters of Part IV; namely, "An Akan Perspective on Human Rights" (chapter 12), "Philosophy and the Political Problem of Human Rights" (chapter 13), and "Democracy and Consensus: A Plea for a Non-Party Polity" (chapter 14). At issue in these discussions are not any internal changes in the mechanism of representation, as in the idea of proportional representation, but a substantially different cast of polity. The fundamental thought is that a consensual approach to statecraft is incompatible with the party system.

A non-party system is, of course, entirely different from the one-party variety. The latter is, in fact, a more drastic negation of the ideal of consensus than the multi-party system. In the first of the three chapters just mentioned, which was written in 1988, there is an attack on the one-party system. At that time one-party regimes, both by constitution and by force, were the order of the day in Africa. As in Eastern Europe, it is amazing with what rapidity events have overtaken those regimes since then. But we must not start counting our blessings too prematurely, for it is all too easy to exaggerate the gains accruing to genuine democracy from the change to multi-party politics. In fact, the evidence from various parts of Africa ought to move anyone not keen on burying his head in the sand, ostrich style, to begin to investigate alternative forms of democracy more suited to the peculiar ethnic diversities of the great majority of African states with their troubled histories. It is hardly necessary to point out the responsibilities of philosophy in any such search.

In the essays in question I have confronted questions of conceptual lineaments and political feasibility in an exploratory manner, though a formal blueprint of the preferred polity is not a specially difficult task. At this stage the greatest need is for the explanation of the concept of consensus as a basis of statecraft, which is not a trivial undertaking. In need of explanation also is how a non-party system is possible without the violation of the people's right to belong to parties of their choice. A skeptic might demand to know, furthermore, why, supposing that a consensual system was possible in the relatively uncomplicated conditions of traditional times, it should be thought practicable in present-day conditions. The second and third of the three chapters mentioned above are devoted to these issues. They make essentially the same case with basically the same armory, but from different angles; the second from the human rights angle, and the third more directly from the angle of democracy. This dual procedure may, perhaps, lend a certain desirable intensity to the plea for a consensual polity.

That consensus is universally desirable among human beings is unlikely to be disputed. What is likely to evoke debate is whether it is a necessary condition for a viable political system. But 'viable' is a broad concept. Some may argue that consensus might be necessary only in order for Western democratic politics to acquire a noble countenance, but insist that it can, and does, get by pretty well without what, after all, may be a utopian objective. Such a suggestion would, surely, be open to debate from many angles, but it does not sound utterly bereft of perception. In Africa, on the other hand, my suggestion is that only so much as a moderate perspicacity should suffice for the realization that consensus in our political arrangements is a necessary condition for our survival in any tolerable social condition.

To sum up the basic message of this book: Human beings cannot live by particulars or universals alone, but by some combination of both.

Part I

General Considerations

2

A Philosophical Perspective on the Concept of Human Communication

Communication is the transference of a thought content from one person or group of persons to another. Such a thought content may be a statement (a semantic unit which invites appraisal in terms of truth or falsity) or the expression of an attitude, an emotion, a wish, etc.—all of which are semantic units that invite evaluation in terms not of truth or falsity but of a variety of normative concepts such as noble, ignoble; beautiful, ugly; good, evil, etc. Language, of course, is the vehicle of this transference, but language can have almost any medium—words, gestures, artifacts, etc. All this is probably unproblematic. But difficult philosophical problems soon arise when one attempts a deeper elucidation of the concept of communication.

Because of the overriding human importance of communication, it is of the greatest consequence to try to gain as deep an understanding of it as possible. No human society or community is possible without communication, for a community is not just an aggregation of individuals existing as windowless monads but of individuals as interacting persons, and an interaction of persons can only be on the basis of shared meanings. Indeed, without communication there is not even a human person. A human being deprived of the socializing influence of communication will remain human biologically, but mentally is bound to be subhuman.

What, then, are the fundamental presuppositions of communication? We have already made reference to shared meanings. But what are meanings and how can they be shared? According to one school of thought, of very ancient ancestry in Western philosophy, meanings are abstract entities which exist in their own right independently of human minds. In this theory, understanding a meaning is conceived on the model of perceiving an object. If this theory were valid, it would secure in a particularly easy way an essential condition of the objectivity of meanings. For something to be subjective is for it to depend in an irregular manner on the peculiarities of individuals. Inversely, to be objective is to be independent of the irregular peculiarities of individuals. If meanings are objects existing independently of individuals, it follows *a fortiori* that they are independent of any peculiarities of individuals defying laws, from which the objectivity of meanings immediately accrues.

Now, the objectivity of meanings is absolutely essential to the possibility of communication, for if meanings were subjective, that is to say, if they depended irregularly on the peculiarities of individuals, there could be no conventions, no socially established rules, correlating symbols to meanings. Accordingly, no one could converse with anyone else. Worse, no one could converse with himself or herself, for any kind of conversation at all presupposes syntactical and semantic rules which, if they are available to any one individual, would argue the existence of regularities of which others, too, could, in principle, avail themselves for the purpose of communication.

Indeed, if meanings were subjective, thinking would be impossible, for what has been said about conversing with oneself applies to thinking itself. A thought is a conceptual construct. And such construction is impossible except in accordance with a certain minimum of rules, and a rule is the very antithesis of subjectivity.

Let us leave off this train of thought temporarily and return to the theory of meanings as independently existing, abstract entities. Here the explanation for the possibility of different individuals entertaining the same meanings is that their individual minds reach out to grasp the same entities that exist "out there" in a special realm of their own. At first sight this seems plausible. Unfortunately, it is very radically invalid. The argument is this. Suppose meanings were entities of some kind, then they would be subject to the following consideration, which applies universally to entities: If one entity is different from another, then that entity has a certain characteristic which the other does not share. To conceptualize such a characteristic one would have to use some meaningful concept. But, by hypothesis, meaning is itself an entity. This entity must be different from the original entity, for it would not make sense to say that an entity is identical with a characteristic it possesses. If the difference here is to be grasped, a new entity will similarly have to be brought into the picture, which would entail having recourse to another entity, and so on, *ad infinitum*. It follows that if meanings were entities, differences between them could never, in principle, be grasped; which is absurd.

Another, and related, argument is this: any entity must be capable of being referred to. Now, referring involves the use of a symbol, a meaningful symbol, of course. If the meaning of the symbol is itself an entity, as it must be on the view under consideration, then understanding the symbol would entail relating this entity to another entity, for to know what an entity is involves knowing it as an **x** rather than as a **y**, which, since it involves the use of presumably meaningful symbols, means a resort to an entity. But knowing what this further entity is, in turn, must involve reference to another entity, and so on *ad infinitum*. Hence if meanings were entities, they would be incapable of being referred to; which is absurd.

Furthermore, if meanings were entities they would lose their generality, which is ironic, since it was partly to account for this very generality that meanings were construed as abstract entities. A meaning can apply to a multitude of objects or situations; this is what is designated by the 'generality of meanings'. On the other hand, an entity—in other words, an object—cannot apply to anything. One cannot even talk of 'applying' in the latter case except in some non-semantical sense. Of course, an entity can signify something; but this means that a rule can be established by which the given entity puts us in mind, in a certain way, of the 'something' in question. We must be careful to note that when an entity signifies something, the signification is neither identical with the entity itself nor with any other entity that may happen to be 'signified'. Suppose, for example, that a certain flag flying over a house signifies that a king is present there. It would be idiomatic to say that the flag signifies the king. But, strictly, what is signified is not the king but the *thought* that the king is present. In fact, in every use of a meaningful symbol or sign, whether it be a word, a variable, or an entity such as a flag or a gesture, what is signified is a thought, never an entity. It is true that symbols do frequently refer to objects, entities. The point, however, is that when a symbol refers to an entity, the entity can never be said to be the signification or the meaning of the symbol. The entity is the referent, not the signification, and it is the signification that directs us to the referent. It should be noted, though, that the signification of a symbol need not always direct us to a referent. The word 'non-existence', for example, is significant; it has a signification, a meaning, but there is, surely, nothing to which it might be said to refer through that signification.

The distinction between referent and signification is an essential semantic distinction because, without recognizing symbol, signification, and referent as separate categories, no adequate analysis of designation is possible. It is not, however, an ontological distinction, for the same kind of element of discourse can be a signification in one context and a referent in another. Consider again the word 'non-existence'. It is an English word, but, of course, what it expresses, i.e., its signification, its meaning, cannot sensibly be said to be English. What it expresses is the concept of non-existence. In my own language, Akan, spoken by an ethnic group in Ghana, the concept of non-existence is expressed not by one word but by the phrase *se ade bi nni ho*, literally, "the circumstance of something not being there." Note, by the way, the non-existence, in Akan, of any temptation to suggest that the concept of non-existence is some kind of entity. Consider now what has just been said in the last sentence. In that sentence the concept of non-existence, in its second occurrence, functions as a referent. In the first occurrence of 'non-existence' the signification of the word is used to make an assertion about the Akan language, whereas in the second the concept of non-existence is not used for the purpose of saying something about anything else, but rather mentioned as a subject of reference about which something is said. Thus a concept can be, now a signification, now a referent; from which it is evident that the categories of signification and referent do not mark an ontological difference.

By contrast, the distinction between an object or entity and a concept is radically ontological, and I would say that the absurdities which we have already seen to be inherent in the theory of meanings as abstract entities arise owing to the theory's construal of concepts, which is what meanings ultimately are, as entities.

There is a tradition in Western philosophy strongly opposed to the theory of meanings as entities of some kind, which latter is a form of realism. I am referring to the doctrine of nominalism. This doctrine denies, quite legitimately, that meanings are any kind of entities whatever. But it goes further to try to eliminate the category of signification from semantic analysis. Thus, a nominalistic analysis of designation recognizes only the symbol and the referent. The trouble is that when no referent is available, as in the case of the word 'nonexistence', no plausible account of its status as a vehicle of communication is forthcoming. If one divests the word 'non-existence' of the concept with which it is associated, there remain only marks on some surface, if written, or a series of sounds "signifying nothing."

The reason why nominalists, and others besides, have shown such distaste for concepts is that, in Western philosophy, concepts seem historically to have been regarded as mental entities by those philosophers best known for their advocacy of concepts in semantic analysis, namely, the conceptualists. Here, semantics is intertwined with the philosophy of mind. It would not be quite in place here to make an extensive excursion into the philosophy of mind, but it is impossible to avoid a remark or two about the nature of mind. There are at least two valid points in conceptualism. First, it is correct to insist on the necessity of concepts in the theory of meaning. It is valid, secondly, to maintain that concepts exist nowhere but in the mind. But to conceive of the mind as a kind of entity is not warranted.

I would, in this connection, like to make a brief reflection on my own language. In the Akan language the word for 'thought' is the same as the word for 'mind'; it is *adwene* in both cases. My own interpretation of this, and also of Akan usage generally, is that the conception of 'mind' implicit here is of mind as a function rather than an entity. Mind, in this conception, is the function of thought. I find indirect support for this interpretation in the fact that there is no mention of mind *(adwene)* in the traditional Akan inventory of the elements that unite to constitute a human person. The constituents of a person, according to a view prevalent among a large section of the Akans, are: (a) *nipadua* (bodily frame), (b) *mogya* (blood), (c) *ntoro* (a genetic factor due to the father), (d) *Sunsum* (basis of personality), (e) *okra* (soul?) (the question mark indicates that the translation is philosophically problematic). There are some subtle problems in the analysis and evaluation of this conception of a person. That, however is not a task to which I am addressing myself here. I wish merely to observe that if *adwene* (mind) is not an entity, but rather a function, then its omission from a list of the entities that constitute a person is just what one would expect. It hardly needs to be pointed out, therefore, that this omission does not imply any diminution in the importance of mind in the Akan scheme of things.

Given this background and my reflective awareness of it, I have never felt drawn to the Cartesian conception of mind as a spiritual substance. Of course, linguistic considerations of the sort mentioned above are not philosophically decisive. But there are independent considerations for thinking that the conception of mind as a kind of entity is faulty. The basic reasoning that seems to lie behind that conception is somewhat as follows: there must be a portion of a person which is responsible for thinking. Since thought is non-material, that which produces thought must be immaterial. Therefore, there must be in a person a non-material substance which is a thinking agency, a *res cogitans*. There is a deep obscurity in the notion of a non-material entity, but let that pass. The exact meaning of the clause "thought is non-material" is no less hidden. But let this too pass. The trouble still is that thought seems to be viewed as some kind of entity. Suppose, on the contrary, that thought is not an entity—I have already given arguments reducing the suggestion that thought might be an entity to absurdity—then the argument falls to the ground. The reason is simply that the claim that thought is non-material determines absolutely nothing about what its nature might be. If thought is not an entity it might well be a state or an aspect of a state of an entity. Suppose it is the latter. Then to say that a certain aspect of a certain state of a material entity is non-material seems hardly idiomatic. Perhaps we can improve it somewhat by saying 'non-physical' rather than 'non-material'. Then, one crucial claim in the argument under consideration may be formulated as follows: if any aspect of a state of an entity is non-physical, then the entity itself must be non-physical. But now, the claim loses plausibility. One can say, at the very least, that no reason has been given for supposing that every aspect of every state of a physical entity should be physical. Nor are there any immediate indications of intelligibility in the notion that an aspect of an entity must be supposed itself to be an entity. In any case, owing to the purely negative character of the notion of a non-physical entity—its whole nature seems to consist in allegedly being non-physical—we have no positive basis for the assumption that such an entity is better adapted to giving rise to thought than, say, the brain. With regard to the brain we have at least the advantage that there are empirically established connections between its states and the occurrence of thought.

I wish to repeat that no definitive treatment of the problem of mind is intended here, but I hope that it emerges from the foregoing remarks that there is no real antecedent implausibility in the hypothesis that a thought may be an aspect of a brain state, and mind an ongoing complex of such states. On this hypothesis, be it noted, the mind is not the brain but rather a certain complicated set of aspects of its states. Concepts, similarly, are no longer conceived of as entities, but aspects of brain states. Concepts, then, are not in the mind, on the model of items in a container, but are of the mind; they are the stuff of the mind. The same is true, of course, of the combinations of concepts called propositions. This is the sort of view of mind to which reflection on my linguistic background and other considerations incline me, and for which I would be prepared to argue at length. (See further, Kwasi Wiredu, "The Concept of Mind with Particular Reference to the Language and Thought of the Akans of Ghana," *Ibadan Journal of Humanistic Studies*, no. 3, October 1983. Reprinted in Safro Kwame, ed., *Readings in African Philosophy: An Akan Collection*, Lanham: University Press of America, 1995).

Meanwhile, it might be asked what relevance this conception of mind has for the elucidation of communication. The answer is that it makes it possible for a viable account of the objectivity of concepts and conceptual constructs such as propositions to be given. As has already been amply emphasized, the objectivity of concepts is an essential condition of communication. A very prevalent error in philosophy, which is committed by the realism with respect to meanings that I have criticized above, is the idea that for something to be objective it must exist independently of the mind. In that theory, meanings were claimed to be abstract entities having an independent existence of their own. I have argued that if meanings were entities it would be impossible ever to grasp them. There are also famous metaphysical difficulties as to how meanings as entities might be related to the rather more mundane entities to which they may apply. From the point of view of communication, the position is gloomier still. According to the opening sentence of this chapter, human communication is the transference of a thought content from one person or group of persons to another person or groups of persons. The notion of 'transference' here will have to be interpreted metaphorically, as will be seen shortly. On the realistic view, however, its interpretation will have to be impossibly literal. We would have to construe the transference as the actual sending forth of an entity from one person to another. But since there is only one abstract entity in the case of each meaning, world-wide communication must precipitate an unspeakable scramble. In any case, any such transference is totally mysterious.

Or suppose it is suggested that communication be viewed not as a sending forth of an abstract entity by one individual to another but rather as a case of an individual directing the attention of another to an independently existing abstract entity. Such a supposition would bring no improvement, for directing another person to attend to something or to do anything is nothing short of communicating with him or her. In the upshot, then, communication is defined through itself.

The circularity in this last suggestion is two-fold, for in addition to the circularity just pointed out it may be noted that any notion of two or more individuals perceiving, apprehending, grasping, attending to, the same entity already presupposes a milieu of communication. The notion of different persons perceiving or apprehending the same entity presupposes a system of interpersonal correlation of inner experiences with external reality, which is inconceivable without communication.

What lies at the basis of the possibility of the correlation of experiences just mentioned? This question brings us to the crux of the whole matter of communication. My suggestion is that the answer is to be found in the basic biological similarity of human beings. It is the biological affinity between one person and another that makes possible the comparison of experiences and the interpersonal adjustment of behavior that constitute social existence.

A human being is born with a biological make-up, but with no concepts. We can say, if we like, that within this make-up, within the brain, specifically, we have the basis of innate conceptual abilities. If the theory of innate ideas, old or new, means more than this, then it takes the conditions of concept-possession too lightly. To possess a specific concept, an idea, entails some linguistic ability, however slight. But such an ability is the result of training. Human life is a learning process, which begins almost immediately on arrival in the world. This learning has to be in the context of a society, starting with the narrow confines of mother or nurse and widening to larger and larger dimensions of community as time passes. This learning process, which at the start is nothing much more than a regime of conditioning, is, in fact, the making of mind. In this sense a new-born baby may be said to have a brain but no mind, a reflection that is in line with the traditional Akan view that a human creature is not a human person except as a member of a community.

The development of mind is the development of communication. We do not first develop a mind which then has to learn how to communicate. The objectivity of concepts is guaranteed by their social provenance. This remark is not meant atomistically. Language is a system, and a concept is necessarily an element of a language. Given the social establishment of a certain minimum of linguistic abilities, individual conceptual inventiveness is possible and its results are interpersonally intelligible because of the rule-governed character of language.

Let us now return again to our initial characterization of communication. "A transference of thought-content," we said. On the suggested view of mind, a thought-content is an aspect of a brain state. It is an empirical fact that patterns of brain processes can be set off by socially directed stimuli. In these terms, language is basically the systematic relating of external stimuli to patterns of brain processes. The transference of a thought content, from one person to another, then, is the inducement by the one in the other of some brain states through appropriate stimuli. So much, for the present occasion, by way of the unravelling of the metaphor of the transference of a thought content.

It is obvious from the last two paragraphs that the study of communication must engage many disciplines. It is probably clear, in any case, that psychology, linguistics, and the biological sciences have an important place in the enterprise. But it is no less the case that disciplines such as anthropology, sociology, and logic are highly relevant, not to speak of all the branches of physical science and technology that must enter when one considers the means for disseminating 'thought-contents' far and wide.

A little reflection will show that cultural factors predominate in the development of the powers of communication in an individual. Hence the great relevance of anthropology and sociology. However, the reference to culture here needs very careful handling. There are elements of both particularity and universality in culture, in any culture. The former account for the comparative ease of communication among the members of a culture. Human beings communicate values as well as facts in their mental interactions, as was noted in the first paragraph. It is well known that some values vary across cultures. Some conceptions regarding factual matters, too, may differ from culture to culture. Nevertheless, the fundamental biological similarity of all human beings assures the possibility of resolving all such disparities, for the foundation of all communication is biological. Cultural particularities are accidental. What defines the human species are the universals of culture. Thus any fundamental elucidation of the concept of communication must dissipate that cultural relativism which is a bar to intercultural dialogue and, hence, to international understanding.

3

Are There Cultural Universals?

Our question is "Are there Cultural Universals?" I propose a *reductio ad absurdum* proof for an affirmative answer as follows. Suppose there were no cultural universals. Then intercultural communication would be impossible. But there is intercultural communication. Therefore, there are cultural universals. Let me now try to unpack this epitome of a proof. I start with the premiss that there is intercultural communication. This is too visible in the present-day world to be disputed; what may need arguing is what it implies. But not everything regarding its implications is open to debate. For example, it is tautologically obvious that for any two persons to communicate at all they must share some common medium of communication. In turn this implies that at some level they must share a conceptual scheme, however minimal its dimensions. Any such scheme of concepts is a universal for, at least, the given participants in the communication. The question now is "Is there any scheme of concepts which can be shared by all the cultures of humankind?"

This last question is equivalent to asking whether there is anything about which all the different cultures of the world *can* communicate. The answer, in fact, is "Everything." But let us start with *vital* fundamentals. I use the word "vital" here to hint at the fact that in certain respects communication is an existential necessity. Without communication there can be no human community. Indeed, in the total absence of communication we cannot even speak of human *persons*; there could, perhaps, be lower animals, but that is another matter. A human *person* is the product of culture. Whatever else goes into the essence of personhood, mind is a *sine qua non*. But we are not born with a mind, not even with one that is a *tabula rasa*; we are only born with the potential of a mind (in the form of a nervous system). This potential is progressively actualized in a certain way through the barrage of sensory stimulation emanating from the purely physical (i.e., non-social) environment; but the person-making attribute of mentality is not attainable without another kind of barrage, namely, the cultural or socializing barrage of sensory stimulation from kith, kin, and kindred. And this means nothing but sundry forms of communication.

We may say, accordingly, that by and large communication makes the mind. That, of course, is from a developmental point of view and is without prejudice to the fact that it is minds that make communication. Two basic factors are involved in communication, namely, conceptualization and articulation. The power to conceptualize is only a development and refinement of the capacity to react to stimuli in a law-like manner which is present in even amoebic forms of life. In the more elementary forms of life, response to the environment is governed by instinctual drives for equilibrium and self-preservation. At this level of existence, instinct ensures uniformity of reaction in a species. In so far as one can speak here of an analogue of communication this will take the form of instinctive gestures and noises, instinctually standardized. I see in both types of uniformity the humble origins of the rules of conceptualization and articulation which are distinctive of human communication. Human behavior is, of course, governed by both instinct and culture. Because of the element of instinct we can be sure of a certain species-distinctive uniformity in human actions and reactions. But because of the element of culture, that is, of habit, instruction, and conscious thought, there will naturally be plenty of room for variation. The first consideration accounts for the possibility of objectivity and universality in the standards of thought and action in our species, the second for various degrees of relativity and subjectivity. The point, however, is that what unifies us is more fundamental than what differentiates us.

What is it that unifies us? The beginning, at least, of an answer is easy. It is our biologico-cultural identity as *homines sapientes*. At the very minimum this status implies that we are organisms that go beyond instinct in the drive for equilibrium and self-preservation in specific ways, namely, by means of reflective perception, abstraction, deduction, and induction. By reflective perception I mean a kind of awareness that involves the identification of objects and events through the conscious application of concepts and which entails, consequently, the power of recall and re-identification. Any being capable of reflective perception is already possessed of a concept of the external world. By abstraction I mean the mental procedure of bringing particulars together under general concepts and the latter themselves under still more general concepts, and so on. Both deductive and inductive capacities are already presupposed in rudimentary forms in reflective perception, for to recognize something as an X is to perceive it as an X rather than a non-X, which implies that it is not both X and not X. Here, implicitly, is the Principle of Noncontradiction, which, paraconsistentism notwithstanding, is the supreme principle of deduction. Further, to bring an object or event under a concept is to be able, in principle, to envisage what would obtain under some hypothetical situations. Hypotheticals loom even larger in the context of action. To embark on an action, that is, a premeditated action, one must have some notion of the consequences of various options and, in any case, of the adjustment or maladjustment of possible means to possible ends. The power of judgment comes into play here, evidently, and, with it, the power of inference.

Action, then, involves judgment and inference, but social action, an essential ingredient of humane existence, involves, besides these, communication. Now, if a being is capable of judgment and inference, then, necessarily, it is capable of communication. Actually, this could possibly be misleading as to the logical order of human mental development, if it were to give the impression that the power of judgment and inference antedates that of communication. On the contrary, it follows from our previous remarks about the making of mind that communication, from the point of view both of giving and taking, is present at very early stages in the development of the thinking powers of a human person. What our immediately preceding remarks were intended to do was to amplify a little the interconnection between thought and communication in preparation for drawing some species-wide implications. At this stage the issue can be framed as follows: "Mind presupposes communication. Granted. But communication with whom? Communication with our own kith and kin can be taken for granted, but can we guarantee the possibility of communication with people of very different climes and cultures?" This question is, in fact, anticipated in the previous paragraph. It was there noted that being a human person implies having the capacity of reflective perception, abstraction, and inference. In their basic nature these mental capacities are the same for all humans, irrespective of whether they inhabit Europe, Asia, or Africa, just as in their basic nature the instinctive reactions of, say, the frogs of Europe are the same as those of the frogs of Africa. In particular, the concept of object in general is the same for all beings capable of reflective perception. The reason is because any beings that need to supplement instinct with wits in their struggle for equilibrium and self-preservation will have to have a regularized way of identifying and re-identifying items in their environment in a manner dictated by both their constitution and the impinging stimuli. On both counts there is a common human identity. The human constitution of flesh and bones, quickened by electrical charges and wrapped up in variously pigmented integument, is the same everywhere; while there is only one world in which we all live, move, and have our struggles, notwithstanding such things as the vagaries of climate. These facts, which underlie the possibility of communication among kith and kin, are the same facts that underlie the possibility of communication among the various peoples of the world. The same facts make all human beings kindred.

Admittedly, communication among widely separated peoples is often more difficult than communication among people living relatively close together. This should be easy to understand. Apart from anything else, there is the babel of languages. Widely separated groups tend to develop different symbolisms for the articulation of thought. Out of the myriads of possible phonetic articulations different peoples will use different subsets through essentially accidental circumstances.[1] Scripts, where there are any, will also differ similarly. Nor are the differences limited to the physical aspects of symbolization. Space and time are implicated in apparently inscrutable ways in the variegation of patterns of thought that are evidenced in disparate grammars. Such disparities do sometimes result in differences in the structure and content of particular concepts. Consider an example. English has the procedure of forming abstract nouns from 'concrete' ones. Thus, from, for example, 'chair' you get 'chairness'. Adjectives also can yield abstract nouns in a similar manner: 'Red', for example, gives you 'redness'. On the other hand, in my own language, the Akan language spoken in parts of Ghana, the thought-transitions represented by these English grammatical transformations are handled quite disanalogically. The word for chair is *akongua*, but what corresponds to chairness is not a single word belonging to a separate grammatical category, but rather a periphrasis. We would say something like "the circumstance of something being a chair" (*se bribi ye akongua*) or if it comes to that, something like "the being a chair" (*akongua ye*). Here now is the point of this example. In a language like Akan, it is obviously going to be very hard for anybody to persuade himself, let alone anybody else, of the plausibility of saying something like "Chairness is an abstract object existing over and above particular chairs." Think what such a piece of discourse would (approximately) boil down to in such a language. One would have to say something which translates back into English as "The circumstance of something being a chair is an abstract object over and above particular chairs." And if this sounds incongruous in English, the situation is compounded by a sizeable factor in Akan. The point is not, as is sometimes absurdly suggested, that Africans don't or can't think in abstract terms, for the phrase "the circumstance of something being a chair" is as abstract in its significance as the word 'chairness'. The point is rather that in English and languages like English in this respect the fact that, in addition to the periphrastic rendering, there is the unitary abstract noun is apt to incline some speakers to objectual deductions, whereas in languages like Akan there is a distinct disincentive to any such objectivization—I do not say hypostatization, for I do not want to beg the question in favor of the Akan language. What I want to do is to emphasize the sharpness of the present contrast between the two languages. To this purpose, one might even characterize the contrast by saying that the sentence "Chairness is an abstract object existing over and above particular chairs" is untranslatable into Akan. One can multiply examples of differences in the conceptual suggestiveness of the grammatical patterns and lexical formations of English and Akan. As is well known, Whorf[2] made relativistic capital out of linguistic contrasts of this sort in his comparisons of Indo-European with American Indian languages. But it is not necessary to go to Whorfian lengths in order to note that differences in languages often reflect and are reflected in differences of world view and that these can exercise the most profound constraints on intercultural communication.

Let all the foregoing be granted; yet no *ultimate* bar to intercultural communication is thereby revealed. No human language is known which non-native speakers cannot, in principle, learn as a second language. The reason underlying this fact is that language is a system of skills fundamental to being human. These are the skills of reflective perception, abstraction, and inference. By means of the first skill one can, in principle, re-identify any symbol and its possible referent; by means of the second, one can, in principle, understand any semantic structures and classifications, analyzing composites and synthesizing units as the case may require, and by means of the third, one can, in principle, map out the bearing of any given proposition on (at least some) close or remote consequences. In sum, a human being is a rule-following animal, and language is nothing but an arrangement of rules. Therefore, barring the impairment of faculties, any human being will necessarily have the capacity to understand and use a language; and if one can understand any one language, one can understand any language. If there be any lingering doubt about this last claim, it might presumably be due to the anticipation of some contingent circumstances that might hamper the learning of a new language. Perhaps, the language manual to hand is pedagogically ineffective? But, surely, one can circumvent all second-hand aids and go and live among the people concerned and, in the words of Quine "learn the native language directly as an infant might."[3]

What, then, of untranslatability? In truth the ability to perceive the untranslatability of an expression from one language into another is a mark of linguistic understanding more profound than the ability to do routine translation. The second ability involves merely moving from the one language into the other, whereas the first involves stepping above both, onto a meta-platform, so to speak, an agility that has not seemed to come easily to some students of "other cultures." Untranslatability, then, can be a problem, but it does not necessarily argue unintelligibility.[4]

But, it might be objected, if some portions of a language can be untranslatable into another, why may not the entire language be so? We shall develop our answer by elaborating on a previous remark. In essence, the answer lies in the fact that the concept of object in general is a common possession of all humans. Operating with this concept is an essential aspect of the human way of interacting with the environment. It is what gives it a cognitive dimension. And because a basic imperative of this cognitive interaction is the drive for self-preservation and equilibrium, the essential discriminations of items of the environment, which the possession of the concept of object in general makes possible, will be of the same basic kind in actuality, if not necessarily in articulation, among all humankind. These essential discriminations will obviously be of the objects of direct perception. The word 'direct' here does not imply the absence of conceptualization. But at this level there is a basic similarity of conceptualization among humans by dint of semi-instinctual constraints. For this reason, the nearer a set of items of discrimination is to direct perception the easier it will be to correlate its elements with the different systems of symbolization obtaining among different peoples. This is what ensures that all human languages are, *at bottom*, inter-learnable and inter-translatable.[5]

But given this basic inter-translatability, no limits can be set to intercultural communication which do not also affect intracultural communication. The difficulties of intelligibility and translation among humans are due principally to the changes and chances to which the twin procedures of abstraction and inference are subject in this world. It is through these processes that human beings make their semantic ascents from the pedestal of direct sensible perception to the heights of sophisticated theoretical conceptions or into the clouds of conceptual obscurity and confusion. The consequent difficulties of understanding occur both across and within cultures, and they need not necessarily be, though they often are, more radical in the first than in the second context. For example, shorn of all epistemological exaggeration, the incommensurability described by Kuhn[6] between alternative scientific positions in certain phases of scientific thought illustrates breakdowns in communication more drastic than at least some of the difficulties that occur in intercultural dialogue. Nevertheless, whether the difficulty in communication occurs within one culture or between different cultures, because human beings are rule-following animals and because we all, by and large, stand on the same cognitive pedestal of sensible perception, such difficulties can sometimes be overcome, or if not overcome, at least, reduced to something less than absolute impenetrability.

It is probably needless to point out that what needs to be shown is not that intercultural or even intracultural communication is always successful, but only that it need not be always unsuccessful. That conceptual understanding is possible in both theaters of discourse should be sufficiently clear from the foregoing considerations. And, as previously noted, this, plainly, presupposes the existence of conceptual universals. Nevertheless, it might be thought that it still remains an open question whether there are epistemic universals. It might still be wondered, in other words, whether the ways of reasoning among the different peoples of the world might not be so incommensurable as to render any cross-cultural evaluation of the truth or soundness of belief systems impossible in spite of the supposed universality of conceptual understanding. In still other words, granted that there is enough mutuality of conceptual schemes for one culture to understand the intimations of another, does it follow that there must be enough commonality of cognitive criteria for the rationality of those intimations to be assessed from the point of view of an alien culture? Questions of this sort have sometimes launched some commentators on the varieties of ways of life and thought among humankind into well-intentioned flights of relativistic fancy. It is thought to be a mark of tolerance and broad-mindedness to view the allegedly disparate standards of reasoning as all equally valid within their own cultural habitat.

But in spite of the recent resurgence of sympathy for relativism, its inconsistency remains as glaring as ever. Here we are dealing with a form of cognitive relativism less sweeping than conceptual relativism, and what needs to be shown is that it is inconsistent to grant the possibility of conceptual universals and deny that of the cognitive variety. The argument is this: To understand a concept is to grasp its possibility of application; but this implies also grasping its criteria of application, that is, the conditions under which *it is true* to say that the concept holds. Two riders should, however, be immediately entered. First, this argument uses a strong concept of understanding. There is, in fact, also a weaker concept of understanding by which one might speak of understanding the concept of, say, a round square without pretending to envisage the *possibility* of something being both round and square. This is a formal concept of understanding which presupposes a substantive concept of understanding at some constitutive level of the given semantic material. Thus, in the present example, one claims, by implication, a substantive understanding of the concepts of 'round' and 'square'. Second, it should be noted that grasping the criteria of application of a concept does not necessarily amount to being able to articulate them accurately or adequately or even coherently. In fact, when the concepts in question are highly abstract and basic to a world view, this lack of equation reveals the root of all philosophy or, at any rate, much of it.[7]

Our argument exploits the connection, not specially recondite, between meaning and possible truth. But we can go further in linking conceptual with epistemic universals. The ground has, in fact, already been prepared for this. As previously argued, the power of conceptualization which yields the idea of the external world involves a basic sensitivity to the principle of non-contradiction and the ability to contemplate empirical hypotheticals. This last definitely implies the capacity to learn from experience. Let us call the principle of all learning from experience the principle of induction (without prejudging any issues about the exact nature of induction). If these two principles, of non-contradiction and induction—principles that are, by any reckoning, basic to human knowledge—are implicit in the power of conceptualization, then it is apparent that together they unite the human activities of understanding and knowing in such a way as to make it impossible that different peoples might be able to communicate, but unable in principle to argue rationally among themselves.

So far I have been arguing about conceptual and epistemic universals. But suppose it is objected that what is required to be proved is the existence of *cultural* universals, not these. It would quickly emerge that the objection is founded on a quite narrow conception of culture. Culture is not just the social forms and customary beliefs and practices of a human group. These phenomena themselves depend on the existence of language, knowledge, communication, interaction, and methods of transmitting knowledge to the born and the unborn. And this is the fundamental sense of the word 'culture'. In this sense, one might sum up the preceding discussion by saying that the fact of language itself, i.e., the possession of one language or another by all human societies, is the cultural universal *par excellence*.

Nevertheless, conceiving of culture as the social forms and customary beliefs and practices of a human group, while not the most fundamental way of conceiving of it, is one legitimate way of doing so. Besides, it is probably the most frequent in non-philosophical discourse. From this perspective, furthermore, there is some initial plausibility in skepticism as to the existence of cultural universals. Culture, in this sense, is a patterned accumulation of contingencies of social consciousness and action in the context of a specific type of physical environment. Here what defines culture, or to be exact, *a* culture, is the humanly contingent, not the humanly necessary. Thus, it is necessary for any human community to have *some* language, but what particular language that might be is a contingent matter. In general, it is necessary for human groups to have some customs but contingent what specific customs they might have.

From such reflections as these, the following train of thought naturally arises. Since customs are contingent facts of particular social formations, so also must be the principles for evaluating them. It proves convenient and reasonable in this connection to view the concept of custom broadly to comprehend such things as usages, traditions, manners, conventions, grammars, vocabularies, etiquette, fashions, aesthetic standards, observances, taboos, rituals, folkways, mores. All these are rules of thought and action, and to say that the basis for evaluating them is contingent is to say that there are no universally valid principles to that purpose. In more positive terms, it is to say that the rightness or wrongness of these rules is culture-relative. If we now view morality as being included under the contingent rules of good behavior, the conclusion appears to follow that it too, along with all other rules of conduct, is culture-relative. By this train of thought, then, we are transported not only to descriptive relativism but also to ethical relativism. It is not just the case, it would seem, that the standards of good and bad vary from people to people or culture to culture but also that their justification consists just in the fact of being adopted at a particular time and place.

Ethical relativism has often been criticized, and justly enough. But when all is said and done it remains unclear by what criteria normative universals of human conduct are to be identified. Interestingly, the narrowly ethical or moral universals seem to be the easiest to characterize. What we need to do is to specify a principle of conduct such that without its recognition—which does not necessarily mean its invariable observance—the survival of human society *in a tolerable condition* would be inconceivable. Let us start with the following minimal premiss. We assume that every human being has a concern for his or her own interests, in whatever way the concept of interest might be defined. The problem of morals arises from the fact that not everybody has a natural inclination to be concerned about the interests of others at all times in their conduct. In consideration of this, the following imperative naturally suggests itself. "Let your conduct at all times manifest a due concern for the interests of others." The question, of course, is: "What is *due* concern?" I propose the following criterion. A person may be said to manifest due concern for the interests of others if in contemplating the impact of his actions on their interests, she puts herself imaginatively in their position, and having done so, is able to welcome that impact. This is obviously reminiscent of what has been called the Golden Rule.[8] If phrased as an imperative, it might be called the principle of sympathetic impartiality. Now, I suggest that it takes little imagination to foresee that life in any society in which everyone openly avowed the contrary of this principle and acted accordingly would inevitably be "solitary, poor, nasty, *brutish*," and probably short. It is arguable—though we cannot stop to argue this here—that this principle suffices for the foundation of morality. It is easy to see, for instance, that the injection of a dose of compassion into Kant's categorical imperative would convert it into a principle of *sympathetic* impartiality. Certainly, whatever one may think of Kant's argumentation in basing morality on the categorical imperative, that effort cannot be dismissed as a triviality. And I might observe—harking back to my own background of indigenous thought—that traditional Akan ethical maxims quite demonstrably converge on some such foundation as the principle of sympathetic impartiality.[9] It seems clear, in any case, whether or not, as a matter of philosophy, people take this principle to be the basis of all morals, that, as a fact of ethical life, it is essential to the harmonization of human interests in society.

On the these grounds it may be asserted that the principle of sympathetic impartiality is a human universal transcending cultures viewed as social forms and customary beliefs and practices. In being common to all human practice of morality, it is a universal of any non-brutish form of human life.

In retrospect one can now easily spot the error in the relativistic train of thought rehearsed earlier. That train illicitly carried morality along with mores in the same bag of contingent rules of good behavior. But moral rules are a class apart. Yet it is so common to confuse morality with other types of rules conduct that, lexicographically, one legitimate sense of the word 'morality' is "conformity to ideals of right human conduct," even though not all such ideals are moral ideals. (Nor do the etymologies of 'moral' and 'ethical' provide any disincentive to the error complained of.) Thus people speak, for example, of the stoic and epicurean moralities, comparing and contrasting them as alternative models of morality. Similarly, one speaks of Christian or Islamic ethics or even of African or European ethics. It then appears that morality itself is something that can vary from group to group.

In fact, however, in the respects in which these systems of rules and ideals of conduct differ, they are customs; that is, contingent norms of life, rather than forms of morality in the strict sense of this word. In this strict sense morality, from the standpoint of conduct, is the motivated pursuit of sympathetic impartiality. Such values as truthfulness, honesty, justice, chastity, etc. are simply aspects of sympathetic impartiality, and do not differentiate morality from culture to culture. At best, what the contingencies of culture may do is to introduce variations of detail in the definition of some of these values. Thus the concept of chastity in a polyandrous society will accommodate more diversified sexual contacts with men on the part of a woman than in a monogamous environment. These differing constraints on definition are, of course, constraints of custom, and do not flow from sympathetic impartiality by any stretch of logical implication. This is true of customs in general, and explains why, though morality, strictly so called, does not and cannot differ from place to place, custom can and does. But since strict morality, at least as precept, is a social constant, and any society will have one set of idiosyncracies or another, what are often called alternative moralities will be found, on examination, to be composites of universal morality and contingent custom. Exactly such is the character of the epicurean and stoic moralities, for example. These systems are ratiocinative celebrations of different life-styles combined with attempts to define justice and moral virtue. For another example: what is referred to as Christian ethics is, in fact, a mixture of pure morality (e.g., Do not steal!) and customs (e.g., Man, you may marry only one woman!) with some taboos thrown in (e.g., Do not work on the Sabbath!).[10]

This insistence on a separation, in thought, between custom and morality does not, most assuredly, carry any suggestion that customs cannot form a basis for discriminations of the good, the bad, and the indifferent. The point is only that there are more grounds for the normative appraisal of conduct than moral merit or demerit. Neither is it implied that the extra-ethical codes are not important. Just think of the importance of traffic rules in places like

New York! And yet it can hardly be said that such a thought experiment yields proof that traffic rules are moral principles.

Two sub-conceptions of morality are implicit in the preceding remarks. Morality has been construed, now as a set of rules, now as a pattern of conduct cognizant of those rules. Sympathetic impartiality represents a fusion of the two conceptions: the impartiality is what the moral rules embody, and the sympathy is what the moral motivation evinces. The two elements underlie a distinction in moral evaluation on which Kant was famously keen: It is one thing to act in accordance with a moral rule and quite another to act out of respect for it (or, from the sympathetic perspective, out of concern for it). Only the latter has moral worth. But here comes an objection: Moral worth may be a precious thing, but it may not be a universal necessity. A society of rational egoists might conceivably get by with an exclusively prudential conformity to the moral rules. This objection does not, of course, threaten the universality of the moral rules, only the universality of the concern for them. But in picturing the rational egoists as a tribe totally bereft of human sympathy, it threatens their very status as human persons.

The objection just noted argues, in effect, that the doctrine of sympathetic impartiality says too much. There is an inverse objection to the effect that it says too little: Far from sympathetic impartiality being sufficient for morality, it may be compatible with the most severe infractions of human well-being. A sadist may cause pain to others without need of special pleading. What this shows, however, is not that sympathetic impartiality is not necessary for the human community, but rather that it is not sufficient for human well-being. And this is important. Being sufficient for morality is not necessarily sufficient for all desirables. Otherwise it would not be necessary to supplement morality with custom in every society. In addition to sympathetic impartiality, human society needs various other things, including common sense and psychiatry.

An even more topical objection perceives the specter of authoritarianism in the very idea of a cultural universal. Suggesting that some rule of conduct has universal validity seems to be interpreted as a prelude to a program of imposition. This feeling exists thanks to the history of intercultural oppression, in which some cultures have sought, sometimes successfully, to force their ideas of good and evil, conceived as universal verities, on other cultures. The practice has, in fact, usually been doubly pernicious; for what the aggressors have imposed have generally been their pet customs, rather than any principles of pure morality. Nevertheless, a little thought should enable one to distinguish between the universality of morality and the arbitrariness of any self-righteous pretenders to universal insight. Judicious claims of universality imply only that contending adults can, in principle, discuss their differences rationally on a basis of equality, whether inside identical cultures or across them.

But granted that moral rules are humanly universal and stand apart from all other rules of conduct, does it follow that all those others are lacking in cultural universality? No premiss or rule of inference seems available for establishing any such necessary implication, but it does seem to be one of the most visible facts about human societies that customs vary greatly from one society to another and, even within the same society, from one era to another. This, indeed, is a matter of fact that we have repeatedly noted. However, on a closer look, qualifications begin to press themselves upon our attention regarding the inscrutability of the variations. First, any custom which violates a moral rule is *ipso facto* condemnable as bad, not *for* this or that society, but *simpliciter*.

Second, customs often rest upon beliefs about the world. In so far as cognitive standards are ultimately universal, as argued in the first part of this discussion, such customs are, by and large, open to cross-cultural evaluation. Thus, for example, prayer to, or in care of, the Virgin Mary is an important custom among Catholics. But, obviously, if a Catholic were, *per improbabile*, to be argued out of her belief in the existence of God, that custom would, barring instinctual inertia, lose its hold on her. And where argument is concerned the principles of non-contradiction and induction unite all humankind. Similarly, were it, for instance, to be proven that our ancestors do not continue to exist in any shape or form, the traditional Akan custom of pouring libation to the departed ancestors would be deprived of its traditional rationale. In short, so long as a custom has a rationale, it has, at least, a qualified universality via its transcultural intelligibility.

But, third, some customs do not seem to have a rationale. We exclude cases of forgotten rationale, for, logically, they belong to the class already dealt with. The relevant cases here are the ones that seem to be born of caprice or pure accident. Paradoxically, these are, perhaps, the easiest to understand transculturally; for caprice is caprice, and accident is accident everywhere. So long as the resultant modes of conduct are objectively harmless, their known variety will, at best, support only a vacuous relativism, since there is, by hypothesis, no real disparity of values. On the other hand, where they are harmful, they are, as argued above, open to cross-cultural evaluation on moral or other rational grounds. In either case, little comfort accrues to relativism, ethical or even descriptive.

Fourth, even in those spheres of human activity, such as art (fine, literary, culinary) or music, dance, games and other recreations, where the historically well-established differences in values and sensibilities among the various peoples of the world have spawned great varieties of form and content, nothing is plainer than that increasing communication and familiarity, made possible by the tremendous advances in media technology and the like, are fast universalizing not only appreciation but also creative assimilation. Thus, where we cannot as yet speak of actual universals we can at least anticipate potential universals.

It is apparent from all this that when, as is often the case, critics of relativism have quickly conceded descriptive relativism in warming up toward the refutation of normative relativism, they have, in fact, unwittingly passed over some quite significant anti-relativistic considerations.

We started this discussion with the question whether there are any cultural universals. We must now begin to wonder whether ultimately there are any cultural non-universals.

4

The Biological Foundation
of Universal Norms

A norm is a rule of thought, talk, or conduct. Thoughts of moral rules come readiest to mind on the mention of norms, but human concerns abound with non-moral norms as well. We can quickly remind ourselves of those norms of work, play, or even idleness that depend on the choices and idiosyncracies of the different peoples of the world. These may be called customs in an enlarged sense of the word. They are extremely important in that, among other things, it is in terms of them rather than of the principles of morality in the strict sense (since the latter are universal) that different cultures may be individuated.

So far, what has come to mind have been rules of behavior—outward behavior. But we need, more particularly, to reckon with norms of thought, for these have the importance of necessary conditions for the very possibility of a human community. The underlying reasoning is this: Without communication community is impossible, and without thought communication is impossible. But without some common norms of talk communication is impossible and without common norms of thought common norms of talk are unavailable. Therefore, without some common norms of thought a human community is impossible. Add to this the fact that the human race constitutes an international community in which communication across borders is not only possible but pervasive and intensive, and it becomes obvious that the whole species must have some norms of thought in common.

Consider the implications of this last result. It cannot be history, culture, or ideology that accounts for this commonality, for these are the causes of the diversity rather than the unity of the species. And, in any case, they all presuppose that very same commonality. Why? Because the norms of thought that make it possible for us to think and make history and everything else are the same conditions that make social interaction with others (of whatever identities) possible. It is, I suggest, nothing other than our common basic biology that underlies the particular mental affinity of all the members of the human race with which we are concerned. But this may be anticipating overmuch.

Let us first attend to a preliminary clarification. Adapting Kantian language, we may distinguish between hypothetical and categorical norms. The first sort do not, in general, occasion speculation as to their basis or justification. If the technical linking of means to end is correct, there is nothing to puzzle over. The reason lies, I think, in what may be called the optional character of hypothetical norms. Such norms are of the form "If you want **A**, do **B**," where it is understood that one may not want **A**. Here what breeds understanding is the unconcealed rationale of the project in question; the rule itself reveals its purpose, its reason. By contrast, a categorical norm or imperative is peremptory. One is required to do **B**, short and simple. In particular, this requirement, this imperative, overrides contrary inclinations. Since human inclinations and tendencies often run counter to categorical imperatives, it is clear that the latter have a disciplinary authority. And while it may be a symptom of an infantile mentality to rebel against discipline, critical curiosity about the basis of so absolute a disciplinary rule as a categorical imperative may well be the beginning of wisdom. In this context 'basis' may mean underlying reason, justification, purpose, or origin. How the question of origin enters the picture will turn out to be closely connected with the biologic orientation of the present discussion.

Meanwhile, given the existence of incompatible philosophical accounts of the basis of the norms of morality, for example, it might be salutary to bear in mind that while it may be easy to initiate the search for wisdom, the road to that objective is not lined with roses. In the matter of the basis or the foundation of ethical norms, that road is littered with a variety of theories that fall into two basic and contrasting classes, namely, the naturalistic and the non-naturalistic. Actually, in its widest meaning the naturalism/non-naturalism antithesis would seem to be suspect. It is questionable whether a coherent demarcation can be made between one realm of processes and existences to be called nature, and another to be called anything else. Naturalism is generally supposed to be firmly anchored to the first side of this divide; and so it is. But insofar as it seems to concede so much as the logical possibility of such an ontological duality, it is problematic.

This last remark is inspired by my understanding and intellectual identification with my African traditional background of thought in which there is no bifurcation between nature and supernature and in which, consequently, the question of the biological foundation of norms does not precipitate any metaphysical puzzles. In my branch of the African tradition we have, on the one hand, a phrase (*Aboa onipa*), encapsulating a whole philosophical outlook, which may be translated literally as "Person, the animal"; but, on the other hand, we also have the phrase "Child as God" (*Akwadaa Nyame*), signifying a sense of the continuity running through all sensitive existence from its biologic base to all the spirals of human potentialities. Although in the conception of this continuum there is the notion of an advance beyond the biological at the human level, there is no suggestion of an ontological transcendence of the biological. Nor is there any pretense of a physicalistic reduction to the sub-human.

However, the question of the biological basis of human norms emerges as a many-sided issue in any intellectual milieu in which the distinction between nature and non-nature, if we may put it that way, is taken to be intelligible. Western philosophy is roughly one such intellectual milieu. It turns out, fortunately for my purposes, that the issue is intertwined with various others of independent interest. In taking up the issue in question, then, I am glad to be able to shift tactically from the traditional African framework to that of Western philosophy, appropriating whatever I find of worth in it. This, by the way, is what I understand by the universality of philosophy. Presumably, the time will come when Western philosophers too will approach African philosophy not just as a curiosity but as a field in which they might find something to appropriate in the modern world.

But, let us return to naturalism with respect to norms. In spite of my reservations regarding the general distinction between naturalism and non-naturalism, a limited appropriation can, I think, be made of the term "naturalistic," in the specific context of an investigation into the basis of norms, to name theories that define and explain norms in terms of the interests, capabilities, and circumstances (present and primeval) of the human species. I will pursue a naturalistic line with respect to norms in this sense without wishing to be held answerable for the metaphysics of naturalism.

A biologic theory of norms is necessarily naturalistic, though a naturalistic theory of norms is not necessarily biologic. Thus Mill's utilitarianism is a naturalistic theory of ethical norms, but he does not follow through to their biological foundations. This unavailability of the converse is even more striking in the study of epistemic norms. Empiricist theories of knowledge are, or can easily be made, naturalistic; but they are rarely biologic. Rarity almost becomes vacuity when we come to the norms of logic. Here naturalistic theories are hard to come by, let alone biologic ones.

John Dewey was one of the few great philosophers who advanced a biologic theory of the basis of logic. In his *Logic: The Theory of Inquiry* (New York: Holt, Rinehart and Winston, 1938) he argued that there is a natural continuity between inquiry and the elementary forms of organic behavior. The former is simply a transformation of possibilities inherent in the latter. Dewey pointed out that "the development of language (in its widest sense) out of prior biological activities is, in its connection with wider cultural forces, the key to this transformation" (44). How does this development occur? According to him, organic life is essentially an interaction with the environment in which there is a continual process of the expenditure of energy and its recovery. In the simpler organisms this interaction generally takes the form of direct contact, but in the more complex organisms, possessing distance receptors and endowed with special organs of motion, this process, which might be called one of trying to resolve a tension with the environment, takes on a serial character in which the earlier phases prepare the way for the later. Here talk of stimulus and response begins to make sense: A pattern develops of initial tension and exploratory activities for reintegration with the environment which modifies organic structures and conditions future interactions. "This modification," Dewey says, "constitutes habit," and "habits are the basis of organic learning" (31).

Given the time lag between tension and resolution, the exploratory activities, perforce, acquire the dimension of prevision, which together with the need to interact with kindred organisms—a cultural circumstance—gives rise to language and communication and thereby to the possibility of a logic of discourse. This possibility is realized through sensitivity to the efficiency of certain methods of inquiry and the inefficiency of others in securing warranted assertibility. And it is in this way that logic establishes *norms* of thought in the actual conduct of inquiry rather than merely proffering 'transcripts' of empirical material (103).

It is to be noted at once that the only sense in which this account might be thought to bring enlightenment as to the basis of logic is genetical. If taken as justificatory, it begs the question in much the same way that inductive justifications of induction beg the question, (all the sophisticated rescue attempts of recent times notwithstanding). This is not intended to be deprecatory of Dewey's theory. On the contrary, it is to emphasize that if one is at all touched by curiosity as to the basis of logical (and epistemic) norms one must disabuse one's mind of any anticipation of a ratiocinative justification. As it happens, the entertainment of such illusory expectations has been the root, if not of all, then certainly of many, of the difficulties that bedevil the study of the foundations of induction (of which more below).

Dewey is, in fact, self-consciously genetical in his approach. But he does not (see, e.g., pp. 21, 103) seek to 'naturalize' the philosophical study of inquiry by reducing it to some empirical discipline like biology or psychology, as some leaders of the contemporary movement for the naturalization of epistemology seem bent on doing, and—in the case of Dewey—with good reason. A genetic account of norms is one that seeks to show that they are founded on the empirical constitution and natural antecedents of the human mind. It is, or should be, evident that the basis of all the norms in a given domain cannot itself be a norm but must rather be an existential fact of a descriptive nature. Yet, norms will remain norms, whether in logic, epistemology, or ethics. Dewey's account could do with some fleshing out, but it is hard to foresee a radically disparate alternative to its basic tendency. Nevertheless, in the broad sweep of his biological theory applications to specific principles of inquiry are not pursued. How, for example is the law of non-contradiction or the principle of induction to be shown to have a biological basis?

These last mentioned canons of inquiry may be called the supreme laws of thought, the first in all thinking, the second in the field of all reasonings from experience. To cast a forward glance at the domain of morals, we might anticipate our forthcoming suggestion that in this field also there is what might be called a supreme principle. If Kant is right—a hypothesis that seems to me, by and large, probable in this particular case—the categorical imperative or something like it is such a principle. This listing of 'supreme' principles should give us a reasonably general and yet sufficiently specific idea of the fundamental norms due for a biologic accounting. Since I have indulged a little in Kantian terminology, I might observe that Kant does not extend his hypothetical/categorical distinction to the norms of thought. Thus the categorical imperative, for him, is just that one principle of good conduct, which serves as the foundation of ethics. For us, on the contrary, each of the domains of thought or conduct mentioned, namely, the logical, the epistemological, and the ethical, has a hierarchy of categorical norms, which are reducible in some sense to those designated as supreme. Again, although I am of the opinion that the supreme norm of ethics might coincide with something resembling Kant's categorical imperative, my biologic motivation here obviously betokens as un-Kantian a mindset in these matters as can be.

Be that as it may, let us go back to the norm of non-contradiction. Of the basis of this principle we can be brief. Any universal liberties with it would be bound to be devastating to human society, for without it there would be no telling when a message is affirmed or denied, and the possibility of communication would be out of the question. Worse, individual *human* survival would be in jeopardy, for if I cannot tell affirmation from denial in communication, neither can I tell the difference between my believing and not believing something. In other words, my powers of thought, and with it my continued membership in the club of humans, would be at an end. Of course, the human mind is weak, and we are all unfortunately subject to occasional involuntary defaults in complying with the principle or sometimes even in acknowledging it—witness, in our time, paraconsistentism. What we will not survive, as humans, is a thoroughgoing abnegating of the norm of non-contradiction. But this immediately earmarks the requisite minimum of actual compliance as a naturally selected factor in our equipment for survival as a species, a selection too crucial evolutionarily to have been left to the tender consistencies of the individual psyche. Evolutionarily antecedent modes of organismic interactions with the environment, like those discussed by Dewey, which eventuate in the use of language are just such as to ensure a sufficient implementation of that categorical imperative of survival. That sufficiency, is, of course, not a sufficient condition for our future survival but only a necessary one, for there are obvious contingencies that could compromise that prospect.

Issues become very much more subtle when we come to the principle of induction. Unlike the case of the principle of non-contradiction, there is not even agreement as to what it is. The most famous discussion of the problem of accounting for the basis of induction in Western philosophy was given by David Hume. Ironically, he does not seem to have used the word 'induction' in his study of 'experimental' reasoning, or at any rate not with the modern signification or assortment of significations. What is more, it is not at all clear that he recognized any *form* of argumentation that might be called inductive in the current acceptation of the word. At the beginning of his discussion of 'matter of fact' reasonings in *An Inquiry Concerning Human Understanding,* Hume asserts unequivocally: "All reasoning concerning matters of fact seem to be founded on the relation of *cause* and *effect.* By means of that relation alone we can go beyond the evidence of our memory and senses" (section IV, Part I, p. 41 of edition by Charles W. Hendel [New York: Macmillan, 1955]). On this showing, he understood the *structure* of all such reasoning to be deductive. Yet, afterwards he seems to suggest that all such reasonings are typified by the following formulation: "I have found that such an object has always been attended with such an effect *and* I foresee that other objects which are in appearance similar will be attended with similar effects" (section IV, Part II, p. 48). This admittedly, gives the impression that Hume did after all recognize a form of reasoning distinct from deduction and appropriately called induction in current terminology. The formula, indeed, sounds very much like what many people would be willing to call the principle of induction. If Hume did intend it in this sense, that would mean that he was guilty of a stupendous inconsistency committed by asserting or implying the contradictory of his position within a very short distance of its formulation. That is, of course, possible.

But a hypothesis that seems to tie together various lines of reflection in the *Inquiry* is that in the formulation just quoted Hume is thinking (not perhaps with the maximum of clarity or rigor) of some kind of process at some level of the human psyche which lies underneath all 'experimental' reasonings rather than characterizing a ratiocinative transition from premiss to conclusion. It might be noted in this connection that, although Hume's writing style was of extreme beauty, it was not marked by unbroken rigor or precision. Moreover, it is pretty clear that the investigation he is pursuing does not have to do with conditions for the soundness of arguments from experience. On this he offers intellectually methodological advice in the *Treatise* (Book I, Part III, section XV: "Rules by Which to Judge of Causes and Effects"). His concern seems, in fact, to be with the foundation of the practice itself of factual inference. Thus the question which he says he is moved by his "sifting humor" to ask is "What is the foundation of ALL conclusions from experience?" (*Inquiry*, 46, my capitals). The considerations already adduced in this discussion show that a question of this sort cannot be answered by exhibiting any sort of step of argumentation or by giving a reason why a certain class of arguments are sound. If the question is answerable at all, it must be, as previously suggested, by some manner of genetical reflection. This is exactly the strategy that Hume adopts.

Seen in this light it begins to be intelligible why Hume, certainly no congenital obscurantist, maintains that "in all reasonings from experience there is a step taken by the mind which is not supported by argument" (ibid., section V, Part I, p. 55). For him, on the contrary, the trait of the human mind that is in question here is a natural, nay, biological one. It is, according to him, found in custom, that ingrained tendency of the mind, which alone moves us "after the constant conjunction of two objects" to "expect the one from the appearance of the other" (ibid., p. 57). The problem with this particular formulation of Hume's point is that in being couched in terms of perceptual objects and propositional attitudes it is made to appear as if custom is a characteristic of the mind that is *consciously* manifested at the level of our cognitive operations. In fact, however, if it is to provide a basis for the procedure itself of factual reasoning in general, then it will have to be an evolutionarily begotten condition of the mind that is responsible for the possibility but not the performance of cognitive activities, just like Dewey's concept of habits which, recall, he says are "the basis of organic learning." That Hume was basically aware of this is discernible in various remarks in Part II of section V of the *Inquiry*, but it comes out clearest in the remarkable section X, entitled, "Of the Reason of Animals," in which, among other revealing things, he says that "experimental reasoning itself"—he surely means the driving principle of the process—"which we possess in common with beasts, and on which the whole conduct of life depends, is nothing but a species of instinct or mechanical power that acts in us unknown to ourselves, and in its chief operations is not directed by any such relations or comparison of ideas as are the proper objects of our intellectual faculties" (116). Common criticisms of Hume's theory of custom have thrived on construing custom, contrary to Hume's intentions, which were biological, as a proposed cognitive procedure conversant with the ideas and operations that are "the proper objects of our intellectual faculties" (116).

Suppose, now, that in the name of the principle of induction one tentatively proposed something like the following: "In a wide and varied experience, constant conjunction of events or characters constitutes a good reason for expecting a similar conjunction in unobserved cases." Our discussion above should, hopefully, preempt any temptation to conflate this with Hume's principle of custom. The present formulation is, in fact, best seen as a kind of definition of empirical reason. It expresses, at the level of conscious cognition, an intellectual norm for which the evolutionary principle of custom provides a biologic basis.

What of the biologic basis of ethical norms? The considerations rehearsed above, particularly in connection with the principle of non-contradiction, enable us to proceed with considerable dispatch here. The need for morality arises from facts of the following kind. Human beings have common as well as conflicting interests. Coexistence in society requires some adjustment or reconciliation of these interests. The possibility of such an adjustment rests on the fact that human beings do have a basic natural sympathy for their kind. The difficulty of the thing, on the other hand, is due to the fact that that sympathy is often quite sparse and in other cases easily extinguishable by a variety of causes. The moral way out of this situation is for individuals to *endeavor* to adopt in their conduct the standpoint of what might be called sympathetic impartiality. The principle of this standpoint is always to act in such a way as to avoid doing things that have effects on others that one would not welcome if one were in the situation of those others in an otherwise identical reenactment of the action. The similarity of this to Kant's categorical imperative, and also to the Golden Rule of the Son of Man, is obvious. It is also the cardinal principle of the ethical thought of my own people. Indeed, insofar as a people have any sense of morals at all (in the strict sense) they must operate, explicitly or implicitly, with some such principle. As in the case of the principle of non-contradiction, the survival of human society is possible in the face of quite a lot of defaults and defections from the observance of the ethical principle, but unless it held a certain minimum of sway in the thought and action of some individuals at least, there would be a collapse of human society. This necessary connection of the principle with the survival of the group and, by and large, of the species, invests it, again as in the case of non-contradiction, with the status of an evolutionary force.

The foregoing findings, which connect our logical, epistemic, and ethical norms with our situation as organisms in necessary interaction with the environment and with our kind illustrate the fact that we are after all a part of 'nature'.

Part II

Religion and Morality

5

Universalism and Particularism in Religion from an African Perspective

Two assumptions that may safely be made about the human species are, one, that the entire race shares some fundamental categories and criteria of thought in common and, two, that, nevertheless, there are some very deep disparities among the different tribes of humankind in regard to their modes of conceptualization in some sensitive areas of thought. The first accounts for the possibility of communication among different peoples, the second for the difficulties and complications that not infrequently beset that interaction.

Is religion a field of convergence or divergence of thought among the peoples and cultures of the world? The obvious answer is that religion is both. There is also an obvious sequel: What are the specifics? But here an obvious answer is unavailable, at least as concerns Africa vis-à-vis, for instance, the West. In fact, it is not at all obvious in what sense the English word "religion" is applicable to any aspect of African life and thought.

This last remark, of course, amounts to discounting the frequent affirmations, in the literature of African studies, of the immanent religiosity of the African mind. What exactly are the features of life and thought that are appealed to in that characterization? In investigating this issue I am going to have to be particularistic. I am going to have particular, though not exclusive, recourse to the Akans of West Africa, for the considerations to be adduced presuppose a level of cultural and linguistic insight to which I cannot pretend in regard to any African peoples except the Akans, whom I know through birth, upbringing, reading, and deliberate reflective observation. This particularism has, at least, the logical potential of all counter-examples against universal claims.

It has been suggested, even by some authors by whose reckoning African life is full of religion, that there is no word in many African languages that translates the word 'religion'.[1] Whether this is true of all African languages or not I do not know, but it is certainly true of Akan, at least in the traditional use of that language. Not only is there no single word for religion but there is also no periphrastic equivalent. There is, indeed, the word *Anyamesom,* which many translators might be tempted to proffer. But the temptation ought to be resisted. The word is a Christian invention by which the missionaries distinguished, in Akan speech, between their own religion and what they perceived to be the religion of the indigenous "pagans." Thus, it means not religion, pure and simple, but Christianity. Ironically, in this usage the Christian missionaries were constrained by linguistic exigencies to adapt a word that the Akans use for the Supreme Being. *Onyame* is one among several names for the Supreme Being in Akan. Another very frequent one is *Onyankopon,* which literally means The Being That Is Alone Great, in other words, That Than Which a Greater Cannot Be Conceived (with apologies to Saint Anselm). The remaining component of the word *Anyamesom* is *som* which means "to serve"; so that the whole word means, literally, "the service of the Supreme Being" or, if you follow Christian methods of translation, "the service of God." In turn, this was taken to mean the *worship* of God.

By way of a designation for what they saw as indigenous religion, the Christians used the word *Abosomsom.* This is a combination of two words, *Obosom* and *som.* Etymologically, *obosom* means the service of stones. Thus, literally, the barbarism means the service of stone service. Still, it served its Christian purpose. But why stones? This is an allusion to the fact that the Akans traditionally believe that various objects, such as certain special rocks, trees, and rivers, are the abode of extrahuman forces and beings of assorted grades.

Religion, however it is defined, involves a certain kind of attitude. If a given religion postulates a supra-human Supreme Being, that belief must, on any common showing, necessarily be joined to an attitude not only of unconditional reverence but also of worship. Some will go as far as to insist that this worshipful attitude will have to be given practical expression through definite rituals, especially if the being in question is supposed to be the determiner or controller of human destiny. There is a further condition of the utmost importance; it is one which introduces an ethical dimension into the definition. Essential to any religion in the primary sense is a conception of moral uprightness. If it involves supra-human beliefs, the relevant ethic will be based logically or psychologically on the "supra" being or beings concerned. Typically, but by no means invariably, a religion will have a social framework. In that case, it will have organized hortatory and other procedures for instilling or revivifying the commitment to moral virtue.

Consider, now, the character of the Akan belief in the Supreme Being. There is, indeed, generally among the Akans a confirmed attitude of unconditional reverence for *Onyankopon,* the Supreme Being. However, there is, most assuredly, no attitude or ritual of worship directed to that being either at a social or an individual level. They regard Him as good, wise, and powerful in the highest. He is the determiner of human destiny as of everything else. But in all this they see no rationale for worship. Neither is the Akan conception of morality based logically or even psychologically on the belief in the Supreme Being. Being good in the highest, He disapproves of evil; but, to the Akan mind, the reason why people should not do evil is not because He disapproves of it but rather because it is contrary to human well-being, which is why He disapproves of it in the first place.[2]

The early European visitors to Africa, especially the missionaries, were quick to notice the absence of any worship of God among the Akans and various other African peoples.[3] They were hardly less struck by the fact that God was not the foundation of Akan morals. On both grounds they deduced a spiritual and intellectual immaturity in the African. Notice the workings here of a facile universalism. It seems to have been assumed that belief in God must move every sound mind to worship. Perhaps, even now, such an assumption might sound plausible to many Western ears. It is, of course, not likely in this day and age that many can be found to suppose that any person of a sound mind must necessarily embrace belief in God. But given the prevailing tendencies in Western, and even some non-Western cultures, it might be tempting to think that if people believe in God, then the *natural* thing for them to do is to worship Him. Yet, consider the notion of a perfect being. Why would He (She, It) need or accept to be worshipped? What would be the point of it? It is well known that the Judeo-Christian God *jealously* demands to be worshipped—witness the Ten Commandments—but, from an Akan point of view, such clamoring for attention must be paradoxical in the extreme in a perfect being, and I confess to being an unreconstructed Akan in this regard.[4]

There is, in their resort to the word *Abosomsom* (the worship of stones) to name what they took to be Akan religion, an odd manifestation of the special importance that the Christian missionaries attached to worship. Having seen that the Akans did not worship God, they were keen to find out what it was that they did worship, for surely a whole people must worship something? They quickly settled on the class of what I have called extrahuman forces and beings, which, as I have already hinted, is a feature of the Akan world view. There is, indeed, a great variety of such entities postulated in the Akan ontology (as in any other African ontology that I know of). Some are relatively person-like; others, somewhat automatic in their operation. The former, it is believed, can be communicated with through some special procedures, and are credited with a moral sense. Commonly, a being of this sort would be believed to be localized at a household "shrine," from where it would protect the given group from evil forces. More person-like still are the ancestors who are thought to live in a realm closely linked with the world of the living.

Actually, the ancestors are conceived of as persons who continue to be members of their pre-mortem families, watching over their affairs and generally helping them. They are regarded as persons, but not as mortal persons, for they have tasted death and transcended it. Accordingly, they are not thought to be constrained by all the physical laws which circumscribe the activities of persons with fully physical bodies. For this reason, they are supposed to be more powerful than mortals. Additionally, they are considered to be more irreversibly moral than any living mortal. All these attributes are taken to entitle the ancestors to genuine reverence. Not quite the same deference is accorded to the first groups of beings, but in view of their presumed power to promote human well-being, they are approached with considerable respect.

More types of extrahuman forces and beings are spoken of in the Akan ontology than I have mentioned, but these are among the most relevant, and they will suffice for the impending point, which is this: the Akan attitude to the beings in question bears closer analogy to secular esteem than to religious worship. The reverence given to the ancestors is only a higher degree of the respect that in Akan society is considered to be due to the earthly elders. For all their post-mortem ontologic transformation, the ancestors are, let it be repeated, regarded as members of their families. The libations that are poured to them on ceremonial and other important occasions are simply invitations to come and participate in family events. Moreover, everybody hopes eventually to become an ancestor, but this is not seen as a craving for self-apotheosis. Ancestorship is simply the crowning phase of human existence.

The nonreligious character of the Akan attitude to the non-ancestral forces is even more clear. Real religious devotion to a being must be unconditional. But that is the one thing that the Akan approach to those beings is not; it is purely utilitarian. If they bring help, praise be to them, and other things besides. On the other hand, if they fail, particularly if that happens consistently, they can fall into disrepute or worse. K. A. Busia and J. B. Danquah, the two most celebrated expositors of Akan thought, have borne unambiguous and, as it seems to me, reliable testimony to this fact. Busia says, "The gods are treated with respect if they deliver the goods, and with contempt if they fail. . . . Attitudes to [the gods] depend upon their success, and vary from healthy respect to sneering contempt" (Busia,1954, p. 205). Danquah goes somewhat further: "The general tendency is to sneer at and ridicule the fetish and its priest."[5] There is an even more radical consideration. According to popular belief, these "gods" are capable of dying. Of a "god" who is finished, the Akans say *nano atro*, that is, its powers have become totally blunted. This may happen through unknown causes, but it also may happen through human design. People can cause the demise of a "god" simply by permanently depriving it of attention. Or, for more rapid results, they can apply an antithetical substance to its "shrine." Such antidotes are known for at least some of these "gods," according to popular belief. It ought, perhaps, to be emphasized that in this matter the thought is not that a "god" has betaken itself elsewhere but, rather, that it has ceased to be a force to be reckoned with at all. In light of all this, it is somewhat of a hyperbole to call the procedures designed for establishing satisfactory relations with the beings in question "religious worship."

The considerations rehearsed so far should be enough, I think, to suggest the need for a review of the enthusiastic, not to say indiscriminate, attributions of religiosity to African peoples. But there are deeper reasons of the same significance. And in studying them we will see the role which the hasty universalization of certain Western categories of thought has played in the formation of the misapprehensions under scrutiny. Take, then, the Akan belief in the Supreme Being. In English discourse about Akan thought the word "God" is routinely used to refer to this being. This has led, or has been due, to the supposition that both the Akans and the Christians are talking of the same being when they speak of the Supreme Being, notwithstanding any divergences of cultural perception. This supposed identity of reference has come in handy to christianized Africans wishing to demonstrate that they can profess Christianity and still remain basically true to their indigenous religions: there is, after all, only one God, and we are all trying to reach Him (see, for example, Idowu, *African Traditional Religion* [London: SCM Press, 1973], p. 146).

Yet, in spite of any apparent similarities, such as the postulation of That Than Which a Greater Cannot Be Conceived in both traditions of thought, the Akan Supreme Being is profoundly different from the Christian one. The Christian God is a creator of the world out of nothing. In further philosophical characterization, He is said to be transcendent, supernatural, and spiritual in the sense of immaterial, nonphysical. In radical contrast, the Akan Supreme Being is a kind of cosmic architect, a fashioner of the world order, who occupies the apex of the same hierarchy of being which accommodates, in its intermediate ranges, the ancestors and living mortals, and, in its lower reaches, animals, plants, and inanimate objects. This universe of being is ontologically homogenous. In other words, everything that exists exists in exactly the same sense as everything else. And this sense is empirical, broadly speaking. In the Akan language to exist is to *wo ho,* which, in literal translation, means "to be at some place." There is no equivalent, in Akan, of the existential "to be" or "is" of English, and there is no way of pretending in that medium to be speaking of the existence of something which is not in space. This locative connotation of the Akan concept of existence is irreducible except metaphorically.[6] Thus you might speak of there existing an explanation for something (*ne nkyerease wo ho)* without incurring any obligation of spatial specification, because an explanation is not an object in any but a metaphorical sense, and to a metaphorical object corresponds only a metaphorical kind of space. The same applies to the existence of all so-called abstract entities.[7] In the Akan conceptual framework, then, existence is spatial. Now, since whatever transcendence means in this context, it implies existence beyond space, it follows that talk of any transcendent being is not just false but unintelligible, from an Akan point of view.

But not only transcendence goes by the board. Neither the notion of the supernatural nor that of the spiritual can convey any coherent meaning to an Akan understanding in its traditional condition.[8] No line is drawn in the Akan world view demarcating one area of being corresponding to nature from another corresponding to supernature. Whatever is real belongs to one or another of the echelons of being postulated in that world view. In that context it has all the explanation that is appropriate to it. An important axiom of Akan thought is that everything has its explanation, *biribiara wo nenkyerease*—a kind of principle of sufficient reason; and a clear presupposition of Akan explanations of phenomena is that there are interactions among all the orders of existents in the world. Accordingly, if an event in human affairs, for instance, does not appear explicable in human terms, there is no hesitation in invoking extrahuman causality emanating from the higher or even the lower rungs of the hierarchy of beings. In doing this there is no sense of crossing an ontological chasm, for the idea is that there is only one universe of many strata wherein God, the ancestors, humans, animals, plants, and all the rest of the furniture of the world have their being.

In this last connection it might, perhaps, enhance understanding to regiment our terminology a little. Suppose we use the term "the world" to designate the totality of ordered existents fashioned out by God in the process of "creation." Then, of course, God, being the author of the world, is not a part of it, in the Akan scheme of things. But we might, then, reserve the term "universe" for the totality of absolutely all existents. In this sense God would be part of the universe. Apart from regimenting our terminology, this gives us the opportunity to reinforce the point regarding the Akan sense of the inherent law-likeness of reality. And the crucial consideration is that God's relationship with the rest of the universe, that is, the world, is also conceived to be inherently lawlike. This is the implication of the Akan saying that "The Creator created Death and Death killed the Creator" (*Odomankoma boo Owuo na Owuo kum Odomankoma*), which, in my opinion, is one of the profoundest in the Akan corpus of metaphysical aphorisms.

But though God's relation with the world is conceived to be lawlike, He is not made the basis of the explanation of any specific phenomenon, for since everything is ultimately traceable to Him, *Biribiara ne Nyame,* references to Him are incapable of helping to explain why any particular thing is what it is and not another thing. Divine law-likeness only ensures that there will be no arbitrary interferences in the course of the world-process. Thus the reason why Akan explanations of specific things do not invoke God is not because He is thought to be transcendent or supernatural or anything like that but, rather, because He is too immanently implicated in the nature and happening of things to have any explanatory value. Still, in facing the cognitive problems of this world all the mundane theaters of being, human and extrahuman, are regarded as *equally* legitimate sources of explanation. Thus, if an Akan explains a mysterious malady in terms of, say the wrath of the ancestors, it makes little sense to ascribe to him or her a belief in the supernatural. That characterization is intelligible only in a conceptual framework in which the natural/supernatural dichotomy has a place. But the point is that it has no place in the Akan system of thought. We may be sure, then, that the widespread notion that Africans are given to supernatural explanations is the result of the superimposition of alien categories of thought on African thought-structures, in the Akan instance, at least. There is nothing particularly insidious in the fact that Western writers on African thought have generally engaged in this practice; for, after all, one thinks most naturally in terms of the conceptual framework of one's intellectual upbringing, and the natural/supernatural distinction is very endemic, indeed, in Western thought. I do not mean by this, of course, that there is a universal belief in the supernatural in the West. I suggest only that this concept, together with its logical complement, is a customary feature of Western conceptualizations, so much so that even the Western philosophical naturalist, in denying the existence of anything supernatural, does not necessarily dispute the coherence of that concept. It is a more striking fact that many contemporary African expositors of their own traditional systems of thought yield no ground to their Western colleagues in stressing the role of belief in the supernatural in African thinking.[9] It is hard not to see this as evidence of the fact that in some ways Christian proselytization and Western education have been over-successful in Africa.

But an interesting and important question arises. Suppose it is granted that, as I have been arguing, the natural/supernatural dichotomy has no place in Akan and, perhaps, African thought generally. Does that not still leave the question of its objective validity intact? And, if it should turn out to be objectively valid, would it not be reasonable to think that it would be a good thing for Africans to learn to think along that line? My answer to both questions is affirmative, which implies a rejection of relativism. This disavowal is fully premeditated and is foreshadowed in the opening paragraph of this essay. However, for reasons of the division of preoccupation, I cannot try to substantiate my anti-relativism here.[10]

Stated baldly, my thesis is that there is such a thing as the objective validity of an idea. Were it not for the recent resurgence of relativism in philosophy, this would have been too platitudinous for words. Furthermore, and rather less obviously, if an idea is objectively valid (or invalid or even incoherent) in any given language or conceptual framework, both the idea and its status can, in principle, be *represented* in, if not necessarily translated into, any other language or conceptual framework.

A corollary of the foregoing contention is that, however natural it may be to think in one's native framework of concepts, it is possible for human beings to think astride conceptual frameworks. In the absence of extended argumentation for this general claim, I will content myself with an illustration with respect to the idea of the supernatural. A relevant question, then, is: "Do the Akans need to incorporate the natural/supernatural distinction into their modes of thought?" I think not, for not only is Akan thought inhospitable to this distinction but also the distinction is, in my opinion, objectively incoherent. If this is so, it follows from our principle that it ought to be demonstrable (to the extent that such speculative matters are susceptible of demonstration) in any language and, in particular, in English. In fact, a simple argument suffices for this purpose.

In the sense pertinent to our discussion, the supernatural is that which surpasses the order of nature. In other words, a supernatural event is one whose occurrence is contrary to the laws of nature. But if the event actually happens, then any law that fails to reckon with its possibility is inaccurate and is in need of some modification, at least. However, if the law is suitably amended, even if only by means of an exceptive rider, the event is no longer contrary to natural law. Hence no event can be consistently described as supernatural.

What of the notion of the spiritual? Again, I begin with a disclaimer on behalf of Akan ontological thinking. As can be expected from the spatial character of the Akan concept of existence, the radical dualism of the material and the spiritual can find no home in the Akan scheme of reality. All the extrahuman beings and powers, even including God, are spoken of in language irreducibly charged with spatial imagery. It is generally recognized by students of African eschatology that the *place* of the dead, the *abode* of the ancestors, is almost completely modeled on the world of living mortals (see Kwasi Wiredu, "Death and the Afterlife in African Culture" in Kwasi Wiredu and Kwame Gyekye, *Person and Community: Ghanaian Philosophical Studies, I* [Washington, D.C.: The Council for Research in Values and Philosophy, 1992]). If the replication is not complete, it is only because the ancestors are not thought of as having fully material bodies. Some analogue of material bodies they surely must be supposed to have, given the sorts of things that are said about them. For example, a postulated component of a person that is supposed to survive death and eventually become an ancestor, all things being equal, is believed soon after death to travel *by land and by river* before arriving at the abode of the ancestors. For this reason, in traditional times, coffins were stuffed with travel needs, such as clothing and money for the payment of ferrying charges. I have never heard it suggested in traditional circles that this practice was purely symbolic. If it were a purely symbolic gesture, that, certainly, would have been carrying symbolism rather far. But, in any case, the practice was of a piece with the conception, and the conception is decidedly quasi-material.

I use the term 'quasi-material' to refer to any being or entity conceived as spatial but lacking some of the properties of material objects. The ancestors, for instance, although they are thought of as occupying space, are believed to be invisible to the naked eye and inaudible to the normal ear, except rarely, when they choose to *manifest* themselves to particular persons for special reasons. On such occasions they can, according to very widely received conceptions among the Akans, appear and disappear at will, unconstrained by those limitations of speed and impenetrability to which the gross bodies of the familiar world are subject. This is held to be generally true of all the relatively personalized forms of extrahuman phenomena.

It is apparent from what has just been said that if the extrahuman beings of the Akan world view are not fully material, they are not fully immaterial either. Further to confirm this last point, we might note that, although the beings in question are not supposed to be generally visible to the *naked* eye, they are widely believed to be perceivable to the superior eyes of certain persons of special gift or training. People reputed to be of this class will sometimes tell you, "If you but had eyes to see, you would be amazed at what is going on right here around where you are standing." And here imagery tends to be so lustily spatial that, but for their selective invisibility, one would be hard put to it to distinguish between the quasi-material apparitions and the garden-variety objects of the material world. Descriptions of human-like creatures gyrating on their heads are not unknown in such contexts. Whatever one may think of such claims, the conceptual point itself is clear, namely, that the extrahuman existents of the Akan ontology do not belong to the category of the spiritual in the Cartesian sense of non-spatial, unextended. The category itself is conceptually inadmissible in this system of thought. Should the reader be curious at this stage as to whether mind too is quasi-material in the Akan way of thinking, the short answer is that mind is not thought of as an entity at all but rather simply as the *capacity,* supervenient upon brain states and processes, to do various things.[11] Hence the question whether mind is a spiritual or material or quasi-material entity does not arise.

The Akan world view, then, involves no sharp ontological cleavages such as the Cartesian dichotomy of the material and the spiritual; what difference in nature there is between ordinary material things and those extrahuman beings and forces so often called "spirits" in the literature is the difference between the fully material and the partially material. I ought, by the way, to stress that the absence of the spiritual, in the metaphysical sense, from the

Akan conceptual framework, does not imply the absence of spirituality, in the popular sense, from Akan life. In the latter sense spirituality is sensitivity to the less gross aspects of human experience.

But let us return to the class of quasi-material entities. A legitimate question is whether there is adequate evidence that such entities exist. Actually, this is not a question which faces Akan thought alone. All cultures, East, West, and Central, abound in stories of quasi-material goings-on. In the West, investigating the veridicality and theoretical explicability of such stories is one of the main concerns of parapsychology. In Africa there are any number of people who would be willing to bet their lives on the reality of such things, on the basis, reputedly, of first-hand experience. Basically, the issue is an empirical one, though probably not completely, for if such phenomena were to be definitively confirmed, their explanation would be likely to have conceptual reverberations. Speaking for myself, I would say that neither in Africa nor elsewhere have I seen compelling evidence of such things, though dogmatism would be ill-advised. At all events, it is worth noting that the plausibility of specific quasi-material claims tends to dwindle in the face of advancing scientific knowledge, a consideration which any contemporary African would need to take to heart.

It is, however, interesting to note that the waning, in Africa, of belief in extra-material entities and forces would leave the indigenous orientation thoroughly empirical, for the African world view—at any rate, the Akan one— makes room for only material and quasi-material existents. The contrary seems to be the case in the West. Here any reduction in quasi-material beliefs has not resulted automatically in gains for empirical thinking in the minds of a large mass of people; for, in addition to the categories of material and quasi-material, there is that of the spiritual, that is, the immaterial, which exercises the profoundest influence in philosophic and quasi-philosophic speculation. Not only is actual belief in immaterial entities widespread in the West, but the intelligibility of the material/immaterial contrast seems to be taken for granted even more widely. Moreover, in spite of the fact that, to say the least, quasi-material beliefs are not at all rare in the West, the tendency is for thinking to be governed by an exclusive disjunction of the material with the immaterial. Thus, for many, though of course, not everybody, in the West, if a thing is not supposed to be material, it is necessarily immaterial. The Europeans who imposed on themselves the "burden" of bringing "salvation" to the souls of the peoples of Africa certainly had this particular "either/or" fixation. Consequently, those of them who made sympathetic, though not necessarily empathetic, studies of African thought could not but formulate their results in terms of that and cognate schemes of thought. A visible outcome of their assiduous evangelism is the great *flock* of faithful African converts who think in the same language, proudly attributing to their own peoples belief in sundry things spiritual and supernatural.

Yet, not only is the notion of the spiritual unintelligible within a thought system such as that of the Akans, but it also is objectively a very problematic one. One searches in vain for a useful definition of the spiritual. The sum total of the information available from Cartesian and many other spiritually dedicated sources is that the spiritual is that which is nonmaterial. But definition by pure negation, such as this, brings little enlightenment. The word "that" in the definition suggests that one is envisaging some *sort* of referent, but this possibility of reference is given absolutely no grounding. How are we to differentiate between the spiritual and the void, for instance? Some negative definitions can be legitimate, but only if their context provides suitable information. In the present case the context seems to be a veritable void.

An even more unfortunate definition of the spiritual than the foregoing is sometimes encountered.[12] It is explained that the spiritual is the unperceivable, the invisible, or, to adapt a phrase of Saint Paul, the unseen. The problem with this definition is not its apparent negativeness, for the conditions of unperceivability are concrete enough; the problem is that it is so broad as to make gravity, for example, spiritual. It is, of course, not going to help to protest that although gravity is unseen, its effects are seen and felt, for exactly the same is what is claimed for the spiritual. Nor would it be of greater avail to add the condition of non-spatiality to that of invisibility, for something like the square root of 4 is neither spatial nor visible, and yet one wonders how spiritual it is. Of the material/spiritual (immaterial) dichotomy, then, we can say the following: It is not a universal feature of human thinking, since the Akans, at least, do not use it. And, in any case, its coherence is questionable. It is not to be assumed, though, that if a mode of conceptualization is universal among humankind, then it is, for that reason, objectively valid. Belief in quasi-material entities, for example, seems to be universal among cultures (though not among all individuals), but the chances are that the concepts involved denote nothing.

After all the foregoing the reader is unlikely to be surprised to learn that the idea of creation out of nothing also does not make sense in the Akan framework of thinking. Avenues to that concept are blocked in Akan land from the sides both of the concept of creation and of nothingness. To take the latter first: Nothingness in the Akan language is relative to location. The idea is expressed as the absence of anything at a given location, *se whee nni ho,* literally, the circumstance of there not being something there. Note here the reappearance of the locative conception of existence. If you subtract the locative connotation from this construal of nothingness, you have exactly nothing left, that is, nothing of the conception remains in your understanding.

The concept of creation in the Akan language is similarly non-transcendent. To create is to *bo,* and the most self-explanatory word in Akan for the creator is *Obooade*. *Ade* means "thing," and *bo* means "to make" in the sense of "to fashion out," which implies the use of raw materials. Any claim to *bo* an *ade* without the use of absolutely any raw material would sound decidedly self-contradictory in the language. Thus the Akan Supreme Being is a maker of things, but not out of nothing; so that if the word "Creator" is used for Him, it should be clearly understood that the concept of creation involved is fundamentally different from that involved in, say, orthodox Christian talk of creation. The Akan creator is the architect of the world order, but not the *ex nihilo* inventor of its stuff.

Interestingly, even within Western philosophy the concept of *ex nihilo* creation was not in the conceptual vocabulary of some of the greatest thinkers. It is well known, for example, that neither Plato nor Aristotle made use of any such concept. Of course, whether it is intelligible is a separate question. On the face of it, at least, there are tremendous paradoxes in that concept, and unless its exponents can offer profound clarifications, its absence from a conceptual framework can hardly be taken as a mark of insufficiency. Be that as it may, it is clear that the word "creation" should not be used in the context of Akan cosmology without due caution. It should be apparent also that considerable semantic circumspection is called for in using the word "God" for the Akan Supreme Being. Any transcendental inferences from that usage are misplaced.

So, then, we have the following picture of the outlook of the Akans. They believe in a Supreme Being, but they do not worship Him. Moreover, for conceptual reasons, this being cannot be said to be a spiritual or supernatural being. Nor is He a creator out of nothing. Furthermore, the foundations of Akan ethical life and thought have no necessary reference to Him. It will be recalled also that although the Akans believe in the existence of a whole host of extrahuman beings and forces, they view these as regular resources of the world order which can be exploited for good or, sometimes, for ill, given appropriate knowledge and the right approach. To all this we might add the fact that the customary procedures in Akan society pertaining to important stages in life, such as naming, marriage, and death, which are well-structured, elaborate, and highly cherished as providing concrete occasions for the manifestation of communal caring and solidarity, have no necessary involvement with the belief in the Supreme Being. These considerations, by the way, explain why some early European students of African cosmology called the African God an absentee God. In my opinion those visitors to Africa had their finger on something real, but the pejorative tenor of the observation can only be put down to a universalistic conceit. As for the ancestors, they are called upon to come and participate in all important ceremonies, but as revered members of the family, not as gods.

If we now renew the question of the applicability of the concept of religion to any aspect of Akan culture, we must be struck by the substantial differences between the Akan setup of cosmological and moral ideas viewed in relation to practical life, on the one hand, and Western conceptions of reality and the good life viewed in the same relation. For the purpose of this discussion the most important disparity revolves around the slicing up of human experience into the categories of the religious and the secular. To start from the Western end of the comparison: Whether we interpret the concept of the religious in a supernatural or non-supernatural sense, it is not a simple matter to discover an analogue of it in the traditional Akan context.

It might be thought that there is substantial common ground between Akan life and thought and that of, say, the Christian religion, since, even if the Akan *Nyame* is not thought of as supernatural, He is still regarded as in some sense the author of the world and determiner of its destiny. But conceptions or beliefs that do not dovetail into the fabric of practical life can hardly constitute a religion in the primary sense.

That the belief in *Nyame* has no essential role in the conduct of Akan life can be seen from a little exercise of the imagination. Imagine the belief in *Nyame* to be altogether removed from the Akan consciousness. What losses will be incurred in terms of sustenance for any institutions or procedures of practical life? The answer is "Exactly zero." Customs and moral rules relating to the critical (or even noncritical) stages and circumstances in the lives of individuals do not have their basis in the belief in *Nyame*. The same is true of the institutions of traditional Akan public life. Thus neither the pursuit of moral virtue and noble ideals by individuals nor the cooperative endeavors of the community toward the common good can be said to stand or fall with the belief in *Nyame;* they all have a solid enough basis in considerations of human well-being, considerations, in other words, which are completely "this-worldly."

To elaborate a little on this last point: To the traditional Akan what gives meaning to life is usefulness to self, family, community, and the species.[13] Nothing transcending life in human society and its empirical conditions enters into the constitution of the meaning of life. In particular, there is not, in Akan belief (in contrast, for instance, to Christian belief), any notion of an afterlife of possible salvation and eternal bliss; what afterlife there is thought to be is envisaged very much on the model of this life, as previously hinted. More importantly, that afterlife is not pictured as a life of eternal fun for the immortals but rather as one of eternal vigilance—vigilance over the affairs of the living with the sole purpose of promoting their well-being within the general constraints of Akan ethics. Indeed, this is what is taken to give meaning to their survival. From everything said (to my knowledge) about the ancestors, they are generally believed never to relent in this objective, which is one reason why they are held in such high esteem. The inhabitants of the world of the dead, then, are themselves thoroughly "this-worldly" in their orientation, according to Akan traditional conceptions.

Basically the same considerations would seem to discourage attributing to the Akans any sort of non-supernaturalistic religiosity. One great difficulty would be how to articulate such a notion within the Akan conceptual framework. Suppose we construe religion as life and thought impregnated by a sense of the sacred. Then, since the primary meaning of the word "sacred" presupposes some conception of deity, we would be duty-bound to give some notification of a broadening of meaning. Accordingly, the sacred might be understood as that in ethical life most worthy of respect, reverence, and commitment. But this, in turn, would presuppose a system of values and ideals, and, in the case of the Akans, would bring us back to their irreducibly "this-worldly" ethic. Now, the remarkable thing is that in this ethic a demonstrated basic commitment to the values and ideals of the society is a component of the very concept of a person. An individual is not a person in the fullest sense unless he or she has shown a responsiveness to those ideals in confirmed habits of life. Not, of course, that an individual failing this test is denuded of human rights, for every individual, simply on the grounds of being human, is regarded as a center of quite extensive rights (see chapter 12). On the other hand, there is a prestige attached to the status of personhood, or more strictly, superlative personhood—for indeed, the status is susceptible of degrees to which all Akans of sound mind aspire. But this is simply the aspiration to become a responsible individual in society, an individual who, through intelligent thinking, judicious planning, and hard work, is able to carve out an adequate livelihood for himself or herself and family and make significant contributions to the well-being of the community. The problem now is that if this is what in the specific context of Akan culture, living a life informed by a sense of the sacred means, then applying the concept of religion to it would scarcely pick out anything in the culture corresponding to what in, say, Western culture might be called a non-supernaturalistic religion. In Western society there are historical as well as conceptual reasons why one might want to organize one's life on the lines of what might be called a non-supernaturalist religion. In Akan society there are really none. In the West, loss of the belief in God, for example, usually results in disengagement from certain well-known institutions and practices. (Think, for example, of the role of Christian marriage or religious funerals in Western society.) The consequent psychological and social void might be filled for some by a "non-theistic" religion. In the Akan situation, on the other hand, no such void is to be anticipated from a comparable belief mutation. Speaking from my own experience, failure to retain the belief in *Nyame*—I make no mention here of the Christian God, the conception of whom registers no coherent meaning upon my understanding—has caused me not the slightest alienation from any of the institutions or practices of Akan culture.

Not unexpectedly, what has cost me some dissonance with the culture is my skepticism regarding the continued existence of our ancestors. The pouring of libation, for example, as previously indicated, is a practice in which the Akans call upon the ancestors to come and participate in important functions and lend their good auspices to any enterprise launched. This is an important and not infrequent ceremony in Akan life. But obviously, if one does not believe that the ancestors are actually there, one cannot pretend to call them, or, what is the same thing, one can only pretend to do so. I cannot personally, therefore, participate in a custom like this with any total inwardness. In this, by the way, I do not stand alone. Any Akan Christian—and there are great numbers of them—is logically precluded from believing such things as the Akan doctrine of ancestors, for it does not cohere with Christian eschatology. As far as I am concerned, however, there is a saving consideration. This custom of libation, and many other customs of like quasi-material basis, can be retained by simply reinterpreting the reference to the ancestors as commemoration rather than invocation. That, of course, would entail obvious verbal reformulations, but it should present no problem. What of customs that prove not to be susceptible to such revisions in the face of advancing skepticism? One hopes that they would eventually be abandoned. The culture is rich enough not to incur any real existential deficit from such a riddance, nor is the atrophy of custom under the pressure of changing times at all rare in the history of culture.

Be that as it may, the fact remains that, as already argued, the Akan belief in the existence and power of such beings as the ancestors, and the procedures associated with that belief, do not constitute a religion in any reliable sense. We are now, therefore, brought to the following conclusion: The concept of religion is not unproblematically applicable within all cultures, and Akan culture is a case in point.[14] Nevertheless, there may be some justification for speaking of Akan religion in a broadened sense of the word "religion."[15] In this sense the word would refer simply to the fact that the Akans believe in *Nyame*, a being regarded as the architect of the world order. Certainly, this is an extremely attenuated concept of religion. As pointed out already, religion in the fullest sense, whether it be supernaturalistic or not, is not just a set of beliefs and conceptions, but also a way of life based on those ideas. What we have seen, however, is that the Akan way of life is not based on the belief in *Nyame*. Hence, if we do use the word "religion" in the Akan context on the grounds of the belief in *Nyame*, we should evince some consciousness of the fact that we have made a considerable extension of meaning, otherwise we propagate a subtle misunderstanding of Akan and cognate cultures under the apparently widespread illusion that religion is a cultural universal.

Yet, surely, something must be universal. Consider the ease with which Christian missionaries have been able to convert large masses of Africans to Christianity by relaying to them "tidings" which are in some important parts

most likely conceptually incoherent or, at any rate, incongruous with categories deeply embedded in indigenous ways of thinking. To be sure, it cannot be
assumed that in the large majority of cases conversion has been total in terms
of moral and cosmological outlook. Still, there are impressive enough numbers of African converts, some in the high reaches of ecclesiastical authority,
whose understanding of and dedication to the Christian religion challenges
the severest comparisons among even the most exalted practitioners of the
same faith in the West. I take this as testimony to the malleability of the human
mind, which enables the various peoples of the world to share not only their
insights but also their incoherences. This characteristic of the mind, being
fundamental to the human status, makes our common humanity the one
universal which potentially transcends all cultural particularities.

6

Custom and Morality

A Comparative Analysis of Some African and Western Conceptions of Morals

Contemporary African experience is marked by a certain intellectual anomaly. The African today, as a rule, lives in a cultural flux characterized by a confused interplay between an indigenous cultural heritage and a foreign cultural legacy of a colonial origin. Implicated at the deepest reaches of this cultural amalgam is the superimposition of Western conceptions of the good upon African thought and conduct. The issues involved here are of the utmost existential urgency, for it may well be that many of the instabilities of contemporary African society are traceable to this circumstance.

But first, to fundamentals. Rules are absolutely essential to human communities. At the very least there must be some linguistic rules—rules of syntax and semantics—for without some interaction you do not have the communion implied by the concept of community, and without language you do not have the communication presupposed by human interaction. Only a little reflection is required to see that there also has to be a whole host of other kinds of rules for defining, regulating and facilitating interactions and relationships. For example, if we drive, we must have traffic rules; if we buy and sell, we must have rules not only to regulate these activities but also to define them in the first place. And so on, indefinitely.

The mention of rules of traffic and of commerce naturally brings to mind the concept of law. Laws are promulgated or acknowledged rules that are enforced or, at least, intended to be enforced by a recognized authority having sanctions, usually physical force, at its disposal. Laws are, of course, a feature of the *modus operandi* of governments. But there are other, more informal, rules such as are prescribed by custom, tradition, convention, fashion, and etiquette. Most likely, any human society will have rules of this sort whether or not it is organized in the manner of political governance. There is still, however, one category of rules of the most extreme importance to human society that we have not mentioned so far, at least, not explicitly. This is the category of moral rules. Morality and law do intersect, for some laws are simply moral rules formalized and backed up with the authority of the state. But there are also laws that are clearly not moral rules. Think of traffic rules, for example.

The question now is: How may we distinguish between moral rules and all the rest? This question is important because moral rules seem to have an *intrinsic* obligatoriness which is lacking in other kinds of rules. In warming up toward an answer, it would perhaps help if we cleared up some points of usage. The word "moral" and its cognates are frequently used with such broad signification as to cover matters that might also be brought under custom, tradition, or even convention, all of which, for the sake of conceptual economy, might be called simply custom. Thus, in discussing the morals of a given people one might mention such things as their rules of marriage and sex conduct generally, their manner of organizing mutual aid, their way of defining and evaluating success in life, their system of reward and punishment, and so forth. Considerations of this kind should certainly reveal a lot about their values, but the point is that not all those values would be moral values.

Consider some particulars. Among the Akans of Ghana a value is placed on beauty of speech that might well appear extraordinary to other people. Beauty of speech here refers not just to beauty of delivery but also, and more particularly, to a characteristic of speech deriving from both logical and rhetorical factors. Beautiful speech is one that develops a coherent and persuasive argument, clinching points—and this is crucial—with striking and decisive proverbs. Anybody not possessed of such a tongue can forget any ambitions of high office at the court of a traditional Akan ruler. There is, surely, nothing immoral in adhering to much less proverbial criteria for this kind of recruitment.

Or consider a somewhat simpler case. In Akan society one just does not address a person or group without first greeting them. Failure to observe this rule is regarded as a very serious lapse from good behavior. Persistent default will cost any individual her or his reputation. A related rule is this. If in the course of greeting people one has occasion to shake hands with or wave to more than one person, one absolutely must always proceed from right to left. Again, nonconformity is regarded as an error so grave as to be capable of radically compromising a person's standing in the society. These rules are motivated by values which are not universal, either generically or in terms of degree; they can hardly be called moral rules.

This should become apparent from the following thought experiment. Compare any of the rules just mentioned with the rule of truth-telling. One cannot contemplate the latter for any length of time without a renewed sense of its unconditional imperativeness. An Akan living in Akanland is expected, as a matter of course, to observe, for example, Akan rules of greeting. It goes without saying that other people living in other lands need not feel any such obligation. On the other hand, whether you are a Ghanaian or an American or a Chinese or of any other nationality, race or culture, truth-telling is an indefeasible obligation. To trifle with such an imperative is, quite plainly, to be immoral in a very strict sense. It seems, then, that if we could elucidate the unconditional or universal obligatoriness of moral rules, we would be able to make at least a start at drawing an illuminating distinction between rules of conduct that are moral in the strict sense and those that are not moral or are so only by courtesy of some linguistic idiom.

In this project it might be useful to start with another thought experiment. Let us revert to the rule of truth-telling and ask ourselves if we can imagine any circumstances in which it might be feasible to base conduct in human society on its reversal. To so much as pose this question is to realize that the answer must be "No!" Any such situation would be a situation of the breakdown of human community; for if truth-telling were, by open common avowal, not binding, and everybody could tell lies without let or hindrance, no one could depend on anyone's word, and social life would become intolerably Hobbesian. By contrast, it is a visible fact that life without rules like the Akan rules of greeting mentioned above is not intolerable. This suggests the following condition for the identification of moral rules in the strict sense: A rule of conduct is not a moral rule unless its non-existence or reversal would bring about the collapse of human community.

It should be observed that the kind of contra-truth-telling situation which we imagined a moment ago is not merely one in which many people tell lies in various circumstances. This, unfortunately, is the actual state of affairs in which we all live, move, and have our struggles. On the contrary, the imagined scenario is the more drastic one in which, to use Kantian language, the maxim "Tell lies whenever convenient" has become a universal rule of conduct. Apart from flirting a little with Kantian terminology, there is an obvious formal analogy between our emerging characterization of moral rules and Kant's use of his "categorical imperative" to the same purpose. In one formulation the principle of the categorical imperative says, "Act only on that maxim through which you can at the same time will that it should become a universal law." Now, for Kant the decisive consideration is that one cannot *consistently* will the maxim of an action which is contrary to good morals to be universalized. This elevation of pure consistency in the realm of morals is quite germane, but still insufficient as the foundation of morals. If it were, the principle of non-contradiction would be the supreme law of morals, but it is not.

It is important, however, to note that the principle of non-contradiction satisfies the condition so far specified for moral rules. Certainly, if that principle were to be generally and studiously discarded—a scale of non-compliance not dreamt of by even the most enthusiastic paraconsistentist—there would no longer be any such thing as a human community, for communication would become impossible; and without communication, as we earlier saw, there is no human community. It follows that the condition in question is not a sufficient condition for a rule being a moral rule but only a necessary one.

How, then, may we attain sufficiency in the characterization of the rules of morality? What we need is, I think, to exhibit the necessary connection between morality and human interests. This connection almost leaps into the eye when we consider what sort of motivation might lead an individual to break a rule such as that of truth-telling. This can only be the desire of the individual to pursue his or her own interests in deliberate indifference to the interests of others. Its short name is selfishness. The point becomes even more clear if we take concrete examples of moral imperatives such as "Do not steal" or "Do not pursue your neighbor's wife." It must dawn on us, from such considerations, that the rationale of a moral rule is the harmonization of the interests of the individual with the interests of others in society, and its motivation the sympathetic appreciation of those interests, a frame of mind which facilitates the mind's ability to contemplate with equanimity the possible abridgement of one's own interests in deference to the interests of others. The rationale discloses the objective, and the motivation the subjective, aspects of morals; both aspects are essential to the constitution of morality. And this accounts for the important distinction between scrupulous action and a merely prudential one. An individual is not deserving of moral approbation merely because he did something which promotes the requisite harmony of interests; he has to have done it in the requisite spirit.

This last remark must again remind us of Kant. The sage insisted that doing your duty is not morally meritorious unless it is done out of respect for duty. But our depiction of morals also has an un-Kantian implication. Kant spurned any suggestion that human well-being could be the motto of the moral life. On the other hand, by our lights, human well-being is an irreducible presupposition of all morality. Not, of course, that every quest for human well-being is a moral enterprise; but every moral endeavor is a certain kind of quest for human well-being. It is the kind which seeks its objective through the empathetic harmonization of human interests.[1] Empathetic or not, a certain minimum of harmonization of interests is indispensable to any tolerable form of human social existence. Hence morality, at least on its objective side, is humanly essential. Herein lies the universal obligatoriness of moral rules.

Perhaps no one can be the ultimate authority on the origins of his opinions, but I find these thoughts on the necessary connection between morality and human well-being totally attuned to the moral thinking pervasive in the culture in which I was born and raised, the culture of the Akans of Ghana. The first axiom of all Akan axiological thinking is that man or woman is the measure of all value (*Onipa na ohia*). And every Akan maxim about the specifically moral values that I know, explicitly or implicitly, postulates the harmonization of interests as the means, and the securing of human well-being as the end, of all moral endeavor.

On the strength of the last remark we may characterize Akan ethics as humanistic. In this, of course, the Akans are not unique. There are humanistic strands in Western ethical thought, too. But it is significant to note that there is also in the West, in contrast to the situation in Akan thought, a highly influential tradition of ethical supernaturalism. Indeed, if you take account of popular as well technical thought, it may justly be said that the dominant bent of Western ethics is non-humanistic. I hasten to point out that I use the word 'non-humanistic' as the strict contradictory of 'humanistic' in the sense just indicated. I do not mean 'non-humanistic' in the sense of wicked, or anything like that. As for wickedness, I suspect that, by and large, it is evenly distributed among all the different tribes of humankind. It is, besides, worthy of note that not all non-humanistic ethics in the West is supernaturalistic. Kant's ethics, for example, is sharply non-humanistic; he expressly disavows any *necessary* connection between morality and human interests. Yet, his conception of morality is equally sharply non-supernaturalistic. He defines moral worth purely by the lights of human reason, in terms of respect for the categorical imperative. God, indeed, has a place in the total scheme of Kant's ethics, but only as the legislative and executive source of compensation, in the afterlife, for virtue unrequited in this life. God's very existence, incidentally, is ("from a practical point of view") established—believe it or not—by the alleged necessity of this eschatological compensation. As distinct from this kind of logically extrinsic status for God in ethics, ethical supernaturalism bases the very essence of morality on the will of God. On that view, what is morally right is, by definition, what is in accord with the will of God. This view of ethics is particularly popular, though not universal, among Christians. I have already remarked on its absence from Akan ethical thinking and will return to the point in due course.

Meanwhile, there is a judicious flexibility in humanistic ethics to which attention should be called at this point. It consists in the fact that from such an ethical standpoint it is easy to see that, although moral rules are uncondi-tionally imperative, they are not necessarily exceptionless. Probably everyone has had his or her moral imagination teased by the following classical poser: What do you do if confronted by a sword-brandishing psychopath who inquires of your mother's whereabouts with the unambiguous purpose of promptly hacking her to pieces? By virtual common consent, moral upright-ness does not require sacrificing your mother on the altar of truth-telling under this kind of duress. But on non-humanistic premisses it is not clear why. On the other hand, if the moral end is the even-handed securing of human interests, then some tempering of the truth in the harrowing encounter imagined is easily recognized as a rational adjustment of principle to special circumstance. The reason why such an adjustment does not smack of opportunistic casuistry is that it is obvious that everybody's interests are, on the whole, best served by withholding the truth in question from a lunatic on the rampage. It might be said, accordingly, that what we have here is only an exception to the rule of truth-telling, not an overturning of it; and if the exception proves this rule, it is because in the very act of seeming to evade it we are, in fact, reaffirming its rationale. It emerges, by an obvious generalization, that moral rules are susceptible to exceptions but not to reversal, and the admissible exceptions can only be ones that uphold their rationale.

In Western philosophy Kant is certainly one of the thinkers who had the strongest sense of the irreversibility of moral rules. But he seems to have conflated this irreversibility with exceptionlessness. He thus made himself an uninviting exception to the apparent consensus in regard to the permissibility of telling a lie to save one's mother in the terrible situation visualized a moment ago. As is well known, he earnestly maintained, in the teeth of this specific example, that one is duty-bound to yield the truth, come what maniac may. I cannot help suspecting that the powerful mind of Kant was trapped into so irrational an inflexibility by the dead weight of his non-humanistic approach to ethics.

But this is speculation. Let us return to the question of the distinction between custom and morality, this time more concretely. In the light of the foregoing discussion it is clear that, for example, the Akan rule of greeting mentioned earlier is a rule of custom rather than of morality, strictly speaking. It is not unimportant on that account, but it lacks the unconditional obligatoriness of a moral rule; an honest person can envisage its absence from human social intercourse with composure. It is only putting the same point in different words to say that the obligatoriness of custom may be relative to a particular culture or society or to an even lesser grouping. Perhaps this might be called a form of relativism. If so, it will have to be recognized as a rather limited and atypical form of relativism which does not really conform to the acceptation of that word, for it does not rule out the possibility that the rationale of a custom might become interculturally appreciated when once it has been situated in the context of its own habitat.

However, the question of rationale does not always arise in connection with custom. It would seem that some customs originate in accidental or even subconscious circumstances. It may well be, for example, that the unique set of phonetic articulations used in a particular language out of the myriads of possibilities owes its origins to a process in which, as Ruth Benedict suggests in her classic "Anthropology and the Abnormal,"[2] accidental and subconscious factors play a decisive role. In regard to customs of such accidental origins, which are, I think, more important in the differentiation of cultures than the cross-culturally explicable ones, propriety or impropriety is even more strikingly relative to culture.

As an example of a cross-culturally intelligible custom, consider the rule of respect for elders. Probably every culture enjoins it with some degree of urgency. But the differences of degree from one society to another in this continuum of urgency can be extremely significant. One of the Ten Commandments says, "Honor thy father and thy mother: that thy days may be long upon the land which the Lord thy God giveth thee" (Exodus 20:12). From other Bible stories, such as, for example, the story of the fate that befell the mischievous infants who made fun of an old man who seemed to be making heavy weather of walking up a trivial hill (the Almighty dispatched wild beasts to devour them) one may safely generalize the quoted commandment into a pretty rigorous requirement of respect for those of ripe age. Now, this particular imperative is a major feature of the traditional Akan ethic. In this respect, therefore, there is an obvious similarity between Akan morals and the morals of ancient Judea, from where both the commandment and the story originate. In this same respect, however, there is a noticeable dissimilarity between the dictates of Akan and Judean morality, on the one hand, and those of, say, American morality on the other. Notice, by the way, that in this paragraph I have used the concept of morals in its broad signification.

To return to the comparison of morals, it cannot be said, of course, that people are not expected to respect their elders in the United States. But the fact is that the deference that is considered to be due to age in Akan traditional society is much greater than is required in the American social environment. The difference is, indeed, so great that one might almost call it one of kind rather than of degree. In consequence, one can foresee quite serious disparities in the moral characterization of relevant actions, reactions and attitudes. Thus a traditional Akan elder freshly transported into American society would be likely to find the attitude of American youth to their elders to be marked, or more strictly, marred, by an unbearable offhandedness; while, for their part, American youth in a converse shift of environment would be likely to feel that traditional Akan society demands nothing short of grovelling docility from the young in their relations with the old.

This difference is, in fact, easy to understand. Traditional Akan society, as, presumably, its Judean counterpart, was a society in which science, technology, and industry had not reached any very high level of development. In such societies knowledge is likely to be, on the whole, more a possession of the old than of the young. Prestige and influence will naturally go along with knowledge, more especially, knowledge of a practical kind. Under such conditions the high respect accorded to age is not gratuitous. The position is apt, however, to change in a highly industrialized, technological society. Respect for age is still in place, but it is unlikely to reach the high levels obtaining in a traditional society; nor, in view of the all-too-human tendency to over-compensation in major transitions of outlook, will it always reach a reasonable level.

In all this what is of crucial significance is that the differences noted, whatever their explanation, appertain to custom rather than morality in the narrow sense. To repeat, this observation does not imply any diminution in the importance of custom as such. Still less does it imply that customs are necessarily inaccessible to transcultural evaluation from either a moral or utilitarian standpoint. Morality, in particular, can override anything, saving only its own rationale. Nevertheless, it is of the last consequence to realize that the merits or demerits of a particular custom may be independent of any specifically moral considerations. Many customs are, indeed, designed to achieve the well-being of given societies, and we may suppose that some do actually succeed in this. But in itself, this is not a moral fact. Furthermore, there is plenty of room for variability in the efficacy of customs. A custom that is good in one society may be the contrary in another. Or it may be good in a given society at a given time without being so in a changed era. Thus, for the same sorts of reasons as those previously rehearsed, the high respect demanded for age in Akan traditional society is giving rise to inter-generational tensions in contemporary semi-industrialized Akan society.

This susceptibility to being overtaken by changing time, place, or circumstance is one of the marks of custom as distinct from morality. Yet, because there is, as already remarked, a broad concept of morality within which custom is a moral topic, it has been easy for some students of the great variety of customs among the different cultures of the world to conclude that all morality is *relative* in the specific sense that moral rightness consists in being approved by a given culture, society, group, or epoch. This, of course, is an egregious error. Even with respect to custom there are quite definite limits to relativity. Any custom that leads to needless suffering, for example, is bad wherever and whenever it exists. True, it may not be easy to show that a particular instance of suffering is needless, for the issue may be entangled in the web of a complex system of cosmological beliefs. But it is a fact of history that even the most entrenched belief-systems can change under the pressure of recalcitrant facts.

An interesting thing about the confusion of the norms of custom, which may be relative to time, place, or circumstance, with the norms of morality, which are not, is that it has two sides of opposite attractions. The first consists in treating morality as if it is of a piece with custom, while the second consists in treating custom as if it is of a piece with morality. The relativist wades into the error by the first side, while a sanctimonious anti-relativist is apt to tumble into the same error by the second.

Relativism seems to be enjoying something of a revival in recent philosophy. This is not due to any intrinsic intellectual merit of that standpoint. It is due, I think, to the fact that, ironically, anti-relativism is liable, through a certain adulteration of logic with psychology, to be transformed into some form of authoritarian absolutism, which turns off many intellectuals who have their hearts in the right place. The transformation is roughly like this. From the fact that morality is not relative to culture or circumstance, it is inferred that it is not dependent on anything human. The way is then open to the anti-relativist, full of a sense of the importance of morals, to suppose that morality is only correctly conceived from a divine or some suitably Olympian perspective. The thinker or non-thinker who thus aligns himself with a point of view so infinitely superior to any merely human point of view easily gains a sense of infallibility (by association) in his own self-perception. Accordingly, his own norms of conduct are seen as ineluctable models of the right and the good in the sphere of all morals. The divergent ways of life of other individuals or peoples, except perhaps the most inconsequential, are therefore wrong, immoral, impermissible; they constitute an execrable affront to righteousness. It should now be clear how anti-relativism, ill conceived, can become a particularly insidious enemy of that open-mindedness in the face of the diversity of ways of life among the different peoples of the world which cultural pluralism seeks to foster.

Two misidentifications are touched upon, explicitly or implicitly, in this diagnosis. There is the misidentification of the point of view of morality with some transcendent point of view, and there is the misidentification of good conduct with moral uprightness. I shall return to the first in more concrete terms later. Let me try, at this stage, to bring some concrete observations to bear on the second. It may be conceded at once, in apparent mitigation of the grossness of the error here in question, that it is not always easy to distinguish between custom and morality in specific cases. A particular case which is of considerable intercultural interest is the question of the legitimacy or illegitimacy of polygamy. It is well known that in Africa and some other parts of the world polygamy is regarded as a legitimate marriage arrangement. On the other hand, the Christian missionaries who came to Africa to "save" our souls, perceiving the practice to be incompatible with their own norms of good conduct, condemned it as immoral and worked assiduously to eradicate it. They have had a measure of success in this. But there has been a certain superficiality about that success which has been responsible for a kind of ethical schizophrenia in the consciousness of many of our people. However sincere the African convert has been in his avowal of the foreign faith, he has too often not been able to erase from all the recesses of his consciousness a predisposition to many of the cultural habits ingrained in him in the course of his domestic and community socialization. As a result, many noble and pious Africans have been known to operate a subtle compromise of an official monogamy supplemented with informal but quite stable and demographically significant amorous relationships. Needless to say, the "pagan" sections of our populations have never been able to view this dual system of behavior as anything but a somewhat amusing form of emergency pragmatism.

Be that as it may, the question is: How are we to analyze this whole situation from the point of view of the philosophy of morals? If, in keeping with our earlier thought experiment, we consider whether circumstances are conceivable in which polygamy might come, everywhere, to be seen as a more reasonable connubial institution than monogamy, little imagination would be needed to conjure up a scenario to motivate an affirmative answer. Suppose, for example, that by some unanticipated combination of persisting causes women were to come to outnumber men by, say, fifty to one. Make it a hundred to one or worse, if you foresee greater resistance to the impending suggestion, which is that in such a state of affairs to insist on a policy of one-man one-wife would mean, as a matter of simple arithmetic, that the overwhelming majority of women will go through life in the most drastic sexual deprivation and, very probably, in deep emotional distress on account of the inevitable frustration of related instincts. Common decency would everywhere recommend polygamy or something substantially similar to that system under such conditions.

Or reverse the experiment. Imagine that, through equally inscrutable changes in the phenomena of our world, men come to outnumber women by the aforementioned factor. Then, by similar and perhaps more urgent considerations, good sense would urge an analogous revision of the marriage system: polyandry in place of monogamy! Rational flexibility would be more urgent in this hypothetical case than in the previous one if only because in the new circumstances, if the principle were to be pressed that only one man could be the recipient of all the married attentions of one woman, you could infallibly predict that the resultant sexual and emotional famine among men would quickly drive them to a war of all men against all men. An obvious general lesson here is that rules of conduct were made for man or woman, not the other way round; but a more particular lesson is that, purely in itself, the issue of polygamy versus its contraries is one of custom rather than morality in the strict sense.

Again, from this last point it cannot be inferred that polygamy enjoys any relativistic immunity from cross-cultural evaluation. On the contrary, it can still, in principle, be scrutinized from, at least, a utilitarian point of view. And, in any case, as a human institution, its actual operation by any given group of persons will undoubtedly generate moral issues. The point is that the self-righteous blanket denunciation of polygamy in Africa by the Christian missionaries was, if nothing else, oblivious to philosophical considerations of considerable practical import. In fact, polygamy, like monogamy to be sure, is open to all sorts of moral abuses from both sides of the relationship, and the Akans are extremely sensitive to this fact, as shown in their folklore. They have also been alive to the sociological implications of a changing economy. The generality of Akans have perceived that industrialization, even such as it has been, has brought in its trail conditions severely uncongenial to polygamy, and the practice is currently on the wane. Practical considerations rather than moralistic preachments are what have proved really decisive. And this is as it should be, having regard both to the true nature of the issue and the humanistic basis of the Akan outlook on the rules of human conduct.

Industrialization, by the way, has made a morally more debatable inroad into another aspect of the Akan ethic. The word "communalistic" might be used to characterize the bent of that ethic. This alludes to the fact that in that outlook the norms of morality are defined in terms of the adjustment of the interests of the individual to the interests of society, rather than the adjustment of the interests of society to those of the individual. The latter way of viewing morality may be taken to be characteristic of individualism. From a logical point of view, pure morality still remains a constant in this variation of outlook; for, however the adjustment of interests is arrived at, its actual existence satisfies the objective conditions of morality. But psychologically the accent on the community in a communalistic orientation can provide an added incentive to the moral motivation. Unfortunately, the apparent concomitants of industrialization are eroding this mechanism for the reinforcement of morals.

The most threatening circumstance in this regard is the urbanization that has attended industrialization. African residents of large cities no longer have the benefits of either the support or the sanctions of the system of caring that was the mainstay of traditional community life. The circles of obligations, rights, and privileges which radiated from the center of household relations of kinship to the larger circumferences of lineage and clan affinities provided a natural school for training in the practice of sympathetic impartiality which, in its most generalized form, is the root of all moral virtue. The integration of individuality into community in African traditional society is so thoroughgoing that, as is too rarely noted, the very concept of a person has a normative layer of meaning. A person is not just an individual of human parentage, but also one evincing in her projects and achievements an adequate sense of social responsibility.[3] Bereft of the traditional underpinnings of this sense of responsibility, the city dweller is left with nothing but his basic sense of human sympathy in his moral dealings with the great numbers of strangers encountered in and out of the work environment. The well-known crime rate in the cities is proof of the limited capabilities of that moral equipment. Thus, by and large, industrialization seems to be proving deleterious to that system of communal caring and solidarity which was a strong point of traditional communalism, and one of the greatest problems facing us in Africa is how to reap the benefits of industrialization without incurring the more unlovable of its apparent fallouts, such as the ethic of austere individualism.

When the Akan or, in general, the African traditional social outlook is described as communalistic it is usual to contrast it with that of Western society by calling it individualistic. There is a certain obvious anthropological validity in this comparison. But some riders are necessary. First, it should be repeated that this does not disclose a difference with respect to the actual content of morality. Aside from the difference in the manner of viewing the adjustment of interests required by morality, the real difference between communalism and individualism has to do with custom and lifestyle rather than anything else. Although the notion of custom tends to evoke imageries of social practice while lifestyle is more readily associated with individual lives, both are, conceptually, of a kind and are distinct from morality in the strict sense. While on this, it might be of some use to note that histories of Western ethics regularly allot generous space to certain classical portrayals of different lifestyles. Aristotle's treatments of ethics, for example, or the discourses of the epicureans and the stoics, consist largely of (reasoned) recommendations of particular lifestyles, and only deal with questions of pure morality when they touch, relatively briefly, on such topics as justice. Had our communalist forebears preserved in print their thoughts on the same range of subjects, we may be sure that mutual aid would have loomed larger in their meditations than most of the concerns of the classical moralists.

Second, the distinction between communalism and individualism is one of degree only; for a considerable value may be attached to communality in individualistic societies just as individuality is not necessarily trivialized within communalism. Finally, the two orientations can coexist in different sectors of the same society. Thus, for example, intimations of a communalist outlook are discernible in the lifestyles of the rural folks of individualistic America.

Perhaps the sphere of conduct in which the conflict between Akan morals and Western morality, or, more strictly, the Christian form of it, has been acutest is the sphere of sexual morality. Christianity, as it came to us in Africa through the missionaries, proscribed premarital sex as totally incompatible with morality. Contrast this with Akan conceptions of marriage. This is conceived of as a union in which the parties are a pair of individuals and their respective families, and the purpose is principally, though not exclusively, procreation. As such it is not a relationship lightly to be entered into.

Considerable mutual knowledge between both principals, including "carnal" knowledge, is regarded as a commonsensical requirement. Indeed, prior intimacy is viewed not only as educative but also as pragmatic. Akan men and women usually seek visible signs of fertility before committing themselves to the union in question. Thus, far from something like pregnancy before marriage being looked upon as a scandal, it is welcomed as an auspicious omen.

But a man does not just fall upon a woman and impregnate her on the off chance of a possible marriage. The thing is governed by rigorous and well-structured rules. A man who takes a comprehensive fancy to a woman, if his advances are reciprocated, has to reveal the fact to his own family and to the woman's. To the latter, he goes in due time in the company of his father with offerings of schnapps and a message of the following tenor: The man has been very strongly impressed with your daughter and would like to see a lot more of her. He has, in fact, been seeing her for a little while. This offering is only an earnest of his sentiments and intentions. All being well, he will come back later in due style. Meanwhile, he begs to suggest that if you look for her and you don't readily find her, you may check with him. Unless the woman's family, who, on their side, would already have done some research on the prospective suitor, have well-founded moral or medical objections to him, they will give their blessing to the association, knowing full well that the two will not stop short of sex, though, at this stage, there would be no absolute guarantee of marriage. Of course, if all goes well, the man will come again to seal the relationship with due ceremony.

On the other hand, if a man, heedless to custom, should unceremoniously put a woman in the family way—reckless individuals exist in all cultures—he would be declared to have "stolen" her, and would be liable to quite severe fines and concerted and equally severe reprimands from all concerned on both kinship sides. The premarital arrangements just recounted are, obviously, radically different from anything that was officially countenanced in orthodox Christian circles. Still, in light of our distinction between custom and morality, there is no question but that what we have here is merely two different customs. To the Christian authorities, however, the Akan system involved living in sin.

It is a fact, of course, that in the last three decades or so orthodox Christian precepts of premarital chastity have been massively overtaken by "permissive" practices in Western society. For the time being, however, the significant difference between the Akan and Christian milieus remains; for it makes sense to speak of permissiveness in this connection only in environments where there is a background of previously authoritative commandments to the contrary. In Akan society the practice in question is not permissive; it is the permitted. At all events this difference illustrates the kind of plurality of ways of life in the world which a reasonable mind ought to be able to contemplate without pique or panic.

So far we have not encountered any difference of morality in the strict sense between Akan and Western ways of life. This is not accidental. If the concern of morality is the harmonization of the interests of the individual with the interests of society, this is exactly what is to be expected; for none but the most brutish form of existence could be foreseen among any group of individuals who standardly disavowed and disregarded any such concerns. It is true that individuals and groups may differ in their degree of inclination or dedication to such aims; but this is a fact of practice, not of precept.

Nevertheless, without prejudice to the last reflection, there may be philo-sophically important differences in the ways in which various individuals, groups, or peoples conceive of morality in the strict sense; and I would like to comment on a difference of this sort between Akan and certain influential Western conceptions of morals. The Western intellectual situation is charac-terized by a great diversity of philosophic persuasions, and prudence dictates abstention from unqualified generalizations. Yet there is a certain recogniz-able meta-ethical orientation in some very important forms of Christian thinking which might approximately be called orthodox. This is the under-standing of ethics which sees its basis in religion. Certainly, the influence of this way of viewing morality is very pervasive in popular Christian thinking and is, surely, not unconnected with the semantical fact that the adjective "un-Christian" imputes some measure of moral degeneracy. That this way of thinking about morality is popular, even if not universal, in Western society is undoubtedly a noteworthy fact about Western moral thinking. And in any case, the Christian evangelism that was brought to Africa was of this outlook.

In regard to this notion of the dependence of morality on religion, we encounter a rather striking contrast, for it does not even make sense in the Akan context. This brings us back to some matters previously touched upon, namely, the antithesis in ethics between humanism, on the one hand, and anti-humanism with its sub-species of supernaturalism, on the other. As noted earlier, in Akan thought what is moral is, by definition, what promotes the well-being of society by way of the harmonization of interests. Logically, the existence of God is irrelevant to the essence of morality as so conceived. It is, indeed, a fact that the Akans, like *most* other African peoples, believe in the existence of a Supreme Being, who might be called God, provided this nomenclature is not taken to imply an identity of attributes with the Christian God. This Supreme Being is regarded as supremely good; but, from the Akan point of view, it would be compounding ambiguity with obscurity to suggest that "good" here means anything other than what it means in mundane semantics. In particular, to say that "morally good" means "in conformity with the will of God" would leave it *logically* possible that the morally good could conceivably be at variance with the harmonious ordering of human interests, a veritable contradiction in Akan terms. Yet in orthodox Christianity, specifically this is the kind of dependence that morality is supposed to have on religion. The relation is not merely a motivational dependence; it is a conceptual one: moral rightness connotes accordance with the will of God.

The only area of Akan thinking where any kind of rightness or wrongness is defined in this sort of way (that is, in terms of the will of an extra-human being) is the area of taboo. A taboo is a prohibition expressing the dislike of some extra-human being believed capable of punishing non-compliance with disasters, sometimes quite severe and widespread. The idea here is that what a taboo prohibits is *ipso facto* bad; it is not supposed to be prohibited because it is bad, rather it is regarded as bad solely because it is thus prohibited.

Two observations are urgent at this point. First, in view of the humanistic conception of morals in Akan thinking, any concept of badness defined in terms of taboo falls outside the pale of morality in the strict sense. Second, there is evidence to suggest that taboo is not an irreducible category in the Akan system of norms of conduct. It is arguable that the taboos are a pedagogical expedient designed by our sages of old to concentrate ordinary minds on the path of desirable behavior.

Consider two frequently cited taboos of Akan society. One is, "Do not work your farm on Thursdays," and the other, "Never have sex in the bush." The taboo-style explanation of the first is that Thursday is the day after which the earth goddess is named. Her name is Asaase Yaa. The word *Asaase* means the earth, and *Yaa* is the first name given to any female born on Thursday. Thus the two words together mean something like "Madam Earth whose day is Thursday," and the madam apparently regards working on that day as an act of disrespect to her. Now, the Akans credit their ancestors not only with wisdom but also with ingenuity. Our ancestors are reputed generally to have had good practical reasons for their prescriptions and proscriptions. If so, one must suspect some lost rationale; in this case, perhaps a communally regularized respite from toil.

We are on stronger ground with respect to the second taboo. The common explanation is that bush sex is a pastime that the earth goddess simply finds insupportable and will punish with soil infertility. But why? After all, sex in the bedroom is as much a kind of commotion on some earth surface as sex in the bush. In fact, a practical rationale is not far to seek and is known to be proffered by those who do not rest content with the ideas of the populace. The freedom of unaccompanied females from unorthodox sexual invasion in isolated areas could hardly have been far from the motivation of the ancestors who laid down this rule. Other taboos would seem to be susceptible to similarly intelligible explanations.

Not only, then, are taboos not a component of the Akan system of morals, strictly so called, but also they would seem not to constitute *as such* any *essential* part of the Akan repertoire of customs and usages. The rules themselves, of course, remain an ingredient of the Akan ethos, but the apparent irrationality of their genesis would seem to be dissolvable.

On the other hand, taboos seem to have quite a secure place in the orthodox Christian ethic alongside the moral rules proper. Take the decalogue again and recall the following injunctions: (1) Thou shalt not kill; (2) Thou shalt not commit adultery; (3) Thou shalt not steal; (4) Thou shalt not bear false witness against thy neighbor; (5) Thou shalt not covet thy neighbor's house, thou shalt not covet thy neighbor's wife, nor his manservant, nor his maidservant, nor his ox, nor his ass, nor anything that is thy neighbor's (Exodus 20:13–17, numbering not in biblical sequence). Subject to reasonable qualifications with respect to the first, and some refinements and updating here and there, these are straightforward moral rules in the narrow sense under our definition of morality. They, obviously, do not differentiate the Christian ethic from the Akan counterpart. In their essential meaning, all these rules can be effortlessly duplicated in the Akan stock of ethical sayings. Indeed, it is difficult to see how such moral truisms could differentiate the moralities of any two human groups.

Recall next the following: (6) Honor thy father and thy mother. . . ; (7) Thou shalt not take the name of the LORD thy God in vain. . . . The first, as we have already discussed, is a custom—one that is invested with comparable importance in both traditional Judean and Akan society but is rather less touted in places such as the United States. The second is perhaps a special case of the first.

But, now, reflect on the remaining commandments, which run as follows: (8) Thou shalt have no other gods before me; (9) Thou shalt not make unto thee any graven image or any likeness of anything that is in heaven above or that is in the earth beneath or that is in the water under the earth; (10) Remember the Sabbath day to keep it holy. These have all the distinctive marks of taboos. They are, as far as one can see, rules whose entire normative force consists in expressing the likes and dislikes of an extra-human being.

What do these taboos look like from the perspective of the Akan traditional world view? Let us begin with the first two, namely, those prohibiting any trafficking in other gods. These are unlikely to convey much meaning to a traditional Akan. In his cosmology he believes that there exist, as *regular* parts of the world order fashioned out (not "created") by the Supreme Being, a great variety of extra-human beings and forces which are capable of aiding humans if properly tapped or approached. The more impersonal of these forces are, on this view, as intrinsic to the scheme of things in this world as electricity or rainfall, and the relatively personalized ones are viewed much like we view other minds, except that they are differently localized and in some cases are supposed to be endowed (by God) with striking powers. Thus it must sound very paradoxical indeed to the Akan to suggest that it could possibly occur to God to take offense at his dealings with those forces. Some of the more remarkable aspects of the Christian conversion of large masses of traditional Akans have to do with how they were induced to make verbal commitments to commandments such as the one now under discussion. The fact, in any case, is that the traditional beliefs usually remained psychologically operative in spite of everything.

What of the taboo relating to the Sabbath? This is likely to make some sense to the Akan, since in some ways it appears analogous to the Akan taboo against farm work on Thursdays. However, an important question immediately arises: Would the orthodox Christian take kindly to any attempt to find a practical, non-supernaturalistic rationale for the Sabbath commandment? If, as I suspect, the answer is likely to be NO, then this Christian taboo and the others are revealed as taboos in a more irreducible sense than the Akan ones.

The foregoing reflection has an even more remarkable implication for the characterization of Christian morals. If the Christian does not shy away from calling moral rules in the strict sense commandments of God, whose moral rightness logically consists in the sheer fact of being the will of God, it would follow, from the definition of taboo, that he reduces morality to the status of taboo. Such a reduction is, surely, unfortunate. It is fortunate, however, that in analyzing a set of rules of conduct, such as the Ten Commandments, one can, if one has a clear criterion for the purpose, separate custom from morality, and, even within custom, distinguish the rationally explicable elements from the normative surds. In this way one is enabled to recognize in the ways of life of different peoples those ethical norms of universal applicability which underlie the possibility of orderly dialogue and interaction between different peoples, groups, or individuals, while, at the same time, understanding the basis of the great variety of norms by which people live.

On the above showing, it is apparent that the distinction between custom and morality is of more than a theoretic interest. Failure on the part of some benefactors of Africa to make or observe the distinction in all its subtlety has not served the continent well. But it is not only in Africa that the distinction can have practical consequences. Inattention to it can result, everywhere, in authoritarian moralism.

Part III

Conceptual Contrasts

7

Formulating Modern Thought in African Languages

Some Theoretical Considerations

In his *African Religions in Western Scholarship*,[1] Okot p'Bitek recounts the following story.

> In 1911, Italian Catholic priests put before a group of Acholi elders the question "Who created you?"; and because the Luo language does not have an independent concept of create or creation, the question was rendered to mean "Who moulded you?" But this was still meaningless, because human beings are born of their mothers. The elders told the visitors they did not know. But we are told that this reply was unsatisfactory, and the missionaries insisted that a satisfactory answer must be given. One of the elders remembered that, although a person may be born normally, when he is afflicted with tuberculosis of the spine, then he loses his normal figure, he gets "moulded." So he said, "*Rubanga* is the one who moulds people." This is the name of the hostile spirit which the Acholi believe causes the hunch or hump on the back. And instead of exorcising these hostile spirits and sending them among pigs, the representatives of Jesus Christ began to preach that *Rubanga* was the Holy Father who created the Acholi. (62)

Let us assume that p'Bitek is right in this account, as he very well might be; then one can expect quite wide-ranging incongruities in the translation of Christian theology into the Luo language. P'Bitek, in fact, went on to illustrate this problem with the translation of the first sentence of St. John's Gospel into Luo. St. John's opening message is, of course: "In the beginning was the Word [Logos] and the Word was with God, and the Word was God." Now, according to p'Bitek, "[T]he Nilotes, like the early Jews, did not think metaphysically. The concept of *Logos* does not exist in Nilothic thinking; so the word *Word* was translated into *Lok* which means news or message. . . . And as Nilotes were not very concerned with the beginning or the end of the world, the phrase 'In the beginning' was rendered, *Nia con ki con*, which is, 'From long long ago.' " In the upshot, the Luo translation read as follows: *Nia con kicon Lok onongo tye, Lok tye bot Lubange, Lod aye ceng Lubanga*, which, according to him, retranslates into English as "From long long ago there was News, News was with Hunchback Spirit, News was the Hunchback Spirit" (85). One might not be able to suppress a chuckle, but one must resist any temptation to pass over this as a mere translational curiosity, for serious problems are involved here about communication across cultures.

One obvious question is this: If the concepts of creation, *Logos*, and of the beginning of the universe do not exist in the Luo language, why may they not be introduced into it? It may be admitted that the particular attempt to do so, which we have just noticed, produces quite comical results, but this, it might be suggested, may be blamed on the accidental circumstances of the Italo-Luo conversation recounted (or re-recounted) by Okot p'Bitek. The general idea of introducing new concepts into a language is very extensively relevant to our concerns in this paper, and so we will concentrate on it awhile before returning to Luo particularities.

Without presupposing any particular theory about the ontological nature of concepts, it may be said that, roughly speaking, in the more unproblematic cases of translation from one language into another, what happens is an interchange of signs for conceptual materials antecedently existing in both languages. On the other hand, where a concept exists in one language, but not in another, there is no longer just an interchange of signs but the creation, so to speak, of a new concept in the latter medium. Two options, at least, are available here. One may devise a new term, which may be a word or phrase, using words that already exist in the language, or resort to a new word altogether, which may be a transliteration into the language of a foreign word. In the latter case, there is not only a translation into the language but also an extension of its vocabulary. It is, however, all too easy to suppose that a given concept does not exist in a particular language on trivial verbal grounds. Observing, for example, that there exists no word for a certain concept in a language, it has sometimes been hastily concluded that the concept does not exist in it. African languages have not infrequently been subjected to such a hasty approach and not only at the hands of aliens. Has not a well-known native writer on African traditional thought suggested that African languages lack a concept of the indefinite future because certain East African languages examined by him did not have any word for expressing the indefinite future?[2] A concept need not be expressed by any one word; it may be expressed by a phrase or even a large set of sentences or, indeed, by a pattern of behavior. Certainly, the absence of a single-word designator does not argue the absence of a periphrasis.

Another side of the error just noted is the attribution of certain concepts (and theories, ways of thought, etc.) to some peoples in a proprietary sense. A concept may be associated with a particular people because it was originated by a person or group of persons belonging thereto, or because it has an important place in their received framework of thought, or simply because it occurs in their popular or even esoteric discourse. In neither sense can it be said that there is anything intrinsically ethnic about the concept itself. Nor can ways of thought also be said to be ethnic in any but an adventitious sense. Accident, ecology, economy, or more mysterious factors may incline a people to ways of thinking strikingly different from those of others, but what we know of the fundamental biological unity of the human species should discourage us from supposing that other peoples might not come, through their own devices or through cultural interaction, to make these ways of thought their "own." Effective appropriation is the only criterion of owner-ship in this case, and there is obviously no implication of exclusiveness.

Consider in this connection the unfortunate suggestion, sometimes heard, that logic is not African but Western. If it is implied by this that logic as a discipline was not developed in traditional Africa, as it was in the West, it can be largely conceded; though it has to be noted that the discipline was cultivated in other places—for example, in the Orient—centuries in advance of the West. With historical hindsight we can now appreciate how hasty it would have been if in those far-off centuries somebody had said, "Logic is not occidental but oriental." This reflection should also expose the hastiness, not to talk of the absurdity, of a rather more alarming idea which frequently lies behind the remark that logic is non-African. I refer to the idea that logical thinking, not just the construction of systems of logic, is not a characteristic of the African. Again, this notion is entertained not only by some foreigners but also by some apparently patriotic Africans, even by some who yield ground to none in execrating Levy-Bruhl for saying (in his early phase) that Africans have a prelogical mentality. If Africans had no taste for logical thinking, they would have to acquire it or else hold themselves ready for eventual recolonization. But, in fact, that is not the case. Anybody who has observed traditional African elders arguing, for instance, in the adjudication of disputes, must be quite radically obtuse not to have noticed their logical acumen. This comes out not only in their dialectical adroitness but also frequently in their explicit enunciation, in proverbs, as a rule, of formal logical principles. If a person were to fall into contradiction before a gathering of Akan elders, for example, he would invariably be upbraided with some such proverb as that there are no crossroads in the understanding, which, obvi-ously, is an epigrammatic formulation of the Principle of Noncontradiction (*Asu mu nni nkwanta*).[3] Or, if one tried to evade both the affirmative and the negative of a proposition, one would invite the contemptuous exclamation: "He will not stand and he will not lie either"—an unmistakable invocation of the Principle of Excluded Middle (*Kosi a nkosi, koda a nkoda!*).

These exhibits, incidentally, refute the well-intentioned but unwelcome plea, entered on behalf of Africa by some of her friends, that although African thinking does not operate with such principles as noncontradiction and excluded middle, it is none the worse for it, since there are alternative logics.[4] The question of excluded middle is somewhat involved,[5] but a quite simple consideration suffices to demonstrate that no coherent logical system or even logical thinking is possible that dispenses not just with some particular formulation but with the essence of the principle of non-contradiction. Any system of logic will have to be such as to allow the valid deduction of some propositions from others. But a valid deduction is, by definition, such that the joint assertion of its premises and the negation of its conclusion is self-contradictory, that is, violates the principle of contradiction. If a given system does not have this principle, even at a metalogical level, then the principle is not there to be violated, and the notion of valid deduction must consequently be absent. It follows that dispensing with the principle of noncontradiction is a logically suicidal abnegation.[6]

The crucial relevance of logic to the concerns of this essay may be seen from the following. Formulating modern thought in African languages will take the form largely, but not wholly, of translating things from other languages. Now, any body of organized knowledge may be viewed in at least two ways: first, as an accumulation of facts; and second, as a method of inquiry. It is only necessary to push the methodology of any subject a little along the path of abstraction to reach the logic of that discipline. A similar exercise on a broader path gives you the philosophy of the discipline. Presupposed by the logic or philosophy of any discipline is logic in the fundamental sense of the principles of correct reasoning. This logic, or aspects of it, can be captured in any number of alternative formalizations; but unless different languages shared basically the same logic, it would be impossible to translate one into another, and any question of translating modern knowledge from, say, French into, say, Luo would lapse. The point is not just that the logic of the disciplines formulated in the medium of a language could not be rendered in another language of a fundamentally disparate logic, but also that not even the facts of the subject concerned could be translated.

The point can be pressed further. Language is not just an *ad hoc* aggregation of sound types and symbols but rather a *system* of these with rules of formation and combination. Unless the Principle of Noncontradiction were at least implicitly acknowledged, one could not even begin to talk of the use of rules, for the idea of a rule involves the intent of consistent application. Logic, then, in the most fundamental sense, is presupposed by language. In this sense logic is appropriately described as the science of consistency, that is, the sustained application of the Principle of Noncontradiction.

Let us take stock of the foregoing reflections. They were triggered by the consideration that some concepts and ways of thinking may exist in one language but not in another. Okot p'Bitek had suggested that the concepts of

Logos and creation did not exist in the Luo language and also that the habit of speculating about the beginning and the end of the world was not found among the speakers of that language. And this, it was suggested, had led to strange results in the translation of Christian theology into Luo. With regard to this, our first priority has been to recommend circumspection regarding such claims in general. Concepts and ways of thought do not belong to particular peoples in any but a historically episodic sense. In the special case of the logical way of thinking, what we have seen is, in effect, that it cannot be absent from any group of articulate beings and that this has a special significance for the possibility of translation.

Nevertheless, with all the circumspection in the world, it still has to be acknowledged that, as a matter of historical fact, there have been, and there are, conceptual and methodological disparities in the thinking of different peoples; and our second priority is to investigate the implications of this for the question of formulating modern thought in our African languages.

Interestingly, the natural and mathematical sciences do not present any intractable difficulties in the present connection. It is true that at present our languages are largely lacking in the vocabulary for expressing modern scientific knowledge. But this is not such a significant disability as might appear at first sight. Language is most fundamentally conceived as a skeleton capable of indefinite fleshing out, or, to change the metaphor a little, as an infinitely flexible framework capable of being bent to any purpose of communication or symbolism in general. If we look at a given language as a set of symbols or types of sound and combination rules, together with a definite aggregate of vocabulary, then we may view the adoption of a new word to designate a new perception or attitude or conceptual formation as an accretion. This is legitimate in some contexts. But from the more fundamental point of view, the continual extension of the vocabulary of a language in response to the imperatives of fresh thought and experience is to be seen as just what language is for. We are to think of it not as the enlargement of an instrument but rather as the extended use of it. Thus in Africa we will need to adopt countless new words and symbolic devices in using our languages to domesticate the sciences. But in doing this we would only be exploiting our languages in the natural way.

Three conditions need to be satisfied for the rational and effective pursuit of this aim. The necessity and importance of the enterprise must be clear. Also the ideas and techniques to be thus rendered in our languages must have universal intelligibility and applicability; and finally there must, in any particular case, be an adequate mastery of the given African, or foreign, language and the body of knowledge concerned. That these conditions are either already satisfied or otherwise easily satisfiable is so beyond dispute that one may be tempted to think it superfluous to state them at all in regard to the sciences.

But, as we shall see in due course, it is by no means clear that they are all met or can be met in other areas of thought.

How exactly, then, may the requisite vocabulary be devised? By the specialization of old words in our languages and the adoption of new ones from other languages. This is, in fact, no different from the way in which technical terms are introduced into any language. A word may be specialized by the restriction or extension of its meaning or by that analogical transformation of antecedent meaning that is familiar in metaphorical language. A very considerable proportion of modern African scientific vocabulary, however, will have to consist of adopted words from foreign languages; for where, as one can foresee in many cases, the phenomenon to be named has no apparent linkages with previous experience, there can be little basis for the specialization of an old word.

As a matter of fact, the vocabulary of science in the languages of the so-called advanced countries is full of adopted and adapted words from the classical languages. Africa can follow suit with good sense. Thus, for example, wishing to express the concept of "electron" in the Akan language of Ghana, there is no reason why we cannot simply say "elɛktron" if an indigenous word does not easily present itself. Our Arab brothers have done this sort of thing quite effectively. The Japanese have thrived on it famously.

It should not be supposed, of course, that articulating scientific knowledge in Africa need always take the passive form of translating things from other languages. Once the program of domesticating the sciences gets under way, Africa, too, can be expected to become a major source of modern scientific knowledge. When we enter the areas of the humanities and the more intuitive parts of the social sciences, however, we encounter distinctly subtle problems. Concepts and theories in subjects such as art, literature, sociology, theology, and philosophy are apt to reflect the cultural affiliations of their authors or exponents. In such cases not even universal intelligibility, let alone universal validity, can be taken for granted. In such cases, indeed, translation is capable of becoming a form of unwitting transacculturation.

A further look at the problem, commented on by Okot p'Bitek, of translating St. John's opening metaphysics into Luo will help to illumine some aspects of our problem. According to p'Bitek, the concept of creation does not exist in Luo. He does not, obviously, mean the concept of creation that is involved when it is said, for example, that a sculptor has created a beautiful piece of sculpture. He is referring to the concept of creation *ex nihilo* (out of nothing). How plausible is it to suppose that this concept might not exist in a particular language? To be sure, the word "language" in this context refers more directly to vocabulary than to the abstract framework which, as we have seen, constitutes language in the fundamental sense. The vocabulary of a language is, of course, closely connected with the thought habits of its speakers. If, as p'Bitek says, the Luo were not disposed to speculate on such things as the beginning and end of the world, then it is not inconceivable that they may not have had so transcendental a concept as that of creation out of nothing.

The concept of creation out of nothing is transcendental in the sense that it cannot be defined in terms of anything within human experience. A people can be highly metaphysical without employing transcendental concepts in their thinking, for not all metaphysics is transcendental metaphysics. The Akans of Ghana, for example, are a highly metaphysical people in that they are very curious about such concepts as God, human personality, destiny, free will, causation. But they are preeminently empirical in their intellectual orientation. In particular, their concept of God (*Nyame*) is nontranscendental. Nyame (or Nyankopon) is conceived as being responsible for the world in a sense appropriate to an "Excavator, Hewer, Carver, Creator, Originator, Inventor, Architect."[7] Such a creator can only be supposed to create, to construct new things out of something, not out of nothing. The Akan word for this creator is *Oboade. Bo* means to construct, hew, fashion out, etc. To render the notion of creation out of nothing in Akan, one would have to say something that translates back into English in some such phrase as "constructing, hewing, fashioning out something without using anything," which carries its contradictoriness on its face.

The Akans, then, would seem to be like the Luo in not having a concept of creation out of nothing. Okot p'Bitek seems to suggest that not thinking in terms of concepts of this sort is a sign of a nonmetaphysical outlook. This, as we have pointed out, is not so, unless by metaphysics one means transcendental metaphysics, as some people unfortunately do. The urgent question, however, is this: If the idea of creation out of nothing does not exist in Luo and Akan, then how can the Christian belief in that idea be translated into these languages? We have noticed one comic result of the translation of "creator" into Luo as *Rubanga,* and one might be tempted, perhaps, to think that no appropriate translation is possible so long as the idea to be translated itself does not exist in the Luo language. Yet, a very great number of Akans and Luos are professed Christians and are, presumably, one way or another, able to effect the requisite translation.

Let us compare this problem of translation with the problem of translating, say, "electron" into Akan. As of now, the concept of an electron does not exist in the Akan vocabulary, and the suggestion I have already made is that we might simply transliterate it as "elektron." To this it might be objected that if the concept does not exist in Akan, then this collection of letters can register no meaning on an Akan mind. The objection is well taken. The point is that the introduction of the word "elektron" would have to be part of a pedagogic package in which the Akan listener is led to form the concept of electron through ostensive or periphrastic procedures. We have so far assumed that the Akan concerned does not speak English or any other language which has the concept of electron. Where, however, an Akan speaks some such language as English, matters are simplified quite considerably. It is then just a matter of his transferring his thinking in English into Akan.

Notice the following assumptions in these last remarks. It is assumed that it is cognitively useful to try to translate a concept such as that of electron into Akan, which presupposes that the concept is transculturally intelligible. We have assumed, furthermore, that the Akan can assimilate this concept into his received body of thought. As we suggested earlier, these assumptions are uncontroversial as far as concepts (and methods of inquiry) in the natural and mathematical sciences are concerned.

The situation is quite different when we come to a philosophical concept like creation out of nothing. Being a transcendental concept, it cannot be introduced into Akan by ostensive methods. Neither can it be introduced by periphrasis, owing to the empirical orientation of the vocabulary of Akan, which produces an apparently contradictory result when this is attempted. Thus we are left only with the alternative of thinking partially in English while ostensibly speaking (or writing) in Akan. Not that this is a difficult thing to do. In fact, it is all too easy; one might simply continue using the Akan word *Oboade* while annexing to it the signification the word "Creator" has in Christian metaphysics as articulated in English. This is actually what many Akan Christians educated in English do.

But why should that be done? To exploit one's English-aided grasp of "electron" in order to transliterate it into Akan—note, by the way, the classical origin of "electron" itself—is legitimate; we need science in Africa. But it is not obvious why an Akan should think in English when talking in his or her mother tongue about cosmic matters. We are not, let it be noted, considering at this stage the belief in the existence of a transcendental creator; we are only concerned with the concept itself. Whether or not one uses the Akan word *Oboade* with a transcendental understanding to affirm or deny his existence, the question of the propriety of the practice must press itself on us with equal force.

One danger in this kind of "translation" is liability to fallacies of ambiguity. Take, for example, the oft-repeated claim that we all—the English-speaking Christian as well as the non-English-speaking traditional Akan—worship[8] one and the same God. In the one context "God" refers to a transcendental creator; in the other, it only refers to a hewer writ large, cosmically speaking. Any appearance of truth in the statement is thanks to the ambiguity. To a large extent, this ambiguity rests on the fact that the transference of the thinking in English into the talking in Akan goes on unconsciously. Any Akan who notices the difference in meaning between the Akan word *Oboade* and the

English term "Creator out of nothing" would, most likely, be chary of the sort of claim commented on in the last paragraph. Moreover, observing that trying to translate the notion of creation out of nothing from English into Akan seems to lead to incoherence, he might be constrained to consider whether the fault is in the vocabulary of Akan or in the notion concerned. The resulting meditation may cause him to suggest that Akan vocabulary is inadequate and in need of transcendental enrichment. On the other hand, he may come to think that the concept is, in fact, incoherent. Were he to come to this conclusion, he would not need to restrict his explanations to just pointing out the difficulties besetting any attempt to render the concept in Akan. The reasons underlying these difficulties might be articulated in English as independent considerations.

Such reasoning might, briefly, be as follows: In common discourse, that is, outside the technical language of philosophy, to create is always to fashion something new by manipulating preexisting materials and potentials. Hence to speak of creation out of nothing is to employ a word while failing to abide by all the conditions of its employment. Moreover, the notion of *causation* implied in creation cannot make sense in the non-context of absolute nothingness, for there can be *nothing* to make the difference between *post hoc* (mere sequence) and *propter hoc* (causal sequence).

Valid or invalid, this reasoning is extremely significant, for it shows that in trying to translate a phrase like "creation out of nothing" into Akan or Luo or any other African language, one is not just trying to translate English, but rather a sub-language within the English language, namely, the technical language of philosophical thought. Technical vocabulary in philosophy is always heavily laden with doctrinal history. Although the vocabulary and grammar of the parent language often does influence the character of the technical language, this influence is never rigidly deterministic. Moreover, its flow is two-way, for the technical language of philosophy has a way of influencing ordinary usage. This makes it all the more necessary that one should be wary in translations in philosophy and cognate fields.

Here again the Luo translation of the opening sentence of the Gospel according to St. John offers a very useful illustration of the problems of translation across cultures. The saint talks of the *Word*. This, of course, is the translation in English of the Greek word "Logos," which has a rather special technical meaning. The philosophical use of "Logos" in Greek philosophy goes at least as far back as Heraclitus (about 500 B.C.). For him "Logos" meant not just rational thought but the ontological "principle" from which the rational order of the universe emanates. In Plato "Nous" is the principle which is the source of the rational organization of the "intelligible" world of Forms. In due time this "Nous" is more or less identified in the tradition with Logos. By the time we reach the stoics we have an all-embracing Logos doctrine according to which Logos is, on the cosmic scale, the creative "principle" that is the source of the rational organization of nature and, on the scale of human individuals, the Reason of the soul. On the cosmic scale Logos was identified with God.

St. John's "the Word was God" reflects the Heraclitean-Platonic-Stoic doctrine surveyed above. The Christian "Word" reflects further the elaborations of this doctrinal tradition by the early Church Fathers. Now, what is a non-English-speaking Luo elder, uninstructed in the semantics of Graeco-Christian metaphysics, to make of the message that "the Word was God" which, by Luo interpretation, retranslates as "News was the Hunchback Spirit"? Perhaps the Luo elders in the Italo-Luo encounter referred to by Okot p'Bitek could have done a better job of translating "God"[9] but it is difficult to see how, without an inkling of the Graeco-Christian philosophy of the "Word" and an ability to think in some language, such as English, already impregnated with that tradition, anyone could possibly make even a preliminary sense of St. John's suggestion.

One perceives in this connection an interesting stratification of the African audience for translations of the sort being considered. From the point of view of intelligibility, the most ill-served stratum is the class of non-Western-educated, traditional Africans for whom we have already by implication expressed our sympathy. There is also the class of those Western-educated Africans who are not initiated into the Western metaphysics of the "Word." To these only a partial apparent understanding is possible. We have, finally, the class of those Western-educated Africans who are at home in the relevant Western traditions of thought. They[10] are capable of as full an understanding of the Western doctrines as the native Westerners themselves, and they have, consequently, no difficulty in understanding the versions of these same doctrines in the pretended translations into the African languages.

But what sort of understanding do they have of the African texts? The answer is that the understanding they have is, in a certain sense, a Western understanding. The mental content created by the African text is not integrated into African categories of thought but rather embedded in Western categories. This is what accounts for the symmetry which exists in the relationship between the English text and the Luo rendition in the mind of the African sophisticate, and is absent in that of the traditional Luo.

Take the specific case of "The Word was God." In the first case, the symmetry consists in the fact that this English sentence translates into the Luo sentence *Lok aye ceng Lubanga,* which, in its Westernized apprehension, translates back into the original English sentence. In the second case, the failure of symmetry consists in the fact that, while the English sentence initially translates into *Lok aye ceng Lubanga,* this Luo sentence in its indigenous meaning translates back into English, not as the original English sentence, but rather as "News was the Hunchback Spirit." Using a downward vertical arrow to stand for translation, we might set the contrast down schematically as follows:

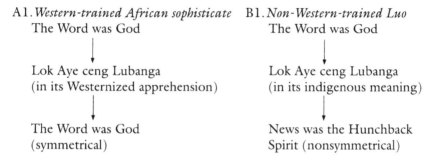

A1. *Western-trained African sophisticate*
The Word was God
↓
Lok Aye ceng Lubanga
(in its Westernized apprehension)
↓
The Word was God
(symmetrical)

B1. *Non-Western-trained Luo*
The Word was God
↓
Lok Aye ceng Lubanga
(in its indigenous meaning)
↓
News was the Hunchback
Spirit (nonsymmetrical)

In an Akan translation the schema would be as follows:

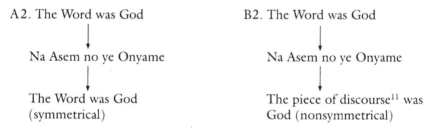

A2. The Word was God
↓
Na Asem no ye Onyame
↓
The Word was God
(symmetrical)

B2. The Word was God
↓
Na Asem no ye Onyame
↓
The piece of discourse[11] was
God (nonsymmetrical)

In *A* what we might call the Western evangelical point of view is operative in each schema from start to finish: There is a Graeco-Christian message to be communicated. An African sentence is chosen to carry the message without a thorough investigation of the conceptual framework within which it has its meaning. Accordingly, in any reverse translation, what is operative is not the original meaning of the African sentence but the evangelical information or apparent information superimposed upon it. If this translational practice is embraced and perpetuated by a significant enough number of Africans, however, it becomes legitimized. What that means is that in the relevant connection Africans would have become Westernized in what I fear would have to be called an unthinking manner.

It is important to stress that this is not just a verbal question. Nor does it concern an isolated piece of translation. In the domain of religion alone—and we shall see in due course that essentially the same issue is encountered in other spheres as well—the translational practices in question betoken a pervasive eclipsing of unexamined indigenous African modes of thought by equally unexamined imported ones. Modes of thought in so vital an area as religion, of course, have sundry implications for action. Since thought and action in such realms constitute an important facet of a culture, the foregoing considerations show how certain forms of translation can become forms of transacculturation, by the nature of their genesis and not necessarily by the impact of their semantic import.

The schemata under *B* may be viewed as a sort of counter to this kind of acculturation. The first segments represent the tendentious translation of the Christian evangelist; the second represent attempts to give the real meaning of the African sentences involved. The point is not that *B*-type translations are literal and the *A*-type metaphorical, but rather that the former take African meanings seriously while the latter do not. A metaphor is a certain way of taking a given meaning seriously; it pays tribute to the suggestiveness of that meaning. Far from paying any tribute to African meanings, *A*-type translations, in effect, take them in vain.

What, then, is the lesson of the schemata under *B2*? The lesson is that translation in such fields as religion ought to be approached with greater conceptual self-consciousness than has been apparent so far. That there is something wrong with the *B*-schemata is certain; for, surely, translations ought to be symmetrical. In fact, if I am right in my earlier remarks about the Akan language in connection with the concept of creation out of nothing, then the word "God" as signifying the creator of the universe out of nothing is simply not translatable into the Akan language, and not into the Luo either, if Okot p'Bitek is right.

Paradoxically, this does not make rendering the idea of God in Akan impossible; it makes it simpler. It would be quite feasible simply to transliterate and write "Gɔd" in Akan. Similarly, we might say "Lɔgɔs" instead of *Asem*. (Here it is obviously better to avoid the English detour of the "Word"). So that "the Word was God" now becomes, in Akan, "Na lɔgɔs no ye Gɔd." There is then no longer any pretense that the Akan language already contains concepts equivalent to "Logos" and "God," and the problem of non-symmetry is effectively and non-tendentiously obviated. Moreover, it would now be easily appreciated that if the intended message is to be received by the non-English-speaking, traditional African,[12] then extensive explanations of "Logos" and "God" will have to be supplied.[13]

How does "Gɔd" as a transliteration into the Akan language compare with "elektron?" They both transliterate untranslatable words into the language. But the prospects of their being understood in the recipient language are different. Unlike "electron," which is an empirical concept, a transcendental concept like "God" can be expected to give rise to difficulties of understanding in an empirically oriented language like Akan, as noted earlier. An English-speaking Akan might have the impression that the idea is easy to understand in Akan, but this is likely to be because in this matter he thinks in English and not in Akan. For an African to think in a Western language in this way is a mark

of what might be called the colonial mentality. By contrast, he may consciously incorporate his Western-acquired concept of "electron" into Akan
without incurring this description, for reasons already given. Accordingly, it
might be said that while a word like "elɛktron" is to be introduced to
encourage the domestication of certain Western concepts and forms of
thinking, a word like "Gɔd" is to be introduced to encourage caution in the
assimilation of Western ideas.[14]

This caution is, indeed, desirable in connection with a large assortment of
Western concepts and categories of thought. In anthropology, history, and
politics, it is well known that the use by European students of Africa of words
like "family," "tribe," "chief," "brother," "cousin," etc., in application to
Africa has often betrayed a Eurocentrism.[15] Ironically, this seems to have
insinuated itself into the discourse of Africans themselves. Sorting out the
intricacies of translation in regard to these and allied concepts is by no means
easy, but matters are much worse when we come to relatively more abstract
concepts like "law," "custom," "morality," "religion," "worship," "punishment," "retribution." When we reach the level of abstraction represented by
logical, epistemological, and metaphysical concepts, the difficulty is to perceive that there is a problem to start with. It would be a major first step toward
the correct formulation of modern thought in African languages if we in
Africa were to cultivate the habit of thinking in our own indigenous languages
as much as possible when talking in one metropolitan language or another
about issues involving concepts such as "God" (which we have already
touched upon), "Mind," "Person," "Soul," "Spirit," "Sentence," "Proposition," "Truth," "Fact," "Substance," "Existence," and about categorical
distinctions such as "the Physical and the Spiritual," "the Natural and the
Supernatural," "the Religious and the Secular," and "the Mystical and the
Nonmystical." Our concern here need not be too narrowly and too directly
focused on translation. Our characterizations, in foreign languages, of African
institutions and modes of thought and behavior, too, ought to be critically
scrutinized, for they have a crucial bearing on our translations.

To start with a simple example. Consider the relation: mother's sister's son.
In Akan a person having this relation to me is called *me nua*. Now *me nua* also
describes the relationship that my mother's son bears to me. In this last case,
me nua translates unproblematically into English as "my brother." The
question is: How are we to translate *me nua* in the first case? The orthodox
translation is "my cousin." But this is quite incapable of expressing the
strength of kinship bonds connoted by the Akan term. To continue to say
"cousin" without a sense of uneasiness is to allow ourselves to be controlled
by a foreign cultural model in our translations. If we do speak of the extended
family, why may we not extend the sense of "brother"? On the other hand, if
we are not careful, an uncritical pursuit of industrialization could so erode our

sense of extended kinship solidarity[16] as to make "cousin" the correct translation, after all. We see, here again, that these issues of translation are not just
a matter of words but also of worth.

Even more interesting conceptual issues arise in connection with the
translation of a term such as "punishment." The standard temptation is to
suppose that there must be an equivalent concept in Akan. In fact, there isn't.
There is no comparable blanket concept for reaction to wrongdoing in Akan.
If a child or an adolescent misbehaves, what is visited upon him is called
asotwe, literally "ear-pulling." This term is never applied to an adult who trifles
with the community's rules. The term used depends on the broad category of
the offense. If the rule involved is just a custom or a convention, what the
misconduct calls for is either an *mpata,* which means pacification or compensation, or *nnwanetoa,* which means apology through an intercessor. Both may
be quite expensive, though frequently a few well-chosen words, reinforced
with the right set of proverbs, will settle the matter. On the other hand, one
who shows himself heedless to a law of the state brings upon himself *amane*
or *adi,* that is, trouble or adversity. This might be a fine, a period in
banishment, or in the gravest type of case, death. Any category of offense
might have an extrahuman dimension, in which case purificatory rituals might
also be incurred.

The following facts are especially worthy of note in regard to the Akan
reaction to error. *Asotwe* is explicitly reformative. Of an erring or fractious
child it is said that *naso nte asem,* that is, his ears do not hear advice; in other
words, he is impervious to moral instruction. His ear is figuratively (and at
times also literally) pulled to open it to edification. Though primarily
reformatory, the exercise is expected, secondarily, to help deter other children. Occasionally, a parent who has temporarily lost his reason through
excessive irritation might set upon his erring child in a spirit of retribution.
Such loss of perspective is, of course, never held up as a model of parental
governance in Akan society. In the case of adult transgression of state laws, on
the other hand, retribution is held to be appropriate; it is, indeed, the primary
reaction, and this is clear from the language used. When the Akan official
announcer proclaims that whoever violates an edict of the "chief" will be
overtaken by adversity (*wunii a wobeye saa adi aye wo; . . . wanya amane;
. . . amane da wo so*), he is unequivocally warning of retribution. Deterrence
does, indeed, enter into the calculation, but as a secondary consideration. The
reformatory motive is more shadowy. The person concerned may very well
"learn sense" (*sua nyansa*) from his troubles, but even if he did not, the
sanction would not be regarded as having proved futile on that account.
Actually, the question of reformation does not always arise. A generally
continent man whose resistance collapses in the face of the oversexy exhibi-
tionism of a married woman is not particularly in need of reformation, for

there is, by hypothesis, no tendency to adultery in his character; nevertheless, he will be dealt with according to law, for he has done wrong. Moreover, even where a misconduct is the manifestation of a settled trait, the principal duty of seeing to the reform of the individual is assigned to his family, rather than to any other institution.

Reformatory motives are, again, quite marginal in those cases in which the wrongdoer (frequently together with his family) is expected to pacify his ancestors or some nonhuman forces ritually in order to restore cherished and beneficial relationships. Ideas of deterrence are equally remote, and those of retribution even more so, if operative at all. The same remarks apply *a fortiori* to the procedures for dealing with offenses that require only an apology or compensation in an out-of-court setting.

Consider now the question, much debated in Western philosophy, of the justification of punishment. Some philosophers have suggested that punishment is only justified by its deterrent and reformative consequences. Others, the retributivists, have maintained that the commission of a forbidden act is the necessary and sufficient condition of punishment. How are we to think about these issues and contentions in the medium of the Akan language? There being no blanket counterpart to "punishment" in Akan, the principal question here has to be raised anew in respect of each of the broad categories of reaction to wrongdoing in Akan society. Suppose, then, that we ask what is the justification of *asotwe*. This would amount to asking for the justification of trying to reform bad children and deter other children from wrongdoing. Whatever one may think of this question, one thing that should be absolutely clear is that you cannot answer it by proposing reformation and deterrence, on pain of an obvious circularity. Nor could one suggest retribution, for to seek to justify reformation by retribution would be to chase after a contradiction. Of course, one can ask whether *asotwe* is the right way of trying to reform children; and this, in fact, is the important question. Yet, were we uncritically to translate *asotwe* as "punishment," we would, most likely, be diverted from this question into debating familiar but not quite pertinent Western issues and proposals.

The point applies equally clearly to the retributive way of dealing with (a certain category of) misconduct. If you think of this simply in terms of the Western concept of punishment, you are likely to be encouraged to pursue the topic along the customary Western lines. But from the Akan point of view, the question that might need investigating is whether retribution is the right way, or, perhaps one should say, the right spirit for dealing with the class of offenses under consideration. It should be noted that this is quite over and above the issue whether a particular concrete form of retribution is fair in relation to a given offense. Now, to ask for the justification of retribution is immediately to transcend the position of the typical Western retributivist; it is, so to speak, to start the inquiry close to where he ends it. The interesting thing here is that this approach is foreshadowed by the preanalytic conceptualizations, in the Akan language, of the phenomena that are studied under what is known in Western philosophy as the philosophy of punishment. It is conceivable that a sustained inquiry into the morality of retribution might lead to the conclusion that, say, reformation is a better basis for dealing with wrongdoing of the type under consideration.[17] If this were then to become the received approach, the chances are that there would be quite a thoroughgoing change, possibly in the direction of greater humanity, in the Akan way of speaking about and dealing with large classes of wrong conduct. That would be a remarkable example of the impact philosophy can have on practical affairs. But the Akan philosopher of today who thinks in English or perhaps French is unlikely to be able to maintain those linguistic links of empathy that will enable him to communicate effectively with and influence his traditional kinsmen on issues such as the ones we have been discussing. If with foreign-oriented thinking he discusses modern thought in this area, as in various other areas, in his own language, the outcome is likely to do violence (though not premeditatedly) to his indigenous categories of thought. Other Africans, Akans and non-Akans alike, are invited to compare their own notes with mine.

In regard to the procedure of settling offenses through purificatory rituals or through compensation or apology, it is even more obvious than in the preceding cases that the (English) concept of punishment and its philosophy are hardly applicable. Accordingly, circumspection is doubly necessary in translation.

I come now to a distinctively metaphysical concept, namely, substance. Nothing is more tempting in this area of reflection than to suppose that the categories of substance and accident or, in more modern language, thing and quality (property), are absolutely essential to all human thought about the world. They have pride of place in Aristotle's list of the categories and are very fundamental in the philosophies of Descartes, Leibniz, and Spinoza. Though the classical British empiricists Locke, Berkeley, and Hume were critical of the notion of substance, they were never completely free of it, since they remained stuck with a notion of quality which was a logical correlate of that of substance. Moreover, Locke never succeeded completely in disabusing his mind of it, being to the last committed to the idea of substance as something *he knows not what*; and Berkeley, though contemptuous of the idea of material substance, was keen on spiritual substance. Hume, the most radical empiricist of all, rejected the notion of substance as an "unintelligible chimera," but in suggesting that things were just collections of qualities, he fell victim indirectly to that notion, for his suggestion suffered from an incoherence deriving from the fact that his notion of quality was a logical correlate of substance.

One way or another, then, the notion of substance has been very influential in Western philosophy.

Aristotle had various ways of characterizing substance, four of which have, in some manner of conflation, become the core of subsequent thought on the topic. Substance was conceived alternatively as a logical subject, that is, as a subject of which predicates could be affirmed or denied but never itself a predicate of anything else, as that in which properties or qualities inhered, as that which had independent existence, and as that which remained the same when something underwent changes in quality. There is here an obvious interplay of grammar, logic, and metaphysics. The organization of the materials of discourse into subject and predicate is a circumstance of speech (and of writing, where it exists) which may not be universal among the human species.[18] Nor need it be an invariable aspect of the structure of all human thought. But even granting the contrary, it is not clear why the structure of thought and discourse has to be duplicated in the structure of reality. Yet this ontological interpretation of a semantic distinction has become widely received into philosophical and semiphilosophical discourse (in the West). In English, for example, one speaks of a thing and its properties or qualities, and it is frequently taken for granted that a thing belongs to an ontological order distinct from that of its properties. A thing is concrete, but its properties are abstract. Thus, for example, when a table is brown, the brownness is said to be a property of the table but not itself a concrete thing like the table, being only an abstract entity. In this form the substance-accident distinction, not necessarily hinged to its Aristotelian or neo-Aristotelian support, is very current indeed in modern English-speaking philosophy.[19] In contemporary philosophy of logic, an added Platonic complication gives rise to a theory of abstract entities in semantic analysis espoused by some of its most prestigious practitioners.[20] The technical language of philosophy, as noted already, is apt to infiltrate common discourse, and much ordinary use of the thing-quality distinction bears the marks of an unconscious metaphysic.

When, therefore, we come to consider how the substance-accident, thing-property distinction might be treated in an African language, we have quite a slippery situation with which to reckon. Although the Akan language, for instance, is not inhospitable to the subject-predicate distinction, the hypostatization of subject into a self-subsistent entity and of predicate into a dependent abstract object is unintelligible in that medium as of now. The word for "thing" is *ade* in Akan, and this is the only word that could possibly be used to render "substance." But the referent of *ade* has to be a full-blooded object; the word cannot be used to express the notion of an existent in abstraction from its properties. The notion of the property of an object may be translated as its "yɛbea" or "tebea," which literally means "way of being," or better, "the way the thing is," or, better still, "the nature of the thing." Two things must be clear at once: first, it does not make sense to conceive of the way a thing is as itself a kind of object, and second, it makes even less sense to envisage the existence of an entity which has no nature. Hence the metaphysical distinction between a thing and its properties cannot be expressed in Akan without unconcealed absurdities.

Of course, the semantic distinction between a thing and its properties can be made in Akan. This just means that one can identify and talk about a thing (*ade*) without giving an exhaustive description of the way it is (*ne tebea*). Thus an Akan, mindful of his indigenous categories of thought, is unlikely to take for granted the intelligibility in Akan of the metaphysical distinction between a thing and its properties. In consequence, when translating any piece of discourse involving that distinction into Akan, he will be likely to adopt cautionary devices, including, presumably, transliteration and periphrasis, complete with explanations. Moreover, in contrast to the case of translations in the field of science, it is improbable that the motive of the exercise will be the desire to domesticate culturally either the thought form or its content.

The same critical approach will be called for in translations of concepts such as "Mind," "Person," "Soul," "Spirit," "Sentence," "Proposition," "Truth," "Fact," "Existence," "Free Will," and category contrasts such as "the Physical and the Spiritual," "the Natural and the Supernatural," "the Religious and the Secular," and "the Mystical and the Nonmystical." These were listed earlier. They do not exhaust the range of concepts regarding which an African would need to be specially open-eyed in his translations. But they are wide-ranging enough to discourage any sense of complacency. Hitherto, complacency has reigned in, for example, Akan translations of terms like "Mind," "Soul," "Spirit." It is usual to find "soul" translated as *okra* and "spirit" as *sunsum* (or, under Christian influence, as *honhom*). "Mind" is rarely directly translated. It may be surmised that this is because in the Akan inventory of the entities that go to constitute a human person nothing that might be called the equivalent of "mind" is mentioned. This is for a very good reason. The fact is that the Akan conception of mind is not of a kind of entity but rather of a capacity and a function.[21] Although "mind" is not often consciously translated in the literature, it is usually, in effect, identified alternatively with the *okra* and with the *sunsum*. The *okra* is supposed to be the entity that accounts for a person being alive. Some authors call it "the principle of life,"[22] others "the life force."[23] Whatever it is called, it is clear beyond peradventure that "mind" cannot mean the *okra*. Nor can it mean the *sunsum*, which is held to refer to something in individuals that gives them the peculiar force of their personality, if for no other reason than that the *sunsum* is thought of as a kind of entity while "mind," *adwane* in Akan, is conceived of simply as the thinking capacity or function. Yet, it has become orthodox to equate the *okra* with the soul, which has the effect, since the soul is more or less identified with the mind, of indirectly equating the *okra* with the mind. The scene is set, accordingly, for entangling the Akan concept of mind in Western problems of dualism, idealism, materialism, etc., which, in truth, do not fit at all into Akan categories of thought.[24]

By a similar circumstance of translation, belief in countless "mystical," "spiritual," and "supernatural" entities has been attributed to the African race. In fact, however, these categories do not exist in Akan thought, for example; they would seem not to exist in the thought of many other African peoples. I would like, however, to see philosophically sophisticated conceptual analyses of the thought of various African peoples by thinkers with an inside understanding of the relevant African languages and cultures before generalizing with any confidence. Still, since one counter-example overthrows a universal generalization, I would like to dwell on the Akan example in briefly considering the universal attributions in question. As I have already observed, the intellectual orientation of the Akan is empirical. To repeat, this does not mean that the metaphysical bent is absent from their thinking. It does not mean, furthermore, that they are unused to thinking with concepts of the highest abstraction. What it means is only that they do not employ in their thinking certain kinds of abstract concepts, namely, those that cannot be defined in terms deriving from human experience.[25] Now, quite clearly, the concept of the "supernatural" goes beyond the world of human experience. It envisages a world over and above this world. By no manner of deduction, extrapolation, or imaginative projection could one arrive at such a concept from empirical beginnings.

The reason why many students of African thought have seen the supernatural, the spiritual, the mystical as being preeminent in the African worldview is because traditional Africans undoubtedly believe in the existence and pervasive influence of a variety of nonhuman beings and powers. But, as far at least as the Akans are concerned, these beings and powers are an integral part of this world. They belong as much to the world as the chairs in this room and the trees outside it. Not even *Onyame* ("God") is supposed to exist outside the universe. That would be a veritable contradiction in Akan terms. To exist is to be there (*woho*) and existence is the being there of something (*sε bribi wo ho*). To exist outside the universe would mean to be there but not at any place, an idea lacking in coherence. Note, incidentally, that the great St. Anselm would have had unmanageable difficulties trying to articulate his ontological argument for the existence of God in vintage Akan, although his definition of the Supreme Being as that than which a greater cannot be conceived is commonplace in that linguistic setting.

There is, then, as Busia puts it, an "apparent absence of any conceptual cleavage between the natural and the supernatural" in Akan traditional thinking.[26] Of a piece with this also is the absence of any conceptual cleavage between the spiritual and the physical. Mbiti observes, speaking of African thought generally, that within it "no line is drawn between the spiritual and the physical."[27] This is assuredly true of Akan thought. No entities are spoken of or even dreamt of in Akan philosophy that are not material to some degree. If we take the maximal limit of materiality to be exemplified by things like chairs and tables, which are subject to all the constraints of space and time and have all the familiar causal susceptibilities, then the difference between such objects, on the one hand, and entities such as *okra* and *sunsum,* on the other, is not that the former are material and the latter are immaterial, extensionless, but rather that the former are fully material, and the latter are thought of as only partially so, being only loosely constrained by space and time and commonplace causality.

The foregoing discussion discloses contrasts between Western categories of thought and those of the Akans, and most likely other African peoples, which have enormous implications for translation. Since a good translation should be symmetrical, both translations from foreign into African languages and the converse are affected. The problems in the second aspect of the matter, namely, those having to do with translations from African, into foreign, languages are especially urgent, since at present very much more of that takes place than the reverse. The translations referred to here are not of the simple and straightforward type in which a composed text in an African language is rendered into a corresponding text in a metropolitan language; they take the form rather of accounts of African thought in foreign languages in which, inevitably, African categories of thought are, so to speak, mapped onto Western ones. We have seen that in some important spheres of thought such mappings have sometimes left much to be desired, conceptually, and that this has led in the past to the uncritical assimilation of Western modes of thought by Africans. Not only concepts and beliefs have been imported in this way but also philosophical problems, some definitely avoidable. Certain forms of the problem of punishment, as we have seen, need not arise in an Akan philosophy of morals. Similarly, the metaphysical problem of substance and quality has no place in the Akan context. Since, as has just been indicated, mind in Akan thought is not a kind of substance or entity, the time-honored problem in Western philosophy of how mind as a spiritual substance can interact with the body as a physical substance also is nonexistent in that intellectual milieu.

The existence of these problems depends on the character of the languages concerned. Not only are the problems not universally ineluctable for the human mind but also they seem to be pseudoproblems. This has not, of course, been established, though there are hints in the above discussion which foreshadow independent considerations in that direction. What needs to be especially emphasized here is that they are not being said to be pseudo-problems simply because they are based, at least in part, on interpretations of language. Many important philosophical problems are of this nature. The trouble only comes when they are based on mistaken interpretations. It is to be noted, furthermore, that the fact that these problems do not arise within the Akan language is not taken as a conclusive reason for supposing that they are pseudoproblems. We will return to a certain implication of this remark soon. Meanwhile, it seems prudent to add that it is not being suggested that the philosophical problems mentioned in the last paragraph are pseudo-problems in all their forms.[28] Only the forms of the problems specifically delineated in our discussion are implicated. It is necessary, moreover, to point out that, when the problems in question are called Western, it is not implied that they are entertained by all Western philosophers. On the contrary, there are important Western philosophers who are not taken in by the metaphysical suggestiveness of their language in these matters.[29] The problems have been called Western simply in the sense that they seem to arise quite naturally in the Western context of thought and language. But in such matters, "language can only incline, not necessitate."[30]

Let us call concepts, problems, and theses that depend on the contingent characteristics of a given language "tongue-dependent." A concept, problem, or thesis that is tongue-dependent is, of course, necessarily language-dependent. On the other hand, language dependency does not necessarily imply tongue dependency. If a problem arises from an absolutely universal feature of language, it is not tongue-dependent. There certainly must be such problems. For example, the idea of message-stating must be inherent in any natural language. It must, consequently be pertinent in any natural language to talk of the equivalence of statements. At least any statement will have to be equivalent to itself. In the systematization of the logic of any natural language, therefore, relating equivalence to other logical concepts, by definition or otherwise, must always be a useful enterprise. The particular way in which this is done in a particular language, however, may not have a translational counterpart in some other language.

Consider the following two definitions:

1. "A is equivalent to B" means by definition "A if and only if B."
2. "A is equivalent to B" means by definition "(if A then B) and (if B then A)."

Both (1) and (2) generate obvious logical truths in English.[31] It turns out, however, that while (2) generates a logical truth in Akan, (1) is not even expressible therein simply for the lack of a counterpart of the phrase "if and only if." Of course, Akan has the concept of a conditional. In fact, any language in which the validity of an argument can be discussed must have this concept and hence must be able to express (2) in one way or another. In Akan, (2) might be expressed as follows:

2. "A ne B kosi faako" kyere se "(Se A a ende B) na (se B a ende A)."

Now, from a logistic point of view, given "(if A then B) and (if B then A)" the phrase "A if and only if B" is superfluous, since the two are definitionally equivalent. And this shows that a logical system in Akan need not be semantically incomplete on account of not having the latter. Actually, in standard presentations of classical logic in English both "A is equivalent to B" and "A if and only if B" are represented by one and the same logical symbol, namely, "↔" or "≡"; which should reinforce our sense of the logistic superfluity of the latter. Nevertheless, the fact that a logical truth, such as (I), may exist in one language and not in another is of considerable theoretical significance. It demonstrates, in particular, that some logical truths are tongue-dependent and, therefore, not universal without qualification. Of course, a relative universality might be secured for (I) by taking cognizance of some such qualifications as "provided that both logical concepts are available in the given language." (This appertains, of course, only to a highly informal level of discussion, such as the present one, for in any rigorous establishment of a logical system there will be an explicit indication of the basic symbols available and of how to obtain new ones.)[32]

It might be of interest, in view of these last remarks, to determine the minimum set of logical concepts for any natural logic whatever. We will not pursue this question here beyond pointing out the dangers of unconscious tongue-parochialism in an exercise of this sort. A case in point is provided by British philosopher David Mitchell in his book *Introduction to Logic.*[33] In the minimum conceptual equipment for logic in any natural language, he cites enthusiastically the distinction between a thing and its qualities or attributes. This distinction, he contends, is not just a linguistic device, "it is rather a *requirement* that the world should present itself to us in this form for it to be thought about" (143; italics in original). It is clear that by "us" he means at least all human beings, including Africans and Chinese. In the light of our earlier discussion, this claim is debatable.[34]

But Mitchell sallies forth onto even shakier ground. He goes on to assert that the equivalence of the active and passive voices in grammar corresponds to a categorial principle inescapable for the human mind: "The *necessary* truth that if A acts on B, B is acted on by A, seems to reflect a categorial distinction between active and passive and not a merely linguistic convention; that is to say, it seems that it is linguistically permissible to substitute 'B is acted on by A' for 'A acts on B'; only because we cannot but think that if A acts on B, B is *necessarily* acted on by A" (146; my italics). Strictly speaking, however, there is no passive voice in a language like Akan. The nearest we can come to "B is acted on by A" is something that retranslates as "What happened to B was due to A," which is not a proper passive. Here then, in Mitchell's "necessary truth," is a tongue-dependent principle, if ever there was one.

An even more interesting example of tongue-dependency in philosophy is the following. In English there is the concept of truth, of fact, and of what is the case, what is so. In Akan, on the other hand, the one notion of what is so (*nea ete saa*) is capable, even at the preanalytical level, of doing duty for all the English notions listed. In consequence, though in English it is quite an important philosophical project to try to elucidate the relationship between truth and fact, no corresponding project of comparable importance discloses itself in Akan. There is the word *Nokware* in Akan, which primarily means truthfulness, though by a turn familiar in linguistic usage generally it some-times means truth in the cognitive sense. But in those contexts in which it has the cognitive sense, the immediate understanding which *eye nokware* ("it is true") engenders is *ete saa* ("it is so"), and it is exactly in terms of what is so (*nea ete saa*) that the notion of fact may be expressed in Akan. "Fact" is to be rendered in Akan by *nea ete saa* or by some variant or synonym of this phrase. Thus, nobody is ever going to be able to pretend to bring enlightenment to an Akan by, for example, informing him or her in the Akan tongue that truth consists in correspondence with fact. The problem of the relationship between truth and fact, then, is another example of a tongue-dependent issue.[35]

We have now seen that tongue-dependency can issue forth in pseudo-concepts, problems, theses, etc., and also in genuine ones. The second sort of case is, perhaps, the more remarkable, for one is apt to assume that problems arising from the peculiar characteristics of a given language cannot be genuine. But this is to confuse genuineness with universality. Be that as it may, it is important to realize that both sorts of tongue-dependency can bedevil translation. It is as gratuitous to embrace other people's pseudoproblems as to tax oneself unnecessarily with their genuine problems. In formulating modern thought in African languages, African thinkers, for their own part, are not only going to have to translate some foreign ideas into their languages but also to formulate in their languages their own syntheses of any insights gained from such sources and those derived from reflection on their languages and indigenous traditional thought. In all this, we are going to have to beware lest our translations and formulations be vitiated by tongue-dependent prepos-sessions from within or from without.

To forestall possible misunderstandings, let me point out that no sort of conceptual relativism is intended or implied by any part of the above discussion. Conceptual disparities between peoples and cultures, even be-tween individuals in limited environs, are a brute fact of the human situation.

Doubtless this is the source of all sorts of complications in translation, particularly across cultures, some of which we have noted. But overriding all such problems is the fact, which is surely one of the most remarkable facts about language, that we can understand even what we cannot translate. This is due to the fact that we can learn languages other than that (or those) in which we were brought up. The fundamental fact here is that, because of the biological unity of mankind, any human being can participate or imaginatively enter into any human life form, however initially strange. The same fact, of course, underlies the possibility of transcultural communication.[36] This, again, is why the well-known insights about the great influence of language on thought obtained by writers like Sapir and Whorf cannot justify relativism of any ultimate sort.[37]

Owing to what has just been said, merely pointing out that a concept, problem, or thesis expressed in a given language is not expressible in another language will never be a sufficient reason for dismissing it as in some way defective. If a notion in English, for instance, cannot be expressed in Akan, the Englishman who has mastered Akan or the Akan who has mastered English can investigate in English why that is so. It may turn out, as we have seen in some cases, that the notion in question needs to be introduced into Akan. In the alternative, arguments intelligible in English can and will have to be given for debunking such a notion. I have tried in the body of this chapter to give at least brief hints whenever such a job of demolition has seemed just in my eyes. In general, this is the only way in which linguistic discrimination, such as I have been advocating, can be prevented from degenerating into ethnic or racial discrimination.

I have been constrained in this discussion to have recourse again and again to my own mother tongue, Akan. Two reasons account for this. First, the considerations I have been urging require a sort of intimate knowledge of an African language, which I cannot pretend to have of any language except my own. Second, I have found in the relevant literature little in the directions that interested me. There is, I think, an urgent need for highly discriminative conceptual studies of our individual languages in preparation for the domestication of modern knowledge in the African context. Such studies obviously will also prove useful if and when Africa achieves a lingua franca and settles down to perfecting it as a carrier and an instrument of modern knowledge.

Earlier writers on the subject of formulating knowledge in African languages, such as Cheikh Anta Diop, had it as one of their principal aims to prove to detractors of Africa that African languages are capable of becoming the vehicles of advanced knowledge. This is no longer in question in any remotely respectable circles. What the present discussion shows is that we need to develop a greater awareness of the conceptual framework of our own languages. Conceptually speaking, the maxim of the moment should be "African, know thyself!"

8

The Concept of Truth in the Akan Language

Ask any group of Akans who speak English what is the Akan word for truth and, unless they have made a special study of the matter, the chances are that they will answer, *Nokware*. In a certain sense they would be right. But a little reflection discloses a complication. The opposite of *nokware* is *nkontompo,* which means lies. But the opposite of truth is falsity, not lies.

What seems to have happened is that the hypothetical Akans have correlated the word 'truth' with a primarily moral, rather than cognitive, concept of truth in the Akan language. But why should they do this? There are, I think, three reasons. First, the main preoccupation with truth in traditional Akan society was moral. Second, the moral concept of truth presupposes the cognitive concept of truth; and third, the English word "truth" itself is ambiguous. When high-minded publicists wax eloquent in praise of the eternal verities of Truth, Beauty, and Goodness, what they have in mind in their reference to truth is truthfulness, rather than truth simply as what is the case! And it is not only in particularly high-minded contexts that 'truth' is used as a synonym for truthfulness; it is quite a common usage. So we have to say that our non-too-philosophical Akans had some excuse for their translation.

It emerges, then, that *nokware* translates as 'truthfulness' rather than truth in the cognitive sense. Naturally we must go on to show how the latter, i.e., the cognitive concept of truth, translates into Akan. But before then let us note one or two things about *nokware*. This word is made up of two words, *ano,* meaning literally mouth, and *koro,* meaning one.[1] *Nokware*, then, means literally being of one mouth. Less literally, it means being of one voice. It is sometimes suggested that this oneness of voice refers to communal unanimity; so that the truth is that which is agreed to by the community. Obviously, the authors of this suggestion have failed to distinguish between *nokware* and the purely cognitive concept of truth. It is intelligible, though extremely implausible, to suggest that truth in the cognitive sense is constituted by communal agreement, but it is not intelligible at all to make the same suggestion about truthfulness. Truthfulness has to do with the relation between what a person thinks and what he says. To be truthful is to let your speech reflect your thoughts. In this what others think or say has no particular role to play. And this was not lost on the traditional Akans. One can conceive of thinking as a kind of talking to oneself without embracing behaviorism; all that is needed is a little flight of metaphor. It then becomes possible to see truthfulness as saying to others what one would say to oneself. This is the oneness of voice that is etymologically involved in the word *nokware*.

The idea that truth (cognitive truth) consists in agreement among the members of a community is, in fact, far from the traditional Akan mind, for there is a sharp awareness of the disparity in cognitive capabilities between the wise individuals of the community (the *anyansafo*) and the populace (*akwasafo*). No elitist contempt for the populace is implied here. The Akans are a communally oriented people, and consensus is one of their most prized values. (On consensus, see further chapters 13 and 14.) Nevertheless, to make communal agreement the essence of truth[2] is an epistemological aberration that cannot be imputed to the Akans.

Of course truth has something to do with agreement, which is evident in the fact that to say of something someone has said that it is true implies agreeing with him. This is agreement between two points of view which does not necessarily involve a whole community. But community-wide or not, agreement cannot be the essence of truth in the primary sense, for when there is agreement in cognition it is about something being so; the agreement is that something is so, i.e., is the case. It is this notion of something being so that connects agreement with truth at all. It is a notion that will loom large in our discussion of the concept of truth in Akan.

It is important to note that *nokware* (truthfulness) involves the concept of truth. To say that somebody is speaking truthfully is to say that s/he genuinely believes what s/he is saying to be *true*. Moreover, it implies that it is, in fact, true. Apparent counter-examples are easily accommodated. If, for example, a man, speaking sincerely, says that there is a cat on the mat when there is, in fact, no cat on the mat, there is a sense in which he speaks truthfully. Certainly, we would not say that he was telling lies. But it would be misleading to say simply that he spoke truthfully when he said that there was a cat on the mat. The most that can be said is that he was being truthful in conveying the impression that he believed that the cat was on the mat.

It is the connection between truthfulness and truth which makes the ambiguity of the English word 'truth' so confusing when it comes to translating into Akan. To say that an *asem* (statement) is *nokware* implies that it is true cognitively. And so long as one is preoccupied with the affirmative, one might be tempted to think that this is all it means.[3] As soon, however, as one considers the negative, i.e., the case in which we say that something someone has said is not *nokware,* it becomes clear that there is also an element of moral comment in the use of *nokware*. There are a couple of words in Akan which have the same significance as *nokware*. These are *ampa* and *ewom*. *Ampa* implies truth, but it has the same excess of meaning over 'truth' that 'truthfulness' has. The word is a unification of the phrase *eye asem pa*, literally "it is a good piece of discourse." *Ewom* means literally "it is in it." This word is somewhat special, for, etymologically, it can be construed in a purely cognitive sense. Thus its meaning is particularly context-dependent.

It is now time to consider the Akan rendition of truth in its purely cognitive sense. And here we meet with a remarkable fact, which is that there is no one word in Akan for truth. To say that something is true the Akans say simply that it is so, and truth is rendered as what is so. No undue sophistication is required to understand that although the Akans do not have a single word for truth, they do have the concept of truth. This concept they express by the phrase *nea ete saa* or *asem a ete saa*, "a proposition which is so." The word *nea* means "that which"; *ete* which is a form of *te*, which, in turn, is a form of the verb *to be* in Akan, means "is" in the predicative sense; and *saa* means "so." *Asem* is an all-purpose word which means, in the present context, statement or proposition.

Notice that in the case of the adjective 'true', the Akans have a single word, *saa*, which provides a simple translation. (*Saa*, you will recall, means "so"). But in English one has both "is true" and "is so," whereas in Akan one has only *te saa* ("is so"). This obviously does not indicate any insufficiency in the Akan language, for if "is true" means the same as "is so," then one can get along as well with any one of them as with both, as far as the making of truth-claims (i.e., is-so claims) is concerned.

Another linguistic contrast between Akan and English is that there is no word in Akan for the English word "fact." A fact in Akan is simply that which is so (*nea ete saa*). Again, no insufficiency is indicated; whatever can be said about the world in English using the word "fact" can be said in Akan using the notion of what is so.

These linguistic contrasts have some very interesting consequences for the theory of truth. Consider the correspondence theory of truth. This is supposed, in one form, to assert something like this: "'p' is true" means "'p' corresponds to a fact." What does this come to in Akan? Simply that "'p' *te saa*" means " 'p' corresponds to *'nea ete saa'*," which in truth is nothing more than saying that "'p' *te saa*" means "'p' *te saa*." In other words, the correspondence definition amounts to a tautology in Akan. In a certain sense, this might be taken as a verification of the correspondence theory, for it might be said that being a tautology is a specially splendid way of being true. Be that as it may, one thing that cannot be pretended in Akan is that the correspondence theory offers any enlightenment about the notion of being so.

This comes out even more clearly in connection with the following variant of the correspondence theory. Some proponents of the theory sometimes formulate it by saying that a proposition is true if and only if things are as they are said to be in the proposition. Now, as pointed out above, in Akan "'p' is true" is "'p' *te saa*," which translates as "'p' is so," and this obviously is an abbreviation for "what the proposition 'p' says things are is as they are." Accordingly, the theory reduces to the tautology that things are as a proposition says they are if and only if things are as they are said to be in the proposition.

Aristotle's famous dictum about truth and falsity which provided Tarski's intuitive motivation in his Semantic Conception of Truth is a close approximation to the formulation commented on in the last paragraph. Aristotle says in his *Metaphysics*:

> To say of what is that it is not, or of what is not that it is, is false, while to say of what is that it is, or of what is not that it is not, is true.

This is very compressed phrasing, indeed. 'What is' in Aristotle's context, is, of course, short for 'what is so'. Translating into Akan and back into English, then, yields.

> To say of what is so that it is not so, or of what is not so that it is so, is not so, while to say of what is so that it is so, or of what is not so that it is not so, is so.

One can, perhaps, derive some lessons about the 'laws of thought' from this piece of discourse, but certainly no insight into the notion of something being so.

It seems, then, that there are some apparently important issues that can be formulated in English but not in Akan. Such, for example, is the question "How are true propositions related to facts?" Since this is not because of any insufficiency in the Akan language, it might be tempting, at least to an Akan philosopher, to suggest that the issues in question are not really philosophical but narrowly linguistic, due to the character of the vocabulary of English. Now, although it is, I think, correct to say that a problem like the one about the relation between truth and fact arises out of the nature of the vocabulary of English, it does not follow that it is not a genuine philosophical issue in English. The concepts of truth and fact are among the most fundamental concepts of human thought. Without the notion of something being a fact or of a proposition being true thinking is inconceivable unless it be a mere succession of ideas, and even that can be doubted. It seems obvious, then, that the relation between the terms 'truth' and 'fact' is a philosophical issue; for, of course, one cannot give a fundamental clarification of any of these foundational concepts in English without relating them one to the other. Yet, since these terms need not be both present in all natural languages, as the case of Akan shows, this task is not inescapable for the human mind. From which it follows that some philosophical problems are not universal. Of course, there must be others that are universal. It must, for example, be apparent from a remark just made that the clarification of the notion of something being so is a universal philosophical problem.

As the point that a problem may be genuinely philosophical and yet dependent on some contingent features of a particular natural language may possibly be controversial, I shall endeavor to reinforce it by analogy with a simple illustration again involving a linguistic contrast between English and Akan. In the English language there occur both the statement form 'p is equivalent to q' and 'p if and only if q'. It seems obvious that any natural language should have the means of expressing the idea of equivalence. And, indeed, in Akan we have a way of doing so, albeit somewhat circuitously. We say of two equivalent statements that they have the same destination: *ne nyinaa kosi faako*—more literally, "they both reach the same place." Since equivalence is distinct from identity of meaning, we might note, parenthetically, that we have a different way of expressing the latter. We say *nsem no mienu ye baako,* the two pieces of discourse are one. The point now is that in Akan we have no such statement form as might be rendered as 'p if and only if q'. We can, of course, assert 'if p then q' (*'se p a ende q'*) and 'only if p then q' (*'se p nkoara a na q'*), and the conjunction of these two forms is equivalent to 'p if and only if q'. But the conjunction is not the same *form* as the biconditional. If we now assert that the statement form 'p if and only if q' is equivalent to '(if p then q) and (if q then p)', we are obviously asserting a logical truth in English. But no such logical truth exists in Akan. There is nothing about the form 'p if and only if q', which makes it necessary that the Akans should have a phrase corresponding to it. Whatever can be expressed by means of that form can be expressed by the Akan way of formulating equivalence as indicated above. It follows that the question whether the relation between 'p if and only if q' and '[(if p then q) and (if q then p)]' is really one of equivalence is a genuine logical issue in English, which is, nevertheless, not universal.

The analogy with the question of the relation between truth and fact is quite complete. Just as the relation between 'p if and only if q' and '[(if p then q) and (if q then p)]' is a genuinely logical question which is dependent on a contingent feature of English vocabulary (and that of any similar language) so is the relation between truth and fact a genuine philosophical issue dependent on the English language. And just as any reasoner in English, whether he be a native speaker or not, will have to be conversant with the logic of the two statement forms, so anybody essaying a theory of truth in the medium of the English language will have to give some attention to the relation between truth and fact. It may well be that there are—indeed, I am sure that there are—ontological pitfalls into which native as well as non-native speakers of English are liable to fall in their thought about this relation. But that is another matter altogether.

There is a fairly obvious lesson that can be drawn from the foregoing observations. If some philosophical and logical problems—actually logical problems are philosophical problems—are relative to particular natural languages, then they cannot be as fundamental as those that are universal to all natural languages. Take, for example, the concept of implication. Any natural language will have to be capable of expressing this concept in one way or another. Furthermore, if we use the term 'entailment' to refer to the relation between the premisses and conclusion of a valid argument, then we can raise the question whether and how entailment can be defined in terms of implication. Such a question would be universal to all natural languages in the sense that it can be posed for any intuitively workable logic that may be constructed in any natural language. In comparison with this, the question of the relation between 'p if and only if q' and '[(if p then q) and (if q then p)]' is of very much less moment for the analysis of human reasoning.

Consider now the issue of the relation between fact and truth, on the one hand, and the problem of clarifying the notion of something being so, on the other. As I have suggested above, no cogent thinking is possible without the notion of something being so. Nevertheless, one can reason to one's heart's content in Akan without recourse to any word or phrase *separately* standing for *fact*, (that is, in addition to the term expressing the idea of being so). It follows that the problem concerning being so is more fundamental than that of the relation of truth to fact.

Suppose the problem of relating truth to fact is solved in the English language. Still, if there is a problem of truth in the Akan language—and there surely is—the position would be that the question has not even begun to be raised. In Akan the question would correspond to: "What is meant by saying that a statement is so, that is, what is meant by saying that things are as the statement says they are?" It is here obvious that certain versions of the correspondence theory of truth can at best only be part of the fundamental problem of truth, not part of its solution. The correspondence theory only begins to shape up as an attempted solution when a certain account of the nature of facts is offered. Some accounts, whether correct or incorrect, will not satisfy this requirement. For example, defining 'fact' simply as 'true proposition' may be correct, but it would leave us exactly where we started in the matter of the more fundamental problem of truth. On the other hand, an ontological interpretation of 'fact' may take us somewhere, though not necessarily in a desirable direction. Suppose, for example, that facts are construed as interconnected objects of a certain sort, then to say that a statement corresponds to fact would mean claiming a certain relation between the statement and the interconnected objects in question. From the point of view of the Akan language this could be interpreted as saying that being so is a relation between a statement and a certain configuration of objects.

In the following passage taken from Russell's *Philosophical Essays* (153) he seems to me to be advancing a theory of this sort:

> When we judge that Charles I died on the scaffold, we have before us, (not one object but) several objects, namely, Charles I and dying and the scaffold. Similarly, when we judge that Charles I died in his bed, we have before us Charles I, dying and his bed. . . . Thus in this view judgment is a relation of the mind to several other terms: when these other terms have *inter se* a 'corresponding' relation, the judgment is true; when not, it is false.[4]

(Note that since Charles I died quite a few years ago, the objects which one is supposed to have before one's mind when one makes a judgment to that effect must be of a rather unearthly nature.) Russell gave a somewhat more refined formulation of the correspondence theory in later life. (See, for example, *Human Knowledge: Its Scope and Limits*, Allen and Unwin, 1948, 170.) However, refined or not, it seems to me that when the correspondence theory is given meat in an ontological fashion it becomes open to fatal objections.

But it is not my intention to discuss the merits or demerits of the correspondence theory. I merely wish to make a meta-doctrinal point that careful attention to the Akan language enables us to see, which is that a theory of truth is not of any real universal significance unless it offers some account of the notion of being so. This some correspondence theories fail to do.

Let me in this connection make one or two comments about Tarski's Semantic Conception of Truth, since it is closely related to the correspondence theory of truth and is, besides, of great independent interest. The apparent intuition which motivates Tarski's theory is the same as that which underlies the correspondence theory at the level at which, as I have tried to show, it has a philosophical interest only relatively to the English language and kindred languages. (Recall, in this connection, our comment on Aristotle's dictum.) Still, Tarski's theory, or a part of it, has the merit of providing a logically precise formulation of the idea of a statement being so, that is, the idea of things being as a statement says they are. A Tarskian 'T' sentence to the effect that 'Snow is white' is true if and only if 'Snow is white' may be taken as a logically precise instantiation of the idea that to say that a statement is true is to say that things are as they are said to be in the statement. In Akan, since 'is true' is *'te saa'* which means 'is so', that is, 'is how things are', the Tarski sentence becomes "'Snow is white' is as things are if and only if snow is white." In this form the sentence sounds trivially truistic, and is indeed so, if it is intended even as partial theory of truth. But it can acquire a more substantial significance if it is made the starting point of an inquiry into the status of the second 'snow is white' in the Tarskian equivalence. This component gives a 'concrete' instantiation of the idea of something being so. If, as I suggest, the puzzle about truth is a puzzle about the notion of something being so, then the use of Tarski's equivalence (in this connection) can only be to provide us, in its second component, with a vivid instantiation of our abstract notion of something being so. Such presentations can concentrate the mind and possibly lead to an illuminating elucidation. However, in itself, Tarski's 'T' sentence, even as completed by the rest of the theory, can only provide a possible starting point in the solution of the problem of truth.[5]

The other main theories of truth traditional in Western philosophy, namely, the pragmatic and coherence theories, do not suffer any trivialization on being translated into Akan, but they take on a new look if they are measured against the task of elucidating the notion of something being so, which reflection on the concept of truth in the Akan language presses on our mind.

9

African Philosophical Tradition

A Case Study of the Akan[1]

I. Introduction

Philosophical thinking is a significant feature of African life. This fact is likely to be hidden from anybody who identifies philosophy with the discipline of academic philosophy, for the latter is, predominantly, an ensemble of written meditations, whereas writing, as a widespread cultural habit, is comparatively recent in most parts of Africa. Not, of course, that writing, as such, or even written philosophy, was historically unknown to Africa. Philosophical conceptions were put into writing in Egypt long before the practice was heard of in the Western world or its antecedents. Moreover, some African peoples south of the Sahara, the Yorubas, for example, are known to have invented scripts of their own. Nevertheless, with few exceptions, such as in the case of Ethiopia,[2] traditional philosophy in Africa south of the Sahara (which, for historical reasons, will henceforward be the referent of "Africa" and its cognates) is an oral rather than a written tradition.

To be sure there is a rapidly developing tradition of written philosophy in Africa today. It is probably recognized by all concerned that an important task of that emerging tradition is the recording and interpreting (in script) of the oral philosophy mentioned above. But, beyond this, what the exact relation between the two types of effort in philosophical thinking should be is, currently, a most contentious issue.[3] In my opinion the agenda for contemporary African philosophy must include the critical and reconstructive treatment of the oral tradition and the exploitation of the literary and scientific resources of the modern world in pursuit of a synthesis. One rationale of this is that the character of contemporary African culture has been determined by the interplay between African traditional modes of life and thought and Christian and Islamic customs and ideas along with the impact of modern science, technology, and industrialization. If in this process of synthesis contemporary African philosophers take critical cognizance of all these strands of the African experience, the resulting tradition of modern African philosophy should be rich in its variety and vital in its relevance to contemporary existence.

This does not mean that every single African philosopher is duty-bound to grapple with all the many sides of contemporary African life. Division of labor is as good a policy in intellectual as in economic production. Thus a contemporary African who specializes in the Philosophy of Mathematics or Natural Science and devotes a lifetime to this field might be making potentially valuable contributions to modern African philosophy even if she does not take up in her work issues arising from the traditional strand of our culture.[4] There is only one proviso, and it is that for her work to become a part of the African tradition it should eventually have a linkage, in some kind of organic manner, with a significant body of African efforts in philosophy; which, *mutatis mutandis*, is the only way in which a thought product could become an integral part of an intellectual tradition.[5] Nevertheless, for a long time to come a study of the oral tradition is going to have a prominent place in the preoccupations of African philosophers, as a class, because of the relative neglect that befell it in the period of Western colonization.

II. Sources of African Traditional Philosophy

An oral tradition of philosophy has both strengths and weaknesses. A major weakness is that it tends not to develop sustained and readily accessible expositions of speculative thought, such as in Kant's *Critique of Pure Reason,* or elaborate and architectural systematizations of thought *forms,* such as in Russell and Whitehead's *Principia Mathematica.* Nor, consequently, do you encounter an *easily observed* dialectic of diverging schools of thought with the excitement of an inevitable variegation of insight and illusion. The readiest sources of an oral philosophical tradition are communal proverbs, maxims, tales, myths, lyrics, poetry, art motifs and the like. These are often single statements or sets (which may be numerous) of relatively brief pieces of discourse as opposed to the lengthy exercises in assertion, explanation, and justification that are so characteristic of developed traditions of written philosophy.

The point is not that an oral tradition is condemned to philosophical superficiality or logical obtuseness. On the contrary, some of the folk sayings of African societies express profound conceptions about reality and human experience. And as to logical acuity, there are conceptual absurdities in the *Critique of Pure Reason* that would be promptly laughed out of court among any group of abstractly inclined Akan elders, for instance. Nevertheless, the lack of writing is a definite handicap in the preservation and enhancement of a philosophical tradition.

The situation just mentioned has been aggravated by the manner in which traditional African philosophy has tended to be researched and studied. Attention has seemed to be principally focused on the kind of sources mentioned. But, although these are the readiest sources, they are not the only ones possible. At least two other sources can be mentioned. The first of these should be obvious on only a little reflection. Proverbs and other folk sayings do not materialize out of the void; they originate in the brains of specific individuals, and although in most instances ascription of authorship is impossible, there still are in Africa today indigenous philosophic thinkers not significantly influenced by foreign philosophies who are capable of expatiating at length on these thought materials or advancing fresh ones through their own reasoning.

This should inspire another thought about the communal philosophies of traditional societies. It should be apparent that these are, to a large extent, the amalgamation in the communal imagination of truncated residues of the thought of the speculative thinkers and wise conversationalists of the group. The word "truncated" is used here advisedly. It cannot be expected that the details of the reasonings of various remarkable thinkers would be retained in the memory of the common people over the course of many generations. It is striking enough that some of their more memorable remarks have been preserved more or less intact in spite of the deleterious possibilities of this form of thought transmission. The fact of this preservation is suggested by the near uniformity of doctrinal report that one frequently encounters in widely separated parts of a traditional society. There is, of course, never a total unanimity; but so high a degree of uniformity with regard to basic conceptions can only be thanks to the extraordinary powers of memory that people are apparently apt to develop in the absence of a reliance on writing.[6]

It develops, accordingly, that in the African traditional setting there are two types of exponents of traditional philosophy. There are the traditionalist reporters of the communal philosophy, and there are the indigenous thinkers of philosophic originality. The former are, as a rule, content with, or even insistent on, the transmission of the heritage through quotation, paraphrase or, at best, exegetical flourishes, and do not take too kindly to the idea of criticism and reconstruction. The latter—a rare species in any society—are usually appreciative of the tradition and cognizant of its rationale, but are not hide-bound to it. They can reject or amend aspects of received conceptions and innovate with their own contributions. As it happens, the former are the ones who have tended to be tapped into service as "informants" by researchers into African philosophy. Of course, *if the results are formulated with due conceptual circumspection,* some insights into one level, namely, the folk level of African traditional philosophy, should accrue. Without at this stage pursuing the question whether this proviso has usually been met, it is worth emphasizing that it is a mistake to proceed as if folk philosophy exhausts the whole range of traditional philosophy, for there is the thought of the indigenous individual thinkers of traditional society. Incidentally, an even more egregious error, replete with atavistic forebodings, is that of equating African philosophy with African traditional philosophy.

But, to return to the individual philosophic thinkers of African traditional society, it is only comparatively recently that their existence or importance has received substantial notice; and it may well be that the book by the Kenyan philosopher H. Odera Oruka, entitled *Sage Philosophy: Indigenous Thinkers and Modern Debate on African Philosophy*,[7] which was published in 1990, is the first publication giving extended exposure to the views of named members of that class. M. Griaule's celebrated *Conversations with Ogotemmeli*[8] was somewhat in this direction, though that author's main interest in Ogotemmeli seems to have been as a depository of the communal (but not common) knowledge of his society. (Be that as it may, the complexity of the combination of empirical cosmology and speculative cosmogony that emerges from the talk of that African sage cannot but raise mind-tickling speculations as to what tomes of scientific and philosophic research his society might have produced had it been wedded to the art of writing.)

The reader will get some idea of the intellectual venturesomeness of the indigenous traditional thinkers of Kenya studied by Professor Oruka from the following brief quotations taken from some of the articulations of their conceptions of God. Oruka Rang'inya (1900–1979) asserts, "It is . . . quite wrong to personalize him. He is an idea, the *idea* which represents goodness itself. God is thus a useful concept from a practical point of view."[9] This thinker had no formal education. His conception of God, by the way, is one that would have warmed the heart of John Dewey, who, in *A Common Faith*,[10] criticized the personalization and generally the 'hypostatization' of the concept of God and proposed using the word 'God' to denote "the unity of all ideal ends arousing us to desire and actions."

In striking contrast to the position of Oruka Rang'inya is that of Okemba Simiyu Chaungo (1914–1987), another of the philosophic sages, as Oruka calls them. He says, "I think that God, in fact, is the Sun. . . . Well, the doings of the sun are big. It heats the land all day and its absence cools the land all night. It dries things: plants use it to grow. Surely, it must be the God we talk about."[11] Similar to this in some ways but also intriguingly dissimilar in others are the views of Stephen M'Mukindia Kithanje (born 1922). This sage explains, "When I try to have an idea of God he appears to me as a *mixture of heat and cold*. When these two merge (fuse) there comes up life. . . . The act of fusion, which brings forth life, is what we call *God*. And that is what we mean when we say that God created the universe."[12] The sum total of his Western education was six months in elementary school.

Even when one of these sages seemed to have embraced Christianity, his perspective on God displayed a personal twist. Paul Mbuya Akoko (1891–1981) had Western elementary school education and professed both Christianity and his indigenous religion (the religion of the Luo of Kenya) in which he was regarded as a spiritual leader. His reasoning in regard to God was as follows. "God in my language is *Nyasaye*. But God is one for all communities. The Luos thought differently. They thought their god was not god over other ethnicities. They were wrong. God is one Supreme Being for all peoples. This I can show by reference to the fact of the uniformity of nature. If there were many gods with similar powers, nature would be in chaos, since there would be conflicts and wars among the gods. But nature is uniform, not chaotic: a dog, for example, brings forth a dog not a cat. And a cat produces a cat not a dog or a hen. All this is proof of One Supreme Mind ruling nature. But what exactly is God? This nobody knows and can know."[13] In this quotation African and Western influences are fused and transmuted by means of a personal dialectic in a manner which deserves, in its appropriate place, a cultural as well as a philosophical analysis.

I will conclude these exhibits from Oruka's *Sage Philosophy* with the thoughts of a Kenyan indigenous skeptic. Njeru wa Kinyenje (1880–1976), who had no Western education at all, regarded organized religion, by which he meant Christianity, as the white man's witchcraft. "This witchcraft," he notes, "has triumphed over the traditional African witchcraft. Today I recognize its *victory* but not its *truth*. . . . I do not pray to God nor do I consult witch doctors. Both religion and witchcraft . . . have no truth in them. My greatest wish is that I should be spared interference from religion and witchcraft."[14]

In 1986 the Nigerian philosopher J. O. Sodipo and his American colleague Barry Hallen published a book on *Knowledge, Belief and Witchcraft: Analytic Experiments in African Philosophy*,[15] in which they also relied on the quoted views of some *onisegun*, i.e., masters of Yoruba indigenous medicine, regarded as philosophical colleagues rather than "informants," in making some interesting cross-cultural comparisons of the Yoruba conceptual framework with the English-speaking one. It turns out, on their showing, that, for example, there is a more uncompromising insistence in Yoruba than in English discourse on first-hand sensible experience in the validation of knowledge claims. Another recent work in which some attention is called to the opinions of individual indigenous thinkers of an African society—with names attached in this case—is Gyekye's *Essay on African Philosophical Thought*,[16] though the main focus of the book is on the communal philosophy of the Akans of Ghana. This is an elaborate study commanding the greatest interest.

Both of these books also evince a notable sensitivity to the philosophical intimations of the languages of the African peoples studied; which brings me to the second type of additional source for African traditional philosophy needing to be noticed. I have in mind here the fact that certain features of the vocabulary and syntax of a language may have conceptual consequences of the highest philosophical interest. In the matter of the influence of language on philosophy, it is well to understand from the outset that language inclines but does not necessitate. Nevertheless, that influence can be tremendous and, moreover, can be to the good or ill.

Considerations of language have a double urgency in connection with African philosophy; for in addition to their basic philosophical relevance, there is a need to unravel, by their means, the conceptual distortions that have accumulated in accounts of African traditional thought through the legacy of years of a self-assumed Western spokesmanship. The early European adventurers, missionaries, and anthropologists, who offered to explain to the Western world how Africans think (or fail to think), naturally formulated their narratives in terms of the conceptual schemes of their own upbringing. The fit between those frameworks and the African thought materials was most imperfect; but, unfortunately, these antecedents in the literature established paradigms of conceptualization which, in basic essentials, remain operative to this day in the work of foreign as well, more remarkably, as indigenous scholars. In many parts of Africa the power of Western formal education and Christian indoctrination over the African mind has been so great that, as one knows from one's experience, it is only by dint of a deliberate mental effort that an educated African can begin to think in terms of the categories of thought embedded in his own language in theoretical matters. That effort does not seem to be a widespread phenomenon among contemporary African sophisticates—not even among those who are most prolific in nationalistic protestations. Yet conceptual sanity, like charity, ought to begin at home.

The assumption is not that truth necessarily resides in the speculative promptings of the African vernacular, but only that an indispensable preparation for cross-cultural evaluations of thought is conceptual clarity at both cultural ends. Because the hoped-for conceptual perspicacity presupposes not a little linguistic competence, I propose in what follows to draw on my native understanding of the Akan language to attempt a brief account of elements of Akan traditional philosophy. Such culturally specific studies seem to me to be a necessary propaedeutic to any future generalizations about African traditional philosophy that shall have substance, depth, and legitimacy.

Let me, as a preliminary, give a list of some of the concepts and conceptual contrasts that have frequently been misapplied in expositions of Akan thought.

> Concepts: God, Nature, Person, Mind, Truth, Fact, Free Will, Responsibility.
> Conceptual contrasts: the Material and the Spiritual, the Secular and the Religious, the Natural and the Supernatural, the Mystical and the Non-mystical.

In a number of articles and public lectures I have tried in some detail to

separate Akan ideas with regard to these topics from foreign-oriented en-
tanglements and to elucidate the former with due attention to their natural
linguistic environment.[17] Here I can only give a selective summary, which, by
reason of its brevity, is likely to give an unintended impression of dogmatism.

III. The Concept of God as a Cosmic Architect (Rather Than an Ex-nihilo Creator) and Its Ontological Affiliations

The religious sphere is that in which there is the greatest misrepresentation
of Akan (and in general African) thought. The Akan, as indeed the African,
cosmos is regularly said to be a preeminently religious universe—a universe
full of spiritual entities at the apex of which God, the *ex-nihilo creator* of
heaven and earth, reigns supreme. It is true that most—but, note, not all[18]—
traditional Akans do believe in the existence of a Supreme Being. In fact, one
of the commonest sayings in Akanland is that no one teaches the Supreme
Being to a child (*Obi nkyere akwadaa Nyame*). But this being is supreme, or
if you like, omnipotent only in the qualified sense that he can accomplish any
well-defined task.[19] By comparison with some well-known Western conceptions of the omnipotence of God, this concept of supremacy might be
thought to be vitiated by too impious a rider, especially considering the sorts
of things that are not regarded by the Akans as well-defined. For example, is
it possible for the Supreme Being to reverse that law-likeness of phenomena
which defines the cosmic order as we know it? The Akan answer is "No!" Thus
the state drummer, a veritable public metaphysician, in the course of rendering condolences, on his "talking drums," to an Akan ruler on the occasion of
a bereavement would "say," among other things, "The creator created death
and death killed him."

The late K. A. Busia, sociologist and once prime minister of Ghana, an
Akan scholar deeply steeped in Akan culture by both royal birth and sustained
research, commenting on this quote, remarks, "Akan drum language is full of
riddles that conceal reflective thought and philosophy . . ." and continues,
"The drummer is emphasizing the inevitability of death. Man must die. The
drummer is saying to the ruler: Condolences; do not mourn; remember the
creator made man to die; and when the destined time comes, it is not only
beyond the skill of the physician to save the sick, but also *beyond the creator
himself* to exercise his power to save this man, for the creator has decreed that
every man must die, and so he is unable to stop death from exacting the
payment due to him"[20] (my italics). It should be stressed that the idea is not
that God just decides not to forestall this or any other death but rather that,
by the very nature of the laws by which he fashioned the cosmic order, *he
cannot do so*. So strong is the Akan sense of the universality of law and its
indefeasibility that the process of creation itself is viewed not as the outcome

of motivated decision-making on the part of the supreme being but as the
necessary result of his nature. This is the point of another famous metaphysical drum text:

> Who gave word,
> Who gave word,
> Who gave word,
> Who gave word to Hearing,
> For Hearing to have told the Spider,
> For the Spider to have told the Creator,
> For the Creator to have created things?

In venturing an interpretation of this text we are following a time-honored
practice of the speculative elders of Akan society. A very well-known saying in
this society is that to a wise person you speak in proverbs, not in literal
language. This is the reason why, as Busia notes, Akan drum language, as
indeed other forms of wise discourse, is full of riddles and paradoxes.
Inevitably, someone has to provide solutions, since, especially in the more
abstract cases, not too many curious people can immediately penetrate such
enigmas. Accordingly, one of the accepted credentials of wisdom is the ability
to offer the needed explanations. But since, even in much less subtle matters,
another Akan consensus has it that "two heads are better than one," no one's
explanation is taken as final. Thus the art of interpretation is a continuing
dialectic.

One contemporary Ghanaian philosopher of Akan extraction who has
devoted considerable effort to the interpretation of the cosmological text
under discussion is G. P. Hagan of the Institute of African Studies at the
University of Ghana, Legon. He suggests that the lesson of the riddle is that
"We must not look for the will to act and the reasons for acting in God's
reliance on other entities. Beyond Odomankoma [the Creator] there is no
other being to which the Akans assign any role in creation."[21] This is correct
as far as it goes. But there is an even more radical lesson to be drawn: Not only
must we not look for reasons beyond God for creation, but also we must not
look for reasons within God for creation, for there can be no such reasons.
Why? Because once we start talking of reasons for creation, we would be en
route to a wild goose chase, for what is to prevent us from pressing for the
reasons behind those reasons, and so on, *ad infinitum*? This, clearly, is the
logic behind the iteration and the rhythmic relay of the thought movement
before us. We are, accordingly, left with the notion that the Creator created
the world by the very law of his own being.

But what sort of creation are we talking about? There are doctrinal as well
as linguistic reasons for thinking that the Akan conception is one of a
demiurgic fashioning out of order from a pre-existing indeterminate stuff

rather than creation out of nothing. Again, the doctrine is "concealed" in a riddle: The Supreme Being is likened to a bagworm, and the question is raised as to how the bagworm got into its case. Did it weave it before getting into it or did it get into it before weaving it? One might easily suppose that this precipitates no real antinomy; for, surely, the bagworm couldn't have gotten into a non-existent case. But suppose now that it wove it before getting into it. Very well, then we had no bagworm to begin with, for without the "bag" you have no bagworm; and how could a non-existent bagworm have woven its case or anything else? The corresponding cosmogonic paradox is this: Either the Creator was somewhere before creating everywhere or he was nowhere while creating everywhere. In either case there is a contradiction. Moral: Creation can only have been a process of transformation. By means of a somewhat different reasoning about this same bagworm paradox Hagan derives a by-and-large equivalent conclusion: ". . . the Akan view is that both he and his creator are part of this world. With such a philosophic assumption the quest for the explanation of the universe reduces itself to the quest for the explication of the *internal structure* of the universe."[22]

Hagan's formulation can hardly be improved. But the thought can be reinforced with the following linguistic consideration. In Akan the concept of existence has an explicitly locative connotation. To exist is to *wo ho,* i.e., to be *there*, at some place.[23] Ultimately the same is true, I believe, of the concept of existence in the English language. But in English there is an appearance to the contrary. Through the so-called existential sense of "is" or "to be" the impression is fostered that "to be there" might be interpreted as "to exist in that place"; from which it then appears that existence in itself (as expressed by the verb "to be") has nothing to do with location. Thus, apparently, something might exist, *be*, without *being* in some place. In Akan there is no such pretence, for there is no analogue of the supposedly pure existential "is" or "to be." To say "Some thing is there," in Akan we say, *Biribi wo ho*. If called upon to translate "Some thing *is*" we must insist on the same locution: *Biribi wo ho,* for if you eliminate the localizer *ho,* the remainder is simply meaningless.[24]

Lest it be thought that an exclusively locative conception of existence must rob the Akan of the wherewithal to call attention to the existence of abstract entities, such as numbers, possibilities, reasons, hopes, fears, etc., it should be observed that a simple option is available. It is open to us to argue that an abstract entity is only figuratively an entity (though not for that reason unimportant); and to a figurative entity corresponds only a figurative location. This, in fact, is the construal of abstract entities that is consonant with the bent of the Akan language, but I must forebear to expatiate on it here.

In the present connection what we need to note is the following cosmological implication of the locative conception of existence. If a Creator exists,

He exists in space somewhere, and His creative activities can only have taken *place* in space. Thus He exists exactly in the same sense, though, of course, not with the same powers and properties, as the things He created. Compare: Jack exists in the same sense in which the house which Jack built exists. Logically, the comparison is not outlandish, for the Creator too, on the Akan view, must have operated on some preexisting raw stuff. True, prior to creation there were no mundane entities *x*, *y*, or *z*, but the existence of the creator entails some cosmological environment, however indeterminate. That He could not have existed in the midst (!) of absolute nothingness is also implied in the Akan word for "create," which is *bo*. To *bo* something is to fashion out a product; and, actually, it is closer to the Akan *intension* to describe the Supreme Being as a cosmic architect rather than as a Creator, given the transcendental conceits of the latter English term in contexts like this.

In Akan the idea of to *bo* something out of nothing carries its contradictoriness on its face. In English the semantical incongruity of creation out of nothing is well enough concealed to allow it to be an orthodoxy among great numbers of people. Yet, if to create is to *cause* something to come into existence, then absolute nothingness must be a logically immovable impediment. Consider a Creator working in such a splendid metaphysical isolation. Suppose He exerts himself and then something appears. The question is: What, in principle, is to make the difference between *post hoc* and *propter hoc* in such circumstances or, more strictly, lack of circumstances? Given the hypothesis, the answer is "Nothing," and with it disappears any simulacrum of causation. Personally, I do not believe in either the Akan or the Christian Creator, but it seems to me that the conceptual problems besetting the former pale into insignificance in the face of those afflicting the latter. I might point out parenthetically that I have not, here or elsewhere, taken the mere linguistic portrayal of an Akan conceptual scheme, in contrast to, say, a Western conceptual set-up, as proof of its truth or validity. Such considerations are germane only to the purposes of conceptual description and comparison, which, when there are significant differences, is a substantial enough objective in itself. But where, as in the present paragraph, I have offered an evaluation, I have endeavored to adduce, or at least hint at, *independent* considerations, whose intelligibility and (therefore) merits or demerits do not depend essentially on the peculiarities of the conceptual framework of a given culture. As surface facts, such peculiarities undeniably exist and can impede intercultural understanding. But at the deeper reaches of human conceptualization, they are not cross-culturally irreducible;[25] and that is why independent arguments are possible. My argument for the incoherence of the concept of creation out of nothing is not based on the fact that it does not make sense in Akan, but rather on the fact that there are logico-conceptual considerations against it which are cross-culturally intelligible, or at least intelligible in both English and Akan discourse.

It might be of some interest, however, to expatiate a little on the reasons for the incoherence of the notion of creation out of nothing within the Akan conceptual framework. It is incoherent therein not only on account of the meanings of *wo ho* (to exist) and *bo* (to "create") but also because of the comparable empirical orientation of the Akan concept of nothingness. Significantly, there is no abstract noun in Akan for this concept. The only available translations are in terms of a gerund in some such formulation as "the circumstance of there not being something *there*" (*se biribiara nni ho* or *se hwee nni ho*). In general, the Akan language, as apparently many an African language, is very economical in abstract nouns, preferring gerundive and other periphrastic devices. From this it has sometimes been inferred—absurdly—that Africans tend not to think in abstract terms. In fact, periphrases can be as abstract as single-word abstract nouns. Besides, against the verbal economy achievable through abstract nouns is to be weighed the tendency of the availability of such words to inspire—I do not say compel—the spinning of webs of ontological fantasy. Consider the thesis that number is a species of object. Now, number is rendered in Akan as the how-many (*dodow*) of things. Accordingly, when the thesis is faithfully translated from Akan back into English it becomes something like "The how many of things is a species of object." Anyone is likely to have problems thinking this to herself let alone selling it to others. Again, considerations of this sort are not decisive as to truth or validity. My own antipathy toward the postulation of abstract entities (in semantic analysis and anywhere else) is based not only on my Akan linguistic sensibilities but also on independent argumentation intelligible in English. The burden of my critique (expounded elsewhere)[26] is that this practice, whose frank name is hypostasis, thrives on a conflation of the categories of signifier, referent, and object, especially the last two.

But let us return to *nothing*. It is clear that in the Akan way of thinking it presupposes *something*; it has an intrinsic spatial context. In consequence, any notions of a total and absolute nothingness devoid of all context can have no accreditation in Akan philosophy. If one now reviews the bagworm riddle, its anti-transcendental message with regard to creation should be even more evident. That message and its framework of concepts have further momentous metaphysical implications. For example, if the spiritual is conceived, in the manner of Descartes, as that which is absolutely non-spatial, no such category of being can have a home in Akan thought; which implies that the question of the spiritual/material antithesis does not arise therein.

The natural/supernatural distinction fares no better.[27] If everything is according to law, even including the creative activities of the Supreme Being, as pointed out earlier in connection with the dialectic of Death and the Creator, then there is no separating one order of being, as nature, from another, above it, as supernature; which means that the ontology entertained is a homogenous one in which the concept of nature itself is otiose. True, there is a conception of a hierarchy of existences, starting with inanimate things at the bottom and climbing through the realms of plants and the lower animals to that of human beings, the ancestors and a variety of extra-human beings and forces up to the Supreme Being at the apex. (Having touched upon inanimate things, let me take the opportunity to debunk the routine attributions of animism to all Africans. The Akans, at least, regard some things as lifeless. For them dead wood is quintessentially *dead*, and what is so tragic about a corpse is that it is lifeless—the life-principle has left it!) Different realms of being, then, are postulated, but the important thing is that all of them are viewed, as Hagan well remarks, as *parts* of one comprehensive universe.

Thus, suppose an event or situation in the human realm seems to resist all the commoner modes of explanation. For example, an illness may be defying all the best herbal and psychiatric treatments. Very well, then the explanation, for a traditional Akan, may be that the patient is being punished by an ancestor for some sins of commission or omission. In having recourse to a hypothesis of this sort, there is no feeling of going out of the "natural" order, for no such concept is germane to the thought system under discussion. As can be understood from our earlier remarks, the Akan starts with the axiom that everything has its sufficient reason. (No shades of Leibniz! That there is a sufficient reason, an appropriate explanation, for everything, *biribiara wo ne nkyerease,* is a commonplace of the Akan oral tradition.) Given this axiom, what more *natural* than to seek the explanation for a given phenomenon apparently inexplicable in terms of the factors of one part of the world from another *regular* part? Pardon the pleonasm. By the Akan definition of the universe, everything is a regular part of the system of reality.

Even more inappropriate than calling the kind of Akan explanation we have just cited supernaturalistic is the application of the term "mystical" to it. This term is often used loosely to mean the same as supernatural. In that case it is subject to the disclaimer already entered. But if it is used with a more serious semantical intent, then we have a bigger mistake on our hands.[28] Mysticism in the stricter sense refers to a special experience in which the subject is supposed to attain unity with the highest reality, directly apprehending everything as identical with everything else and yet as distinct, with an associated sense of purest bliss. Nothing is farther from traditional Akan modes of thought and experience than mysticism in this sense. Apart from anything else, the contradictory language, apparently beloved of mystics, is likely to get on Akan nerves and elicit the traditional admonition that there are no crossroads in the ears (*asumu nni nkwanta*), an aphoristic advocacy of the principle of non-contradiction. Here again, let it be conceded, in principle, that mysticism may, after all, be an avenue to higher truths; only many Akans, including the present writer, will take a lot of convincing.[29]

That the concept of the mystical is so inapplicable to the world view of the

Akans is due to the extensively empirical character of their conceptual framework. This is not the same, by the way, as saying that their beliefs necessarily have empirical warrant. The proposition that our departed ancestors are alive and kicking in the world of the dead and can punish the errors of the living may not be empirically justifiable, and I, for one, have the gravest doubts. Yet, the conception itself of the ancestors and their habitat is empirical in orientation.

It has not escaped any moderately attentive student of Akan thought—and of African thought in general—that the ancestors and their world are conceived very much on the model of the living and their world.[30] For example, access to the *post mortem* world is believed to be by land travel during which there is a river-crossing involving the payment of a toll; which was the reason in olden times for the stuffing of coffins with money and other traveling needs. In fact, the Akan world of the ancestors is so like this world that our political order is supposed to be continued there (in perpetuity) in terms not only of structure but also of personnel. Take away the temporal imagery of the conception and nothing is left. The reader who recalls the empirical character of the Akan conception of existence is unlikely to be surprised by this.

But though the ancestors are conceptualized in terms of a this-worldly imagery, they are not supposed, in their interaction with the living, to be constrained by all the laws that govern human motion and physical interaction. Thus they are normally not perceivable, though the initiated are supposed to be capable of entering into communication with them. Again, although they are conceived in the image of persons, they are not vulnerable to the physical perils of this fleeting world. I have elsewhere[31] called entities conceived in this way quasi-material. Entities of this sort—material in image but not in dynamics— are obviously very important in the Akan world view. Actually, they are also important in various brands of Western thought. The Christian belief in the resurrection of the body clearly involves quasi-material conceptions. So too do parapsychological narratives about poltergeists and other apparitions, spiritualist claims of human communication with the dead, and occult theories of astral *bodies.* The interesting and important difference between Akan thought and all these varieties of Western thinking in this regard is that in the West quasi-material ideas coexist with Cartesian notions of spiritual substance while, as previously indicated, conceptions of spiritual entities in the Cartesian sense simply have no place in the Akan ontology.

IV. The Concept of a Person As Both Descriptive and Normative

What has just been said has a substantial implication with respect to the Akan concept of a person. One can straightaway rule out any prospect of a Cartesian dualism of body and mind. In the Akan language the word for mind (*adwene*) does not signify any kind of entity, except in some figurative uses when it denotes the brain (as when we comment on the *adwene* in someone's head). The regular word for the brain is *amene*, and there is little temptation to identify the mind, the *adwene*, with the brain, the *amene*. But there is not even the possibility, short of a linguistic revolution, of identifying the *adwene* with a Cartesian spiritual substance. In our (Akan) conceptual scheme mind is primarily the capacity to think thoughts, feel emotions, construct arguments, imagine things, perceive objects and situations, dream dreams of both night and day and so on.[32] A difference of considerable interest between the Akan concept of mind and many Western conceptions of mind is that sensations viewed in isolation from conceptualization or, if you like, from intentionality, do not count as mental, i.e., as having to do with *adwene*, whereas some very famous discussions of mind in Western philosophy are full of earnest meditations on sensations.[33] The Akan way of viewing this matter prompts the hypothesis that, perhaps, there is no one uniform theory that will illumine the nature of both thought and sensation, though they all, as the Akans are very much aware, depend on the brain. Incidentally, except in regard to the reference to the brain, this is a suggestion to which Aristotle would probably have resonated more readily than many of his spiritual descendants in contemporary Philosophy of Mind.

It would be an agreeable exercise to enlarge upon the advantages of the Akan view of mind but that belongs to another place. Here it might be of greater immediate interest to see what, in addition to mind, the Akans conceive to be involved in the constitution of persons. There is, most visibly, the assemblage of flesh and bones that form the body (*nipadua*, literally, person tree). But, reason the Akans, something must make the difference between a dead, inert, body and a living one. This they attribute to an entity called the *okra*, which they consider an actual particle of the Supreme Being. Since in respect of this divine constituent all persons are exactly alike, they all are deserving, in equal measure, of a certain dignity and respect—a notion which motivates a strong ideology of human rights. However, in all other respects every individual is different from every other; they differ not only in terms of spatio-temporal specifics but also in terms of moral, psychological, and social circumstances, which, in combination with humanly imponderable contingencies, produce achievements and failures, fortunes and misfortunes, and shape individual lives in myriad ways. We might, in light of this thought, sum up one aspect of Akan thinking on human personhood by saying that destiny is the principle of individuation of the *akra* (plural of *okra*), the divine specks that constitute the principle of life in the human frame.

A principle of individuation for the *akra* in terms of mundane circumstances is needed because otherwise they would, from a human point of view, be indistinguishable, being all specks of the divine substance. Prior to incarnation, a given *okra* is, by definition, the *okra* of a person envisaged in a determinate life-story, which the Creator knows in its full completeness *ab initio* but we, humans, can only learn by empirical installments as the individual concerned plays out his or her destiny on this earth day by day. There is here some analogy with Leibniz' individual concept of a person, which, in the mind of God, "includes once for all everything which can ever happen to him."[34] Both conceptions are faced with the problem of human responsibility. Of this problem the Akans are acutely aware. Yet, interestingly, the very notion that each individual has her own antecedently defined destiny is often appropriated in Akan discourse as a basis for the right of individuals to make their own decisions unhindered by others. Since the Akans—and Africans generally—are strongly communalistic in outlook, this stress on what might be called the metaphysical right of decision is significant as indicating a certain balance between the sense of communal dependency and the belief in individual rights. Such metaphysical proclamations of individuality take the form of pointing out that when one was receiving one's destiny from the Supreme Being no one else was there.

It is important to understand that the doctrine of pre-appointed destinies is, logically, integral to the Akan belief in the universal reign of law encompassing even the process of divine creation. The class of facts and events constituting the destiny of an individual is only an instantiation in miniature of the cosmic order. The idea that individuals have each their own unique destinies is expressed in Akan communal thought in the following dramatic form.[35] In the making of a human individual, God (the Akan cosmic architect, not the Christian *ex-nihilo* creator) apportions a part of himself in the form of an *okra* for dispatch to the earth to be born of man and woman. Before the departure there is a ceremony at which the *okra*, alone before God, takes leave of his or her maker. (In fact, the Akan word for destiny, which is *nkrabea*, means, literally, manner of taking leave.) The high point of the proceeding is the announcement of destiny. God reveals to the *okra* what career awaits her or him on earth and how it shall be brought to a conclusion. Thereupon, the *okra* descends to be incarnated into human society to fulfill that blueprint. (When a person descends from on high, says an Akan maxim, she or he lands in a town.)

The incarnation is, of course, in large part a biological process which starts with the intimacy of man and woman. Accordingly, the physiologic make-up of a person is attributed to both partners. To the mother the Akans ascribe the origin of a person's *mogya* (literally, blood). Socially, this is the most important constituent of a person, for it is taken as the basis of lineage or, more extensively, clan identity. Since the Akans are a matrilineal people, it is this kinship status that situates a person in the most visceral relationships and brings him into the most existential of the networks of obligations, rights and privileges that characterize Akan communalism. To the father is attributed the origin of an aspect of human personality which is, conceptually, somewhat elusive. The father's semen is held to give rise to something in a person which accounts for the degree of impact which that individual makes upon others by his sheer presence. Both the inner cause and the outer effect are called *sunsum* in Akan. This is a human characteristic to which the Akans are especially sensitive.

Descriptively, then, the highlights of the Akan conception of a person are the life principle (*okra*), the "blood" (*mogya*), and the distinctive personality ingredient called *sunsum*. Ontologically, there is a greater affinity between the *okra* and the *sunsum*, for they are both quasi-material. But the *okra* survives death to become an ancestor whereas the *sunsum* perishes with the demise of its possessor. Indeed, an individual may die because his *sunsum* has been attacked and destroyed or even devoured by some extra-human agent such as a witch. Only a constitutionally weak *sunsum*, though, is supposed to be susceptible to this kind of attack; a strong *sunsum* will withstand it. Of a person with a strong *sunsum*, the Akans say: *Ne sunsum ye duru*, literally, "His *sunsum* is heavy"; and a weak *sunsum* is said to be light (*hare*). The locution is metaphorical, but the quasi-materiality of the conception of the *sunsum* is evident. Indeed, for the Akans the *sunsum* is, as W. E. Abraham puts it in his classic exposition of Akan philosophy, "that second man who is a *dramatis persona* in dreams,"[36] a temporary duplication of a person which *actually* sallies forth from a sleeping person to indulge in all the goings-on of the dream state.

The difference in ontological character, then, between the *okra* and the *sunsum*, on the one hand, and the *mogya* and the bodily frame as a whole, on the other, is only one of degree of materiality, the body being fully material and the other constituents only partially material in the sense already explained. Carefully to be distinguished from this conception is the Cartesian notion of a material body and an immaterial soul. On this latter conception, any talk of the incarnation of the soul is simply self-contradictory; on the former, there is at least a preliminary coherence. If one is going to talk of an embodiment, it is, surely, a conceptual requirement that the thing to be embodied should be spatial, which is what a Cartesian soul diametrically is not. Both the *okra* and the *sunsum*, being spatial in conception, satisfy this condition, though whether there actually are such entities is severely open to question. This skepticism, by the way, is without prejudice to the utility of a non-hypostatic construal of these two concepts in the analysis of human personhood. One thing, in any case, should be absolutely clear: Neither the *okra* nor the *sunsum* can be identified with the immaterial soul familiar in some influential Western philosophical and religious thinking (with all its attendant paradoxes). This Western concept of the soul is routinely used interchangeably with the concept of mind while the concepts of *okra* and *sunsum* are categorially different from the Akan concept of mind (*adwene*), as our previous explanations should have rendered apparent. Thus Descartes (in English translation) can speak indifferently of the soul *or* the mind and appear to make sense. In Akan to identify either the *okra* or the *sunsum* with *adwene* would be the sheerest gibberish.

Our remarks about the Akan concept of a person so far have been occupied, broadly speaking, with its descriptive aspect, even though some very significant normative consequences have been shown to flow from it, as, for example, the idea that every human being has an intrinsic worth because of the divine element in her being. But it is of the utmost importance to note that in addition to such normative implications there is a normative layer of meaning in the concept itself. In Akan thinking, as indeed in the thinking of many other African peoples, a person in the true sense is not just any human being, but one who has attained the status of a responsible member of society.[37] The characterization of this status will also be the characterization of the Akan system of values. Only the baldest statement is possible here. A responsible member of society, from the Akan point of view, is the individual whose conduct, by reason of a sense of human sympathy, shows a sensitivity to the need for the harmonious adaptation of her own interests to the interests of others in society and who, through judicious thinking and hard work, is able to achieve a reasonable livelihood for himself and family while making non-trivial contributions to the well-being of appropriate members of his extended kinship circles and the wider community. The first component of this conjunction of necessary conditions provides, in fact, the essentials of a definition of morals in the strictest sense, while the second gives intimations of the communalist ethos of Akan society.[38] That ethos also holds the key to Akan political philosophy, which we must leave unexplored due to space limitations.[39] On the question of ethics in the strict sense, let me point out in the briefest possible manner that Akan ethics is a humanistic ethics in the precise sense that it is founded exclusively on considerations having to do with human well-being and, contrary to widespread reports, has nothing to do, except very extrinsically, with religion.[40]

On the above showing, personhood is susceptible to degrees. Moreover, it is not an attribute that one is born with but rather an ideal that one strives to achieve in life. In the path of improvement there are, theoretically, endless vistas of higher personhood. But the downward path has a certain critical line of demarcation. In reflecting on this matter we will be brought back to the problem of destiny and human responsibility in Akan thought, to which the makings of an Akan-inspired solution will be proposed.

V. Free Will As Responsibility

Within Akan canons for the appraisal of behavior an individual may fail to be a person (*onipa*) through, for instance, irresponsible habits. Such an individual is sure to be the recipient of advice and inspirational prodding from kith and kin and from friends and peers; which, incidentally, should allay any fears that the denial of personhood to a human being might be a prelude to some form of maltreatment. Every human being, as previously noted, has an intrinsic value, since he is seen as possessing in himself a part of God. But suppose the individual in question proves utterly impervious to counsel and slides steadily into the depths of social futility. The typical Akan approach at this stage is to substitute a (solicitous) search for treatment and rehabilitation for moral critique and verbal persuasion. Reason? Irresponsibility has passed into non-responsibility. The individual is no longer himself. The critical line of human self-identity has been passed. (*Enye onoa*, literally, "It is not himself" or *Enye nania*, literally, "it is not his eyes.") There is no exact equivalent of the English-speaking notion of free will or, in this specific case, lack of free will, within the Akan framework of concepts, but this may be taken as its Akan counterpart.

But notice five things about the Akan understanding of what in English is called free will. First, neither free will nor the lack of it is a universal feature of the human condition; some people have free will, others do not.[41] Second, one and the same individual may have free will with respect to one sphere of conduct but not some other. Third, since there are degrees of personal and social maladjustment, we can speak of degrees of free will. Fourth, the concept of free will has normative as well as descriptive components. Fifth, and, perhaps most interestingly, both free will and responsibility refer to the same aspect of human consciousness and conduct, namely, the ability of an individual to retain his human self-identity in conduct. As is clear from the context, the self-identity in question is not logical self-identity, which even the most confirmed idler must necessarily retain, but a normative species-identity. We are talking, in other words, of whether the individual has the ability to act as a *normal* human being should. (Behold the normative significance of free will writ even larger.)

When, then, is an individual responsible? We can derive the following answer, which I believe to be the correct one, from the brief sketch given above of the Akan approach to the appraisal of human conduct. An individual is responsible (or free) if and only if she is amenable in both thought and action to rational persuasion and moral correction.[42]

Two philosophical consequences of the conception of free will (or responsibility) just advanced should be rapidly noted. First, determinism does not have the slightest tendency to compromise human responsibility in the present conception. Indeed, rational persuasion is a form of determination: it is the form of determination appropriate to normal human behavior. Second, it follows from the conception in question that there can be only one problem of free will *or* responsibility, not two problems, one of free will and the other of responsibility.[43] This is probably the most interesting difference between the Akan-inspired view of free will and soft determinism or compatibilism in Western philosophy. The soft determinist also does not think that determinism imperils free will, but he speaks of the problem of free will *and* responsibility as if there are two problems here; which accounts, I think, for the persistence of a certain residual sense of mystery when all the admirable compatibilist arguments have been rehearsed. In spite of the abandonment in many Western philosophical circles of the facultative concept of *the will* that may be supposed to be free or unfree, it remains a veritable postulate in much Western thought that freedom is a descriptive attribute that is either present in the human condition or absent from it independently of normative considerations. It becomes then a truly intractable problem how to establish its existence or non-existence. This matter requires infinitely more argumentation, but it seems to me to be a distinct advantage of the conceptual economy of the Akan view of 'freedom' that it is exempt from this problem.

What of the problem of free will and predestination? The difficulty is that any pre-appointing of destiny might seem to smack of a freedom-negating manipulation, and it is not at all difficult to imagine a kind of subtle manipulation that might look in principle like divine pre-appointing. (Think, for example, of a *Brave-New-World* type of pre-conditioning updated with all the technical resources for manipulation that have been developed since this classic was written.) It is appropriate, in answer to this problem, to recall that in the Akan cosmology the predetermination of human destiny (as of everything else) is an integral part of the intrinsically law-governed demiurgic process from which the world order results. The very possibility of such a thing as indoctrination or manipulation presupposes that order, and it is therefore a categorial error to compare any freedom-eroding technique of manipulation that might be devised by humans with the divine preappointing of destiny in the above manner, in spite of the possibly over-suggestive drama of the Akan traditional articulation of the doctrine of destiny. The reason why manipulative conditioning is prejudicial to free will is that it is disruptive of the human way of development on which the Akan conception of free will or responsibility is predicated. That way of development is through nursing, nurture, and the kind of training of the mind that is aimed at producing individuals capable of acting on the basis of judicious reflection—all which, of course, also presupposes the same world order discussed. In my opinion, the

validity of this defense of free will within the context of a worldview based on
the universal reign of law remains intact even when shorn of the belief in a
supreme being.

There is still, however, the problem of fatalism. It might be wondered
whether the Akan doctrine of destiny does not entail a fatalistic policy of life.
There is, actually, a fatalist strain in Akan thought, due, I suspect, to the
tempting conflation of "what will happen will happen" with "what is ordained
by God will happen." But the two suppositions are logically independent; the
first is a logical truth, the second obviously is not. The first is a premiss in the
constitutive argument of fatalism, the second a premiss in the doctrine of
divine predestination. Fatalism argues: "What will happen will happen,
therefore whatever happens happens of necessity," while predestination
argues: "What is ordained by God will happen; God has ordained everything,
therefore whatever happens is ordained by God." The latter is what is
germane to the Akan doctrine of destiny; but the Akan mind, like many minds
everywhere, has not been immune to the deceptive allurements of the former.

It should be observed, in any case, that, logically, fatalism does not imply
a fatalistic policy of life. That policy is premissed on pessimism, which is no
part of the philosophical thesis of fatalism. From fatalism all that one can
deduce is that if success will come, it will come of necessity; and if failure will
come it will come of necessity. The person who supposes, for whatever reason,
that success will come in his life is unlikely to adopt a policy of resignation.
Only those who somehow come to acquire the feeling that what is in store for
them is failure are at all likely to develop that attitude. The underlying
reasoning then is: "Failure will come; whatever will come will come of
necessity, therefore, failure will come of necessity. So why bother?" It is
obvious, by the same considerations, that the doctrine of destiny does not
imply a fatalistic attitude to life. One has to add to that doctrine the logically
independent information that one is destined to fail before any pretense of an
argument for fatalistic inactivity can be made.

It should come, then, as no surprise that although the traditional Akans
are, as a rule, believers in the predetermination of destiny and are, to boot,
frequently fatalists, they are not generally fatalistic. Some Akans are known to
sink into passivity, citing bad fate; others assume a bright destiny and live and
work with high motivation even in the face of adversity.[44] Statistically, the
optimists would seem to be more typical.

This last reflection brings us to a characteristic of an oral tradition of
philosophy, which, I believe, is an advantage. In such a context philosophy
tends to have a very direct and palpable effect on practical life. When
philosophy becomes a written discipline there is always the danger that some
might (though, certainly, they need not) be tempted to pursue technical
virtuosity as somewhat of an end in itself. Such diversions are remote to the

concerns of an oral tradition. The Akan doctrine of destiny and how it is played out in daily life provide a particularly conspicuous illustration of this remark.

This same circumstance probably accounts for the possibility of speaking of the communal philosophy of a whole people. The doctrines involved are not necessarily accepted or even dreamt of by all and sundry, but the close interplay of life and doctrine in an oral tradition of philosophy ensures that in the normal course of socialization one's intellectual sensibilities are attuned to certain kinds of doctrine. In some this attunement amounts to nothing much more than an inchoate predisposition; but in others it takes the form of highly articulate conceptualizations. The foregoing has been a brief report, interpretation, and critical reconstruction of some of the high points of this intellectual phenomenon as far as the Akan communal tradition is concerned. The potentially more exciting exploration of the individual philosophies of the indigenous thinkers of Akan traditional society remains a thing of the future. But the time is obviously ripe for extensive particularistic studies of both types across the continent of Africa.

VI. Contemporary Akan Philosophy

Meanwhile, there is a growing Akan tradition of written philosophy which is very conscious of its heritage of oral philosophy. By a happy historical circumstance, some of the most industrious scholars among the nineteenth- and early-twentieth-century missionaries and anthropologists who studied our culture (from a mixture of motives, facilitation of colonial governance not excluded) were much taken with its philosophical dimensions. Thus the works of Christaller,[45] Rattray,[46] and Westermann[47] on Akan culture give various degrees of exposure to the philosophical conceptions of the Akans. These foreigners were meticulous scholars who lived among our people, learned their language and their ways and tried to empathize with their psyche. Their insights have been appreciated, though their limitations have not gone unnoticed by indigenous Akan scholars[48] (many of them trained philosophers), who, since the beginning of this century, have taken in their own hands the task of expounding their culture and its philosophy. The most celebrated of these was J. B. Danquah (1895–1965),[49] lawyer, politician, philosopher, poet, playwright, whose *The Akan Doctrine of God* is a classic of Akan philosophy. An earlier lawyer-politician and scholar, who, though not as technical a philosopher as Danquah, wrote books relevant to Akan philosophy was J. E. Casely Hayford (1865–1930). His books, especially *Ethiopia Unbound*,[50] are among those that sowed the seeds of twentieth-century Pan-African nationalism. Internationally, of course, the most important Ghanaian political leader was Kwame Nkrumah (1901–1972), first president of Ghana.

Also an Akan, Nkrumah studied philosophy, among other things, in the United States and Britain. In Britain his thesis supervisor (at London University) under whom he wrote a doctoral dissertation on *Knowledge and Logical Positivism*[51] in the mid-forties was A. J. Ayer. This supervisor notwithstanding, Nkrumah was heavily Marxist-Leninist, and published in 1947 a manifesto of African radicalism called *Towards Colonial Freedom,* in which he adapted Marxist-Leninist philosophy to the purposes of African liberation. Later on, in *Consciencism: Philosophy and Ideology for Decolonization with Particular Reference to the African Revolution* (1964),[52] he argued that Marxism agreed in many points with the indigenous philosophy of his own society. Another Akan scholar-statesman, the sociologist K. A. Busia, prime minister of Ghana after Nkrumah's regime, who also had some philosophical background, wrote a number of expositions of Akan culture and philosophy among which the most important, at least from the point of view of Akan traditional political philosophy, was his *The Position of the Chief in the Modern Political System of Ashanti* (1951).[53]

Current Akan workers in philosophy are generally professional philosophers.[54] Of these W. E. Abraham, an all-round philosopher, as much at home in mathematical logic as in the history of philosophy, is something of a pioneer in the exposition of Akan philosophy. His *The Mind of Africa* (1962),[55] integrates a survey of Akan traditional philosophy with a discussion of the political and economic problems of Africa. Gyekye's *An Essay on African Philosophical Thought* (1987)[56] is the latest full-length work on Akan traditional philosophy. It is both expository and reconstructive. Contemporary Akan philosophers, as indeed many contemporary philosophers of other parts of Africa, in spite of their attachment to their tradition of oral philosophy, are not parochial in their philosophical interests, and the corpus of their work displays a variety which reflects a sensitivity to both their own tradition and the intellectual environment of the modern world.[57] There is also another kind of variety in their work. There are differences in the way they interpret and build upon their oral tradition, as is to be expected in any enterprise of philosophy undertaken by different minds.[58]

It is apparent from all the above that the Akan tradition of philosophy includes a traditional and an emerging modern component. The reference of "traditional" here is different from that of the same word as it occurs in a phrase such as "British traditional philosophy." In the latter context it refers to the writings of the historical philosophers of Britain. In the former, that is, in relation to a pre-literate society of the past, "traditional" refers to the body of thought orally transmitted from generations long past. This asymmetry of reference arises from an asymmetry of importance. As remarked earlier, in Africa, owing to the intervention of colonialism, the resources of the oral tradition remain either untapped or only insufficiently tapped. That tradition therefore has a contemporary importance not matched in various other places. This is why there is a need for the kind of particularistic investigations to which attention has been drawn more than once in this discussion. But, certainly, as this situation is more and more attended to and contemporary African philosophers exploit their background of traditional philosophy to construct philosophies suited to modern existence, sub-African categorizations of philosophy, such as Akan, or Yoruba, or Luo philosophy, will increasingly lose their rationale in the arena of contemporary concerns. I leave the question of the possibility of an analogous melting-down of racial categorizations in the global theater of philosophy to the rational imagination of the reader.

10

The Need for Conceptual Decolonization
in African Philosophy

In June 1980 at the UNESCO conference on "Teaching and Research in Philosophy in Africa" in Nairobi I advocated a program of conceptual decolonization in African philosophy.[1] In the present discussion I wish to pursue the idea further. I write now with an even greater sense of urgency, seeing that the intervening decade does not seem to have brought any indications of a widespread realization of the need for conceptual decolonization in African philosophy.

By conceptual decolonization I mean two complementary things. On the negative side, I mean avoiding or reversing through a critical conceptual self-awareness the unexamined assimilation in our thought (that is, in the thought of contemporary African philosophers) of the conceptual frameworks embedded in the foreign philosophical traditions that have had an impact on African life and thought. And, on the positive side, I mean exploiting as much as is judicious the resources of our own indigenous conceptual schemes in our philosophical meditations on even the most technical problems of contemporary philosophy. The negative is, of course, only the reverse side of the positive. But I cite it first because the necessity for decolonization was brought upon us in the first place by the historical superimposition of foreign categories of thought on African thought systems through colonialism.

This superimposition has come through three principal avenues. The first is the avenue of language. It is encountered in the fact that our philosophical education has generally been in the medium of foreign languages, usually of our erstwhile colonizers. This is the most fundamental, subtle, pervasive, and intractable circumstance of mental colonization. But the two other avenues, though grosser by comparison, have been insidious enough. I refer here to the avenues of religion and politics. Through these have been passed to us legacies of long-standing religious evangelization, in the one case, and political tutelage, in the other. I can only touch the tips of these three tremendous historical icebergs in one discussion.

Take first, then, the linguistic situation. By definition, the fundamental concepts of philosophy are the most fundamental categories of human thought. But the particular modes of thought that yield these concepts may reflect the specifics of the culture, environment, and even the accidental idiosyncrasies of the people concerned. Conceptual idiosyncrasy, although an imponderable complication in human affairs, probably accounts for a vast proportion of the conceptual disparities among different philosophical traditions, especially the ones in which individual technical philosophers are deeply implicated. Think, then, of the possible enormity of the avoidable philosophical deadwood we might be carrying through our historically enforced acquisition of philosophical training in the medium of foreign languages. Of course, a similar pessimistic soul-searching is altogether in place even among the natives of any given philosophical tradition vis-à-vis their historical inheritance. This is, in fact, much in evidence in contemporary Western philosophy, for example. But the position is graver in our situation of cultural otherness, for even ordinary common sense would deprecate needlessly carrying other peoples garbage.

What exactly are the concepts I am thinking of here? There are many of them, but let me mention only the following: Reality, Being, Existence, Thing, Object, Entity, Substance, Property, Quality, Truth, Fact, Opinion, Belief, Knowledge, Faith, Doubt, Certainty, Statement, Proposition, Sentence, Idea, Mind, Soul, Spirit, Thought, Sensation, Matter, Ego, Self, Person, Individuality, Community, Subjectivity, Objectivity, Cause, Chance, Reason, Explanation, Meaning, Freedom, Responsibility, Punishment, Democracy, Justice, God, World, Universe, Nature, Supernature, Space, Time, Nothingness, Creation, Life, Death, Afterlife, Morality, Religion.

In regard to all these concepts the simple recipe for decolonization for the African is: Try to think them through in your own African language and, on the basis of the results, review the intelligibility of the associated problems or the plausibility of the apparent solutions that have tempted you when you have pondered them in some metropolitan language. The propositions in question may be about topics that have no special involvement with Africa, but they may well be about the internalities of an African thought system.

By the sheer fact of our institutional education, we are likely to have thought about some, at least, of these concepts and problems framed in terms of them using English or French or some such language. The problem is that thinking *about* them in English almost inevitably becomes thinking *in* English about them. It is just an obvious fact, in philosophy at least, that one thinks most naturally in the language of one's education and occupation. But in our case this means thinking along the lines of conceptual frameworks which may be significantly different from those embedded in our indigenous languages. By virtue of this phenomenon, we are constantly in danger of involuntary mental de-Africanization, unless we consciously and deliberately resort to our own languages (and culture). It turns out that this form of self-knowledge is not easy to attain, and it is not uncommon to find highly educated Africans proudly holding forth on, for instance, the glories of African traditional religion in an internalized conceptual idiom of a metropolitan origin which distorts indigenous thought structures out of all recognition.

There is no pretense, of course, that recourse to the African vernacular must result in instantaneous philosophic revelation. The chances, on the contrary, are that philosophical errors are evenly distributed among the heterogeneous races of humankind. Suppose, for example, that a concept, much employed in, say, English philosophical discourse, seems to lose all meaning when processed in a given African language. This consequence may conceivably be due to an insufficiency in the African language rather than to an intrinsic defect in the mode of conceptualization of the foreign language or culture concerned. How does one determine whether this is so or not? The only way, I suggest, is to try to reason out the matter on *independent grounds*. By this I mean that one should argue in a manner fathomable in both the African and the foreign language concerned. With that accomplished, it would be clear that the considerations adduced are not *dependent* on the peculiarities of the African language in question. In general, failure to heed this requirement is one of the root causes of the kinds of conceptual idiosyncrasies that, in part, differentiate cultural traditions of thought.

Notice that if such independent grounds can be adduced, relativism is false. In many of the things I have written elsewhere, I have argued against relativism.[2] Here I will take it for granted that the theory is false and proceed to give some illustrations of the procedure of conceptual decolonization that I have been talking about, so far in a rather general way. Let us attend, to start with, to the cluster of epistemological concepts in the list of basic concepts given above. We mentioned Truth, Fact, Certainty, Doubt, Knowledge, Belief, Opinion and some more. Now, one very powerful motive for the persistent wrestling with these concepts in Western epistemology has been the desire to overcome skepticism, and one very influential form of skepticism has been the clear and simple form of it encountered in Descartes' methodological skepticism. Interestingly, classical Greek skepticism was more complex in its argumentation than the Cartesian version. But, possibly, partly because of its devastating simplicity and lucidity, it is the latter that has become the driving force of epistemological inquiry. At peak, the skeptical problem *à la* Descartes is simply that so long as my cognition is subject to the possibility of error, it is uncertain; and so long as it is uncertain, it falls short of knowledge. In the *Meditations* the program of doubt starts with the observation that the senses have proved deceptive in the past and consequently cannot be trusted to give us knowledge. This consideration is reinforced with the reflection that, in any case, all our perceptual beliefs might very well be dream illusions.

These two degrees of doubt still leave simple *a priori* propositions, such as those of elementary school arithmetic, unscathed. But not for long, for soon Descartes invokes the hypothesis of an all-powerful God, or for fear of the impiety of the idea, "some malicious demon of the utmost power" who might make me "go wrong every time I add two and three or count the sides of a square."[3] Aside from the dramatic imagery of the hypothesis, what it means is simply that none of our cognitions, or at least none of those considered up to that point, are exempt from the possibility of error. And this is the sole reason why all claims to certainty must be suspended. As is well known, the only thing that proves capable of breaking the suspension is the *Cogito*, the contention that "I think therefore I am," which, in the eyes of Descartes, is guaranteed against not just error but indeed the very possibility of it. From all which it is apparent that for Descartes certainty means the impossibility of error.

It is important to note that this conception of certainty is not peculiar to Descartes in Western philosophy. It has held sway in that tradition, before and since Descartes, over the minds of innumerable philosophers of differing persuasions. For example, the logical positivist position that empirical knowledge is incapable of certainty was predicated on the single consideration that such cognitions are perpetually open to the *possibility* of error. This notion was also entertained (very notably) by C. I. Lewis, the 'conceptual pragmatist' and other non-positivists in contemporary philosophy.[4] Yet, on a little reflection this understanding of certainty is, or should be, seen to be rather surprising, for exemption from the possibility of error is nothing short of infallibility. Accordingly, the quest for certainty[5] becomes the quest for infallibility—as chimerical a quest as ever there was. Certainly, neither Descartes nor the logical positivists and others are known to have laid explicit claims to infallibility in any part of their knowledge. How, then, has this quest for infallibility gone on in actual practice for so long and exercised so controlling a force in Western epistemology? The answer is that this is probably due to the fact that it has almost always—not quite always, because it is explicit in Plato[6]—gone on concealed under the designation of certainty.[7]

But, now, that concealment seems to be at all possible only in a language like English. I find it hard to think that anyone could so much as make a beginning of such concealment in my own language, Akan. In this language to say 'I am certain' I should have to say something which would translate back into English in some such fashion as 'I know very clearly' (*Minim pefee* or *Minim koronyee*) or 'I very much know' (*Minim papaapa*). For the more impersonal locution 'It is certain' we would say something like 'It is indeed so' (*Ampa*) or 'It is true' (*Eye nokware*) or 'It is rightly or very much so' (*Ete saa potee*)[8] or 'It is something lying out there' (*Eye ade a eda ho*). None of these turns of phrase has the slightest tendency to invoke any intimations of infallibility. To suggest that in order to say of something that *ete saa potee* I must claim exemption from the possibility of error would strike any average or above average Akan as, to say the least, odd in the extreme. (The Akans are given to methodological understatement.) Any Akan will tell you, even at a pre-analytical level of discourse, that just because it is possible for me to go wrong, it does not follow that I can never go right. A popular adage says "If you look carefully, you find out" (*Wo hwehwe asem mu a wuhu mu*).

This is not, by any means, to imply that skepticism is unknown in Akan society. But in that environment a skeptic is not one who is moved to doubt the possibility of knowledge through viewing certainty under the pretensions of infallibility. S/he is simply an *akyinyegyefo*, literally, one who debates; in other words, one who is apt to question or challenge received beliefs. And the challenges are ones that are inspired by more stringent criteria of justification (whether in perceptual or conceptual discourse) than is customary. This form of skepticism is akin to the variety which is manifested in the disputing of, say, the belief in God on the grounds that good reasons are lacking. That is a well-established usage of the concept of skepticism in English discourse. In comparison with it, the skepticism of Descartes, even as a methodological foil, seems highly misconceived. And the essential reason is not because it is not supportable by Akan linguistic categories or epistemologic intuitions, but rather that it involves a fallacy; namely, that of confusing certainty with infallibility of which all judicious thinking should steer clear, whether in the medium of Akan, English, or Eskimo. The relevance of Akan language here is this: that (in my opinion) any Akan who reflects on the matter from the standpoint of his or her own language is very unlikely to be drawn into that fallacy.

I will illustrate this relevance further by means of another example, still involving Descartes. His *Cogito* has already acquired quite a place in African philosophy, dialectically speaking. Mbiti has commented, by implication, that 'I think therefore I am' betrays an individualist outlook, to which he has counterposed what he takes to be the African communalist axiom: "I am because we are, and since we are, therefore I am."[9] Before Mbiti, Senghor had expressed a characteristic 'participatory' reaction to the *Cogito* on behalf of the African: Spurning "the logician's conjunction 'therefore'" as unnecessary, "the Negro African," according to Senghor, "could say, 'I feel, I dance the Other; I am'."[10] But by far the most conceptually interesting African comment on Descartes' claim was that by Alexis Kagame, who pointed out that throughout the Bantu zone a remark like 'I think, therefore I am' would be unintelligible for "the verb 'to be' is always followed by an attribute or an adjunct of place: I am good, big etc., I am in such and such a place, etc. Thus the utterance '. . . therefore, I am' would prompt the question 'You are . . . what . . . where?"[11] Kagame's point holds very exactly in the Akan language also, and I would like to amplify it a little and explore some of its consequences for the *Cogito* and other philosophical suppositions.

For our present purposes the most relevant fact regarding the concept of existence in Akan is that it is intrinsically spatial, in fact, locative; to exist is to be there, at some place.[12] 'Wo ho' is the Akan rendition of 'exist'. Without the 'ho', which means 'there', in other words, 'some place', all meaning is lost. 'Wo', standing alone, does not in any way correspond to the existential sense of the verb 'to be', which has no place in Akan syntax or semantics. Recur, now, to 'I think, therefore I am', and consider the existential component of that attempted message as it comes across in Akan. In that medium the information communicated can only be that I am there, at some place; which means that spatial location is essential to the idea of my existence. It is scarcely necessary to point out that this is diametrically opposed to Descartes' construal of the particular cogitation under scrutiny. As far as he is concerned, the alleged fact that one can doubt all spatial existences and yet at the same time be absolutely certain of one's existence under the dispensation of the *Cogito* implied that the 'I', the ego, exists as a spiritual, non-spatial, immaterial entity. The incongruity of this sequence of thought, quite apart from any *non sequiturs*, must leap to the Akan eye. There is, of course, nothing sacrosanct about the linguistic categories of Akan thought. But, given the *prima facie* incoherence of the Cartesian suggestion within the Akan conceptual framework, an Akan thinker who scrutinizes the matter in his or her own language must feel the need for infinitely more proof of intelligibility than if s/he contemplated it in English or some cognate language. On the other hand, if on due reflection the Akan thinker becomes persuaded of the soundness of Descartes' argumentation, that would not necessarily be a loss to conceptual decolonization, for that program does not envisage the automatic refusal of all foreign food for thought. I might mention, though, for what it is worth, that in my own case the exercise proves severely negative.

Negative or not, the implications of the Akan conception of existence for many notable doctrines of Western metaphysics and theology require the most rigorous examination. It is well known that inquiries into the explanation of the existence of the universe enjoy a high regard among many Western metaphysicians and is one of the favorite pursuits of philosophical theology. However, a simple argument, inspired by the locative conception of existence embedded in the Akan language, would seem, quite radically, to subvert any such project: To have a location is to be in the universe. Therefore, if to exist means to be at some location, then to think of the existence of the universe is to dabble in sheer babble. This reasoning does not, by the way, mean that it is so much as false to say that the universe exists. More drastically, it means that it does not make sense to say of the universe either that it exists or that it does not exist. But this same impropriety must obviously afflict any idea of a being

who supposedly brought the universe into existence. If one cannot speak of
the universe either as existing or not existing then neither can one speak of its
having been brought into existence. Since the Akans, in fact, generally believe
in a Supreme Being, it must occur to the student of Akan thought that the
Akan conception of that being cannot be of a type with, say, the *ex-nihilo*
creator of Christianity, but rather must be of the character of a quasi-
demiurgic cosmic architect.[13]

Here now comes the challenge of conceptual decolonization. Have Akan
Christians, of whom there are many, confronted the conceptual disparity thus
revealed and opted for the Christian notion in consequence of critical
reflection, or have they perhaps unconsciously glossed over them or, worse
still, assimilated the Akan conceptions to those of Christianity or vice versa?
One answer that any of them would be exceedingly ill-advised to attempt
would be to say that religious matters are not a subject of argument or analysis
but, instead, of faith. For where two incompatible faiths are available through
indigenous culture and foreign efforts of proselytism, to go along with the
latter for no conscious reason would be the quintessence of supine irrationality. It would, besides, betray a colonized mentality. Again, the suggestion is
not that profession of the Christian persuasion on the part of an African is
automatically a mark of the colonial mentality. In general, only the unreasoning profession of a religion with a historical association with colonialism
merits that description.

Actually, if it comes to that, the unreasoning profession of any religion,
indigenous or foreign, is not a model of intellectual virtue. The Akans believe
traditionally that the existence of the Supreme Being, *as conceived by them*, is
so obvious that no one need teach it to a child. (Hardly any Akan adult
brought up in Akanland can be ignorant of the Akan saying *Obi nkyere
akwadaa Nyame*, which means "No one teaches the child the Supreme
Being.") The implication is not that no reflection goes into the acquisition of
the belief, but rather that it takes only a little of it. If so, the least an Akan
thinker who embraces a foreign conception of the Supreme Being can do, if
s/he is mindful of the Akan tradition, is to make sure that there are good
reasons for that metaphysical belief mutation. Otherwise s/he cannot escape
attributions of the colonial mentality. I myself do not believe either in the
Akan or the Christian or any kind of supreme being, though (a) I find the
Akan concept more intelligible than the Christian one (which, in truth, I find
of zero intelligibility), and (b) I am of the opinion that the locative concept
of existence found in the Akan language is more conducive to sound
metaphysics than its rivals.[14] Although my convictions in these matters are
quite stout, I enjoy no sense of infallibility, and I do not rule out the possibility
of being argued out of them in one direction or another. I might stress in the
present connection, though, that on any appropriate occasion I would be
prepared to try quite industriously to offer rational justifications for these

intellectual commitments or avoidances. Hopefully, I might thereby be able to make some little progress toward freeing my own mind of any vestiges of the colonial mentality. It is, at all events, impossible to overemphasize the necessity for the rational evaluation of religious belief in contemporary African philosophy, for the unexamined espousal of foreign religions, often in unleavened admixture with indigenous ones, is the cause of some of the severest distortions of the African consciousness.

It is equally obvious that Africa has suffered unspeakably from the political legacies of colonialism. Unhappily, she continues in this sphere to suffer, directly or indirectly, from the political tutelage of the West. This is due to a variety of causes, frequently not of Africa's own making. But it is impossible not to include in the inventory of causes the apparently willing suspension of belief in African political traditions on the part of many contemporary African leaders of opinion. After years of subjection to the untold severities of one-party dictatorships in Africa, there is now visible enthusiasm among many African intellectuals and politicians for multi-party democracy. Indeed, to many democracy seems to be synonymous with the multi-party system. This enthusiasm is plainly not unconnected with foreign pressures; but there is little indication, in African intellectual circles, of a critical evaluation of the particular doctrine of democracy involved in the multi-party approach to government. Yet that political doctrine seems clearly antithetical to the philosophy of government underlying traditional statecraft. The advocates of the one-party system at least made an effort to link that system with African traditional forms of government. That linkage was uniformly spurious, and in some cases, perhaps disingenuous.[15] But there was at least an intent to harmonize the contemporary practice of politics in Africa with what was considered viable in the traditional counterpart. The lack of evidence of any such intent in more recent times must raise legitimate fears of a new lease of life for the colonial mentality in contemporary African political thought.

What, then, can we learn from the traditional philosophy of government that might be of relevance to the contemporary quest for democracy? Traditional African governments displayed an interesting variety of forms. But amid that variety, if the anthropological evidence is anything to go by, there was a certain unity of approach, at any rate among a large number of them.[16] And that unity consisted in the insistence on consensus as the basis of political decision-making. Now, this conception of decision-making is very distinct from that which makes the will of the majority, by and large, decisive. Since majorities are easier to come by than consensus, it must be assumed that the decided preference for consensus was a deliberate transcending of majoritarianism. Assuredly, it was not an unreflecting preference; it can be shown to have been based on reflection on first principles. The most fundamental of these principles may be stated as follows: In any council of representatives—traditional councils usually consisted of representatives elected by kinship units—the representative status of a member is rendered vacuous in any decision in which s/he does not have an impact or an involvement. And any such voiding of the will constitutes a deprivation of the right of the representative, and through him, of his constituency to be represented in the making of a decision that affects their interests (broadly construed). By any reckoning, that should be considered a violation of a human right.

It is or should be well known that majoritarian democracy, that is, the form of democracy involving more than a single party in which, in principle, the party that wins the most parliamentary seats forms the government, is apt to render the will of a substantial minority of no effect, or almost of no effect, in the making of many important decisions affecting their interests. It is, then, from a consensus-oriented standpoint, a system that is frequently dele-terious of genuine representation, that is, representation beyond parliamen-tary window-dressing. It is obvious, by the same token, that a democracy based on consensus must of necessity be of a non-party character, not in the sense that political associations must be proscribed, which, of course would be authoritarian, but simply in the sense that a majority at the polls need not be an exclusive basis of government formation. Perhaps some proponents and practitioners of the one-party system confused the one-party with the non-party concept. May the former never return to Africa!

The detailed and systematic working out of a system of the sort barely hinted at above in the contemporary world, as distinct from the comparatively simpler circumstances of traditional times, must encounter many difficulties. But its serious exploration would at least show some sensitivity to the need for intellectual decolonization in African political life. Besides, it might conceiv-ably lead to a system that might bring peace and the possibility of prosperity. (See further chapters 13 and 14.)

Most of the considerations relating to the need for decolonization urged in this discussion were derived from facts about language. I was, accordingly, constrained to focus on the only African language about which I am some-what confident. Africans from other linguistic areas are invited to compare and, if appropriate, contrast, using their own languages. The principle of decolonization will, however, remain the same. My own hope is that if this program is well enough and soon enough implemented, it will no longer be necessary to talk in terms of the philosophical conceptions of the Yoruba or the Luo or the Akans. Instead, we would feel able to advance our philosophi-cal views on independent grounds.

Nor is the process of decolonization without interest to non-African thinkers, for any enlargement of conceptual options is an instrumentality for the enlargement of the human mind everywhere.

11

Post-Colonial African Philosophy

The post-colonial era in African philosophy is the era of professionalism. Yet paradoxically, in this same period philosophical doctrines have been propounded by non-professionals more than by professionals.[1] Moreover, the philosophies produced by the non-professionals have shaped the destinies of millions of Africans since independence, while those emanating from the professionals might well have remained locked up in their brains, as far as these teeming masses are concerned. Why?

The reason is not hard to find. The non-professional philosophers in question were the first wave of rulers in post-independence Africa. They had led successful anti-colonial struggles which were as much cultural as they were political. At independence they were faced with extremely urgent challenges of political and cultural reconstruction. The question facing them was: What form of government or, more generally, social organization is best suited to the requirements of (a) the social and economic development that had become stunted under colonialism and (b) the restoration of the cultural identity that colonialism had eroded? Serious consideration of this question inevitably led to reflection on first principles. And so we find leaders like Nkrumah of Ghana, Senghor of Senegal, Sekou Toure of Guinea, Nyerere of Tanzania, and Kaunda of Zambia putting forward blueprints of politics and development based on general conceptions of community, polity, and the general good.[2] Not all of these men were philosophers by original bent. Some, indeed, like Nkrumah and Senghor had technical training in philosophy. But others, such as Kaunda, had only their own enlightened intuitions to rely on; necessity, to be sure, was the mother of their philosophical inventions. Nevertheless, in every case it was historical circumstance that made them philosopher-kings.

Interestingly, Nyerere's theory of Ujamaa (Familyhood) socialism was more refreshing intellectually and, certainly, more relevant to African traditional society than the thinly Africanized varieties of Marxist socialism that were offered by Nkrumah and Sekou Toure or the romantic negritude of

Senghor's supposititious socialism. I will come back to the question of Africanity in due course, but it should be noted at once that whatever one may think of the content of their theories, these leaders produced genuine philosophies with the most time-honored of motivations; in the words of Serequeberhan, that of the "critical and explorative engagement of one's own cultural and historic specificity."[3]

But how were the philosophies of our philosopher-kings disseminated in their respective countries? In trying to answer this question one is painfully conscious of a certain encompassing negativity. As is well known or can otherwise easily be verified, the process usually took the form of sloganized propagation by a party machine in a one-party environment in which dissent was equated with subversion. This was as true in Tanzania, notwithstanding all the noble and kindly appearances to the contrary, as it was in Ghana or Guinea. This is one of the causes of some of the disappointments that have overtaken our pre-independence assumptions and aspirations which Serequeberhan[4] notes with obvious anguish. I do not want to overemphasize this causal remark, for other causes are probably more profoundly implicated in our continental misfortunes, such as the inequitable terms of international commerce or even communication and the very fact of our relatively recent subjection to a racist colonialism, which has injured our sense of self and largely forestalled our mastery of our situation in the world.

But let me return to the role of philosophy *ex cathedra* in our post-colonial experience. The authoritarian mode of propagation, of course, ensured that the philosophies in question would affect the lives of millions of our people. But that did not necessarily imply widespread acceptance or even comprehension. Except, perhaps, in East Africa, where Swahili offered possibilities of mass understanding, this discourse, often phrased in choicest English or French, was a closed book to the great majority of the African populations, however well versed they may have been in their own vernaculars.

Professional African philosophers may be pardoned if they should contemplate with mixed feelings this aspect of the philosophical activities of the statesman philosophers, who may be called their spiritual uncles with a certain cultural pertinence. But how does the work of the professionals compare with that of their spiritual uncles in regard to genesis, content, and mode of dissemination? One obvious difference relates to genesis. The statesmen were under the pressure of historic leadership to produce positive theoretical and normative underpinnings for their programs of urgent national reconstruction. The imperatives of doctrinal productivity were not and still are not as peremptory for the professionals, though no less historic. At one level they, or more frankly, *we* face the same enigmas about God, mind, destiny, meaning, morality, freedom, justice, etc. that tease the philosophical consciousness everywhere. It is probably through the tantalizing inquiries arising from these intellectual problems that many of us were drawn into the discipline in the first place.

But on a second level we face special problems deriving from our history and contemporary plight. We belong to nations oppressed in the past by foreign domination and ravaged in the present by indigenous misgovernment. And our cultures have been distorted through long-standing foreign blandishments, importunities, and outright impositions.

No extraordinary sagacity is required to realize the necessity for change on many fronts. Such changes call for a comprehensive rethinking of fundamentals. But what sort of thinking are we equipped to do? And how germane is it likely to be? By our academic training, we are products of foreign institutions of education, whether these are located at home or abroad. It is only through our informal upbringing that we get any manner of acculturation to our indigenous heritage. In consequence, the very conceptual frameworks of our lucubrations are in many ways those that are embedded in the foreign languages in which we have been trained. Who and what, then, are we?

It is this problem of self-definition that lies behind the intense debate among African professional philosophers on the question of just what African philosophy is, a debate that once seemed to eclipse the will to tackle substantive philosophical issues. The question, to adapt Kwame Appiah's phrase, is indeed a necessary question.[5] It is not one that is likely to be disposed of shortly, and so it is important that, amid this legitimate methodological soul-searching, we devote some attention to some of the other necessary questions of our discipline.

Fortunately, such an apportionment of time and effort is increasingly in evidence in recent publications in African philosophy. Serequeberhan's *African Philosophy: The Essential Readings*[6] is as good a testimony as any to the intensity, persistence and, not infrequently, the acrimony of the controversy. But Kwame Gyekye, in his *Essay on African Philosophical Thought: The Akan Conceptual Scheme*,[7] though not neglecting to have his say on that contentious problem of definition, directs most of his efforts to the exposition and elucidation of a traditional African system of philosophy encompassing perennial issues such as the nature of God and of human personality, the problem of fate and freedom, the basis of morality and its sanctions, and the place of individuality within the quest for the social good. Segun Gbadegesin, also besides doing all these, offers a passionate, and at the same time rational, discussion of some concrete social and political problems of contemporary Nigerian society from a philosophic standpoint in his *African Philosophy: Traditional Yoruba Philosophy and Contemporary African Realities*.[8] Serequeberhan, too, in his *The Hermeneutics of African Philosophy* has recently offered a sequel of substantive African philosophy to his methodological anthology. And these are by no means the only waters flowing under our bridge. The time, surely, is not too far distant when a student of modern African philosophy will be besieged with an overwhelming wealth of materials on both method and substance from professional sources.

Actually, a lot more substantive philosophizing goes on in contemporary Africa than the quantity of easily accessible publications might suggest. Anybody who attends, say, an annual meeting of the Nigerian Philosophical Association, perhaps the most ample theater of philosophical exchanges on a regular basis in Africa, is bound to be impressed by the vitality and the rich variety of available contributions.

Also, of course, the student or researcher in post-colonial African philosophy can usefully explore the philosophical output of the philosopher-kings of early post-independence Africa. In terms of content that work was not as metaphilosophical as that of the professionals. It would certainly have seemed like playing games while Africa was burning if, having led their countries to independence, they spent time wondering what sort of animal African philosophy was. Moreover, their focus was more directly political. And, as is well known, they proposed varieties of socialist philosophy and ideology, which were sometimes called "African Socialism" to signalize their indigenous orientation or inspiration. Serequeberhan, in the paper already cited, says that in our case, referring to contemporary African philosophy, "it is not the theoretic exigencies of modern science, but the politico-existential crisis interior to post-colonial Africa which brings forth the concerns and originates the theoretic space for the discourse of African philosophy." This characterization of thought context is true without qualification to the case of the philosopher-kings. In our case, too, adverting now to African academics working in philosophy today, there is something political about our concerns, since whatever we do involves, directly or indirectly, some settling of accounts with our colonial history. However, among our concerns we can distinguish between some that are narrowly political and others that are political only in a very broad sense. In the latter sense I would concede, or even insist, that philosophy is ultimately political, for the understanding of reality that we seek is for the betterment of human existence. Accordingly, within the gamut of contemporary concerns in African philosophy we can accommodate, among other things, efforts inspired by developments in logic, mathematics and the sciences. Thus, for example, an African moved to explore the philosophical implications of the cosmological theory of the Big Bang need not be thought to be straying from the confines of acceptable or intelligible motivation in African philosophy in this day and age.

As a matter of fact, many contemporary African philosophers have done work on issues of general philosophic interest not *specially* linked to Africa's traditional thought or to her colonial or post-colonial experience.[9] This has generally been in addition to work specifically grappling with Africa-oriented issues. A little over ten years ago, in an almost random listing of work of this sort among contemporary African philosophers, I noted articles by various authors on Descartes' *Cogito*, Greek Science and Religion, Logic and Ontology, the Bundle Theory of Substance, the Problem of Evil, the A-logicality of Immortality, Transcendentalism, the Is-Ought Controversy, Formal Logic and the Paradox of the Excluded Middle, the Fallacy of the Arrow Paradox, the role of the Hypothetical Method in the *Phaedo*, and Modal Metalogic.[10] As yet, however, no very definite groupings, in terms of philosophical denominations, have materialized in work on substantive issues of this general sort, or even of the sort directly occupied with matters specially relevant to Africa.

By contrast, in the controversy on how best to do African philosophy, which is sometimes misperceived as centering on the rather vexatious question of whether there is any such thing as African philosophy, there has seemed, at least in one layer of discussion, to be a polarization of opinion between those who see African philosophy as coterminous with philosophical investigations having a special relevance to Africa and those of a 'universalist' outlook. The latter do not yield ground to the former in proclaiming the importance of a serious study of African culture and its philosophical heritage, but they insist that such a study ought to be critical and reconstructive and, further, that among the concerns of contemporary African philosophers *as a class* should be a program to domesticate any modern resources of philosophical insight not already exploited in our culture. This insistence has sometimes brought upon them accusations of complicity in logical positivist thinking.

Those contemporary African philosophers who look askance at the 'universalist' predilections of the last-named group tend to regard philosophical work not having special links with Africa, such as those listed two paragraphs back, as a dabbling in foreign philosophy, quite forgetting that the same work can, for reasons of history, come to belong to two traditions at once. It escapes them also that the mere fact that a particular discovery (if so it be) did not emerge from a given culture does not imply that it is not relevant to it in terms of truth or practical consequence. Let them think of penicillin, for example. This general point would fail to apply to philosophy only if there were no such thing as truth in that discipline. But, presumably, an African philosopher is not debarred from supposing, say, that the Yoruba or Akan conception of a person captures some truths about human personality and thus teaches us something about the ontological make-up not only of Yoruba or Akan persons but also of Eskimos, Americans, Chinese, or whoever. If so, it might be thought that non-Africans too would be wise to incorporate those truths in their philosophies with due acknowledgment. And one supposes that no African philosopher would think any the less of them for doing that. These comments do not, by the way, discount the existence of conceptual roadblocks to intercultural communication, especially in abstract matters (of which, more below); they only assume the possibility of breaking through them.[11]

Human experience in itself has its own 'theoretic exigencies', and a study of traditional African philosophy shows that our traditional thinkers were acutely sensitive to these exigencies in pre-colonial and colonial times and remain so to this day. In Akan traditional philosophy, for example, the fact of death inspired some incomparably profound metaphysical reflections. Nor, incidentally, if you consider some Akan apothegms about 'creation', would the big-bang theory have rendered our metaphysicians of old speechless. Thus in investigating our traditional philosophies we will also be responding to elemental promptings to philosophical reflection which are 'interior' to the human condition. Works such as those by Gyekye and Gbadegesin give grounds for optimism in this connection. It is still probably not superfluous to emphasize that the motivation of such studies should be not just expository and clarifying, though clarification, insofar as it leads to the correction of erroneous interpretations of African traditional thought, which are legion, is a mighty enough task; it should be reconstructive as well, evaluating our heritage in order to build upon it.

Mention of the necessity for the critical appraisal of our heritage is apt to get on the nerves of some contemporary African scholars. Yet, our heritage of oral philosophy is, albeit indirectly, the creation of the individual philosophic thinkers of our traditional societies, who must themselves have been critical and original. Any reader of Odera Oruka's *Sage Philosophy*[12] can verify that there are even now among our traditional folks in Africa original philosophic thinkers not unduly influenced by foreign philosophies. They can criticize aspects of the communal philosophy and of any foreign philosophies they have encountered; and they can put forward fresh ideas of their own. Those of them who seem to have come under foreign influence in any degree, as for example, by way of conversion to Christianity, still demonstrate a clear capacity to make a creative synthesis of the foreign with the indigenous. These are the present-day exemplars of our ancestral philosophers, and the research into their thought that Professor Oruka of the University of Nairobi, Kenya, has been spearheading is, I believe, one of the most important developments in post-colonial African philosophy. It hardly needs to be pointed out that in contemporary professional philosophy, too, it is to thinkers of the same type that we can look for the advancement of African philosophy.

But it is time to return to our philosopher-kings. Although they did not, as we have seen, debate the question of African philosophy, their thought was impregnated by the same motivation of self-definition that underlies that debate. This is seen in the extent to which they all went in claiming links between their philosophies and African traditional thought. The links were sometimes real, sometimes largely illusory. But, actually, that does not matter much. Although the presence of such links in the thought of a contemporary African philosopher is precious, their absence is not necessarily invalidating. In describing Nkrumah's Marxism as "thinly Africanized," some criticism was implied, but it was a very limited criticism. Marxism, contrary to *Conscientism*'s claim, has little affinity with African traditional thought, but that does not mean that it may not be relevant to contemporary African conditions. I happen to think that Ghana benefitted little from Nkrumah's Marxism, but it does not follow that there was anything wrong *in principle* in a contemporary African leader adopting a Western theory of social reconstruction. The proviso, of course, is that such a choice should be on the basis of a critical investigation establishing the genuine applicability of the theory in question to African conditions and its superiority to any available African options.

Thus we are brought back to the need to exorcise the misapprehension that if a philosophy does not have links with African traditional thought then it cannot have a place in contemporary African philosophy. This fallacy is one thing which some present-day African professional philosophers have in common with some of our statesman philosophers. On occasion it seems to be generalized to imply that it is inappropriate for an African philosopher to make use of any Western results. In this form it sometimes takes quite a comic form. Thus, it is not unknown for, say, an African Marxist to chide another African, who betrays a sympathy for some non-Marxist Western conception, with domination by Western thought on the ground that, as Marx showed, the truth was something different. It hardly seems to be an item of vivid remembrance in the consciousness of such an African that, as far as it is known, Marx did not hail from any part of Africa! Serequeberhan exposes just such a case of gross illogicality when he notes the "boomerang" possibilities in Wamba-Dia-Wamba's Marxist-inspired exasperation with those Africans who see some truth in some forms of Western thought other than the particular version of Marxist-Leninism that is music to his ears.[13]

There is, indeed, the possibility—I would even say the rampant reality—of the domination of African philosophical minds by Western thought. But an African's acceptance of some Western ideas does not in itself amount to his being dominated by them; he is only dominated if his acceptance is not duly reflective. But what is due reflection? The following conditions for due reflection are implicit in remarks already made. The African concerned should satisfy herself that there are no better or equally good African alternatives to the proposed Western idea. More radically, she should consider whether the categories of thought in terms of which the propositions in question are framed are intelligible within the scheme of categories embedded in her own vernacular. Should this turn out not to be the case, she would then have to investigate whether the problem lies with her vernacular or with the foreign medium. That would be an exercise in cross-cultural conceptual analysis—a difficult but not impossible project. So, there is a condition of intelligibility and also a condition, in a nutshell, of truth.[14]

If these conditions seem inconsequential, I am persuaded that the appearance must be deceptive. On these conditions we would have to say, for example, that many African Christians are dominated by Western philosophical ideas, which is another way of noting that they are afflicted with the colonial mentality. The following is the reason why. Many African Christians, including some who are philosophically sophisticated, are quite happy to say that their belief in the Christian God and his son Jesus Christ is *simply* a matter of faith. Now, the Christian doctrine of God as a creator of the world out of nothing and of Christ as one with God involves a tremendous package of metaphysical conceptions which, in my opinion, is incongruent at many points with the conceptual frameworks of at least some African peoples. Consider, then, an African of some such indigenous conceptual background. If she says that she takes her Christianity on faith, this means that she has not and does not intend to confront any possible conceptual or doctrinal incongruities between Christianity and her indigenous religion, not to talk of any questions of epistemic justification. Grant, for the purposes of argument, that it makes sense to suppose that religious belief is a matter of faith (as opposed to rational reflection). It still does not emerge why an African should betake herself to the faith of other peoples to the abandonment of that of her own culture. We have to conclude, accordingly, that the African who "confesses" to a faith in Christ—that is, to an unreasoning belief in Christ—is also confessing to her colonial mentality. On the other hand, an African who believes in Christianity in premeditated preference to the beliefs of her own people on some rational grounds is not to be debited with the colonial mentality, whether the grounds are cogent or not. What makes the difference? Due reflection.

The fact that, for historical reasons, we have to express our philosophical thought in foreign languages, at least most of the time, has some very sobering consequences. Earlier, we noted the social infelicities, in Africa, of these media of expression in the specific case of the propagation of the philosophies of our first group of post-independence political leaders. Lack of widespread comprehension did not seem to hamper them, since they had the facilities to *enforce* adherence to the programs based on their philosophies so long as they remained in power (a status, however, that history has shown to be ephemeral in the extreme in post-colonial Africa). The academic philosophers of Africa have neither the power nor, presumably, the will to compel. But we cannot engage, let alone persuade, our people unless we can reach them in languages they can understand. In this respect our situation is basically like that of our spiritual uncles. Until Africa can have a lingua franca, we will have to communicate suitable parts of our work in our multifarious vernaculars, and in other forms of popular discourse, while using the metropolitan languages for international academic communication. However, this is a problem that the professional philosophers, in common with other classes of contemporary African intellectuals, have not quite begun to confront.

But this problem has an even more intractable aspect, which is connected with the fact, hinted at previously, that the problem on our hands is not just of articulation but also of conceptualization. Philosophical training and continuous professional work in a foreign language can predispose the mind toward foreign conceptual formations. The English language, for instance, may, by virtue of the special character of its syntax and vocabulary, create certain initial philosophical prepossessions in the minds of the philosophers who speak it and think in it. It seems to me, for example, that the metaphysic of abstract entities (Platonistically construed) or of substance and attribute or of mind-body dualism owes any preliminary plausibility it may appear to have to contingencies of this sort.[15] Insofar as such prepossessions may be different from those of our own languages, any unexamined use of a foreign language in philosophical work is a mark of the colonial mentality. Language, it is true, can only predispose; it cannot compel, but nothing is easier than to see the structure of reality in the accidental structure of a language. To counterbalance this possibility the African philosopher will have to practice thinking things out in his language as well as in the foreign ones, a program that is easier prescribed than implemented, but to which there is no alternative.

The dangers of mental colonization await the African philosopher in all the varieties of Western philosophy—analytic philosophy, hermeneutics, pragmatism, Thomism, Marxism, etc. But if we approach these, along with the philosophic suggestions of other cultures (as, for example, those of the Orient), in the spirit of due reflection, being always on the lookout for any conceptual snares, perhaps we can combine any insights extracted from these sources with those gained from our own indigenous philosophical resources to create for ourselves and our peoples modern philosophies from which both the East and the West might learn something. Post-colonial African philosophy, when not caught up in a regressive traditionalism, is a drive toward this destiny.

Part IV

Democracy and Human Rights

12

An Akan Perspective on Human Rights

A right is a claim that people are entitled to make on others or on society at large by virtue of their status. Human rights are claims that people are entitled to make simply by virtue of their status as human beings. The question naturally arises, what is it about a human being that makes him or her entitled to make the latter kind of claim? I intend to explore the answer to this question by looking principally at the Akan conception of a person.

The word "Akan" refers both to a group of intimately related languages found in West Africa and to the people who speak them. This ethnic group lives predominantly in Ghana and in parts of adjoining Côte d'Ivoire. In Ghana they inhabit most of the southern and middle belts and account for close to half the national population of 14 million. Best known among the Akan subgroups are the Ashantis. Closely cognate are the Denkyiras, Akims, Akuapims, Fantes, Kwahus, Wassas, Brongs, and Nzimas, among others.[1] All these groups share the same culture not only in basics but also in many details. Although the cultural affinities of the various Akan subgroups with the other ethnic groups of Ghana are not on the same scale as among themselves, any divergences affect only details. Indeed, viewed against the distant cultures of the East and West, Akan culture can be seen to have such fundamental commonalities with other African cultures as to be subsumable under "African culture" as a general cultural type.

The Akan Conception of a Person

The Akan conception of a person has both descriptive and normative aspects that are directly relevant not only to the idea that there are human rights but also to the question of what those rights are. In this conception a person is the result of the union of three elements, not necessarily sharply disparate ontologically, though each is different from the other. There is the life principle *(okra)*, the blood principle *(mogya)*, and what might be called the personality principle *(sunsum)*. The first, the *okra*, is held to come directly from God. It is supposed to be an actual speck of God that he gives out of himself as a gift of life along with a specific destiny. The second, the *mogya* (literally, blood) is held to come from the mother and is the basis of lineage, or more extensively, clan identity. The third, the *sunsum*, is supposed to come from the father, but not directly. In the making of a baby, the father contributes *ntoro* (semen), which combines, according to the Akans, with the blood of the mother to constitute, in due course, the frame of the human being to come. The inherited characteristics of the new arrival are, of course, taken to be attributable to both parents. But the father's input is believed to give rise to a certain immanent characteristic of the individual, called the *sunsum*, which is the kind of personal presence that he or she has. This is one meaning of the word *sunsum*. In this sense, *sunsum* is not an entity; it is, rather, a manner of being. But it is assumed that there must be something in the person that is the cause of the characteristic in question. It is in this sense that *sunsum* names a constituent of the human person.

By virtue of possessing an *okra*, a divine element, all persons have an intrinsic value, the same in each, which they do not owe to any earthly circumstance. Associated with this value is a concept of human dignity, which implies that every human being is entitled in an equal measure to a certain basic respect. In support of this the Akans say, "Everyone is the offspring of God; no one is the offspring of the earth." Directly implied in the doctrine of *okra* is the right of each person, as the recipient of a destiny, to pursue that unique destiny assigned to him by God. In more colloquial language, everyone has the right to do his own thing, with the understanding, of course, that ultimately one must bear the consequences of one's own choices. This might almost be called the metaphysical right of privacy. It is clinched with the maxim, "Nobody was there when I was taking my destiny from my God."

Through the possession of an *okra*, *mogya*, and *sunsum* a person is situated in a network of kinship relations that generate a system of rights and obligations. Because the Akans are matrilineal, the most important kinship group is the lineage, which may be pictured as a system of concentric circles of matrilineal kinship relation that, at its outermost reaches, can include people in widely separated geographic regions. In these outermost dimensions a lineage becomes a clan. Its innermost circle comprises the grandmother, the mother, the mother's siblings, her own children, and the children of her sisters. To this group, with the mother as the principal personage, belongs the duty of nursing an Akan newborn. The Akans have an acute sense of the dependency of a human being. On first appearance in this world, one is totally defenseless and dependent. This is the time when there is the greatest need for the care and protection of others and also, to the Akan mind, the time of the greatest right to that help. But this right never deserts a human being, for one is seen at all times as insufficient unto oneself. The logic of this right may be simply phrased: a genuine human need carries the right to satisfaction. The right to be nursed, then, is the first human right. In the fullness of time it will be transformed dialectically into a duty, the duty to nurse one's mother in her old age. "If your mother nurses you to grow your teeth," says an Akan adage, "you nurse her to lose hers." But there is another aspect to the nurturing of a human being—he or she needs to be instructed in the arts of gainful living—and this function the Akans ascribe to the father. To the father, then, attaches the duty to provide the child with character training, general education, and career preparation.

Through an individual's *ntoro*, the element contributed to each biological makeup by the father, one acquires a certain social link to a patrilineal kinship group, which, however, is much less important than one's matrilineal affiliations except for this: from the father's sister the child has the right to receive sexual education.

Earning a livelihood in traditional Akan society presupposed the possession of one basic resource: land. In an agricultural society like traditional Akan society, education profited a person little unless he could count on some land—land to till and land to develop. It is in this connection that we see an Akan person's most cherished positive right, the right to land. This right one has by virtue of membership in a lineage; it is a claim that one has primarily on one's lineage, but because of the state-wide significance of land, it is also, as I will explain later, a right that might be claimed against the state.

We have already mentioned some quite important rights. These are rights, in the Akan perception of things, that people have simply because they are human beings. They are entitlements entailed by the intrinsic sociality of the human status. In viewing a human being in this light, the Akans perhaps went beyond Aristotle's maxim that human beings are political animals. To the Akans, a human being is already social at conception, for the union of the blood principle and the personality principle already defines a social identity. A person is social in a further sense. The social identity just alluded to is a kinship identity. But people live, move, and have their being in an environment that includes persons outside the kin group. They live in a town or city and they have to relate to that environment in definite ways. A well-known Akan maxim asserts that when a human being descends upon the earth from above, s/he lands in a town. Membership in town and state brings with it a wider set of rights and obligations embracing the whole race of humankind, for the possession of the *okra,* the speck of God in man, is taken to link all human beings together in one universal family. The immediate concerns here, however, are with the rights of persons in the context of Akan society. In that society an individual's status as a person is predicated on the fulfillment of certain roles that have a reference to circles of relationships transcending the kin group. There is an ambiguity here in the use of the word *person,* the resolution of which will bring us to the normative conception of a person.

In one sense the Akan word *onipa* translates into the English word *person* in the sense of a human being, the possessor of *okra, mogya,* and *sunsum.* In this sense everyone is born a person, an *onipa*. This is the descriptive sense of the word. But there is a further sense of the word *onipa* in which to call an individual a person is to commend him; it implies the recognition that s/he has attained a certain status in the community. Specifically, it implies that s/he has demonstrated an ability through hard work and sober thinking to sustain a household and make contributions to the communal welfare. In traditional Akan society, public works were always done through communal labor. Moreover, the defense of the state against external attack was the responsibility of all. Good contributions toward these ends stamped an individual in the community as an *onipa*. Inversely, consistent default distanced him from that title. In this sense, personhood is not something you are born with but something you may achieve, and it is subject to degrees, so that some are more *onipa* than others, depending on the degree of fulfillment of one's obligations to self, household, and community.

On the face of it, the normative layer in the Akan concept of person brings only obligations to the individual. In fact, however, these obligations are matched by a whole series of rights that accrue to the individual simply because s/he lives in a society in which everyone has those obligations. It is useful in this regard to recall the fact, noted earlier, that the Akans viewed a human being as essentially dependent. From this point of view, human society is seen as a necessary framework for mutual aid for survival and, beyond that, for the attainment of reasonable levels of well-being. A number of Akan sayings testify to this conception, which is at the root of Akan communalism. One is to the effect that a human being is not a palm tree so as to be sufficient unto himself. (The Akans were highly impressed by the number of things that could be got from a palm tree, not the least memorable among them being palm nut soup and palm wine.) A second saying points out that to be human is to be in need of help. Literally it says simply, "a human being needs help" *(onipa hia moa)*. The Akan verb *hia* means "is in need of." In this context it also has the connotation of desert, so that the maxim may also be interpreted as asserting that a human being, simply because he is a human being, is entitled to help from others. A further saying explains that it is because of the need to have someone blow out the speck of dust in one's eye that antelopes go in twos. This saying obviously puts forward mutual aid as the rationale of society.

Although the rights deriving from the general human entitlement to the help of their kind did not have the backing of state sanctions, they were deeply enough felt in Akan society. In consequence, such rights may be said to have enjoyed the strong backing of public opinion, which in communalistic societies cannot be taken lightly. However, at this stage rights that appertain to political existence too must be looked at. If, as the Akans said, when a human being descends upon the earth, s/he lands in a town, the point is that s/he becomes integrated into a particular social and political structure. The specifics of that structure will determine his or her rights and obligations.

The Akan Political System

The importance of kinship relations in Akan society has already been noted. This grouping provides the basic units of political organization. These units are the lineages. A lineage, to be sure, is all the individuals in a town who are descended from one ancestress. A clan includes all the lineages united by a common maternal ancestry. It is too large and too scattered to be the unit of political organization in spite of the real feelings of brotherhood and sisterhood that exist among its members. In every town there would be quite a manageable number of lineages. Each of them had a head, called *Abusuapanyin* (elder of the lineage), who was elected by the adult members of the group. Age was an important qualification for this position—just reflect on the title "elder"— but so also was wisdom, eloquence, integrity, and, in earlier times, fighting competence. The last qualification calls for a word of explanation. Every head of lineage was, ex officio, a military leader who led his lineage in a particular position in the battle formation of the Akan army. This was not a professional army but rather a citizen force. In battle formation the Akan army had the following pattern. The first line consisted of a number of small units of scouts. Behind them was a large column of advance guard. Next to it came the main body of infantrymen grouped in two large columns. Following after them came the rear guard, which was a very large column. If the chief himself was taking the field, his company occupied the position between the second main infantry column and the rear. Flanking this array of forces on both sides were the left and right wings, which were long columns of fighting men.[2] In view of the military significance of the lineage headship it was natural, in electing someone to that position, to bear in mind the question of his probable prowess in battle. More recently, however, this particular consideration has lost its urgency. The military-sounding names of the headships persist, though, to the present day. (For example, the head of one of the lineages is called *Kyidomhene. Akyi* means rear, *dom* means troops, and *hene* means chief; thus the title means chief of the rear guard.)

It is clear from this description, by the way, that not just military service but military service in a particular battle position or war capacity was a birth obligation in Akan society. Everyone had a part in the war effort. Even those able-bodied men who stayed behind in times of war while others marched to the front did so for a military reason—namely, to guard home. The chief of the home-guard lineage, called *Ankobeahene* (literally, did-not-go-anywhere chief), was quite an important leader. It did not escape the Akans that to commit every able-bodied man to the fray would be to guarantee a field day to any band of marauders on the home front. Also it struck them very forcibly that a situation in which a group of healthy men remained together with a very great number of women, temporarily unattended by their husbands, required wise governance. Women, as a rule, did not go into battle, though it should be recalled that at least one major Ashanti war with the British, the Yaa Asantewaa War of 1900, was fought under the inspiration of a woman. For their part, the women prayed for the success of their men in the field, a function that was quite appreciated. Besides, they could act beforehand as motivators for their men, especially for any reluctant warriors among them.

If every Akan was thus obligated by birth to contribute to defense in one way or another, there was also the complementary fact that he had a right to the protection of his person, property, and dignity, not only in his own state but also outside it. And states were known to go to war to secure the freedom of their citizens abroad or avenge their mistreatment.

The ruling body of an Akan town was a council consisting of the lineage heads with the chief of the town in the capacity of chairman. The functions of the council were to preserve law, order, and peace in the town, to ensure its safety, and to promote its welfare. The office of a chief is hereditary but also partly elective. Some sort of an election is necessary because at any one time there are several people belonging to the royal lineage who are qualified by birth to be considered. The queen of the town (strictly, the queen mother) has the prerogative of selecting the best-qualified candidate, all things considered. But the final decision does not come until the council has assessed the candidate and indicated its approval. Such an approval, if forthcoming, seals the election, provided an objection is not voiced by the populace.

This last proviso is of special significance for the question of human rights, as will be shown later. In every town there was an unofficial personage recognized as the chief of the general populace. He was called *Nkwa-nkwaahene* (literally, the chief of the young men) and functioned as the spokesman of the populace. His position is described here as unofficial simply because, unlike most Akan political offices, it had nothing to do with his lineage; moreover, he was not a member of the chief's council. However, he had the right to make representations before the council on behalf of the young men of the town. In particular, if there were objections to a proposed chief among the populace, he made very forthright representations that, as a rule, prevailed. This is in conformity with the Akan principle that royals do not install a chief; it is those who have to serve him who do.

Beyond the political organization of the Akan town, a certain collection of towns constituted a division *(Oman,* literally, state) with a divisional council consisting of paramount chiefs. In an Akan territory of the proportions of Ashanti, paramount chiefs from a number of divisional councils served also as members of a confederacy council, which held sway over the whole nation.

Rights of Political Participation

This brings us, naturally, to political rights. It is clear from the foregoing that in principle citizens had a say, first in the question of who would exercise political power over them, and second in the issue of what specific policies were to be implemented in the town and, derivatively, in the state and nation. They had two avenues in this matter. They could work through their lineage head, who was duty-bound to consult them on all matters due for decision at the council, and they could work through the spokesman of the populace. The chief had absolutely no right to impose his own wishes on the elders of the council. On the contrary, all decisions of the council were based on consensus. The elders would keep on discussing an issue till consensus was reached, a method that contrasts with the decision by majority vote that prevails in modern democracies. The rationale of decision by consensus, as can easily be inferred, was to forestall the trivialization of the right of the minority to have an effect on decision-making.

Once a decision had been reached in council by consensus, it became officially the decision of the chief, regardless of his own opinion. That opinion would already have been given consideration at the discussion stage, but no one encouraged him in any illusions of infallibility. Nevertheless, the chief was never contradicted in public, since he was a symbol of the unity of the council and was also perceived as the link between the community and its hallowed ancestors. Because of the great pains taken to achieve consensus, the council took a very severe view of a member who subjected any of its decisions to criticism in public. The leader of the populace was in a different position. Not being privy to the deliberations of the council, he had the fullest right to criticize any decisions unacceptable to his constituency, as did the members of that constituency. One thing then is clear here. The people's freedom of thought and expression went beyond the devices of any chief or council.

Nor was there ever a doubt about the right of the people, including the elders, to dismiss a chief who tried to be oppressive. A cherished principle of Akan politics was that those who served the chief could also destool him. (The stool was the symbol of chiefly status, and so the installation of a chief was called enstoolment and his dismissal destoolment.) This was a process governed by well-defined rules. Charges had to be filed before appropriate bodies and thorough investigations made before a decision to destool or retain a chief was reached. Actually, as W. E. Abraham remarked, among the Akans "kingship was more a sacred office than a political one."[3] The chief was regarded as the "spiritual" link between the people and their ancestors and was for this reason approached with virtual awe. But this did not translate into abject subservience when it came to political matters. Here the chief had to play the game according to the rules, and the rules were that he was always to act in conformity with the decisions of the council and eschew any wayward style of life. So long as he did so, he was held to be sacrosanct, but as soon as he violated this compact, he lost that status and could experience a rough time. When this factor is taken into account, the representative character of the Akan system looms even larger. The real power was in the hands of the elected elders of the various lineages. This conforms to the principle that people have a right to determine who shall exercise political power over them and for how long.

That principle links up with another important feature of the Akan constitution: its decentralization. At every level of political organization, the groups involved enjoyed self-government. Thus the lineage, together with its head, conducted its affairs without interference from any higher authorities so long as the issues did not have town-wide or statewide reverberations. Similarly, the town and the division handled all issues pertaining exclusively to their domains. Apparent here is the Akan conception of a right due to all human beings, the right of self-government.

This right of self-government was particularly important in the administration of justice. Because all kinds of cases arising in the internal affairs of a lineage, or sometimes in inter-lineage affairs, were left to lineage personnel to settle on a household-to-household basis rather than in the more formalized and adversarial atmosphere of a chief's court, many potentially divisive problems between people could be solved painlessly, often through mere verbal apologies or minor compensations. A salutary by-product of this personalized way of settling cases was that it often brought a reinforcement of neighborhood good will. This is not to suggest, though, that the official, state-level reaction to issues of wrongdoing and the like was excessively retributive. On the contrary, often the aim was to reestablish satisfactory relations between person and person or person and ancestors through compensatory settlements and pacificatory rituals.

The Right to a Trial

There are some interesting aspects of the Akan approach to punishment and related issues that could be gone into here, but from the point of view of human rights, the most important observation is that it was an absolute principle of Akan justice that no human being could be punished without trial. Neither at the lineage level nor at any other level of Akan society could a citizen be subjected to any sort of sanctions without proof of wrongdoing. This principle was so strongly adhered to that even a dead body was tried before posthumous punishment was symbolically meted out to him. The best-known example of this sort of procedure was the reaction to a suicide apparently committed to evade the consequences of evil conduct. The dead person was meticulously tried. If guilt was established, the body was decapi-tated. If the motive behind the suicide remained obscure, it was assumed to be bad and had the same result.[4] If the right of the dead to trial before punishment was recognized, could the living have been entitled to less courtesy? The modern misdeeds, on the part of certain governments both inside and outside Africa, of imprisoning citizens without trial would have been inconceivable in a traditional Akan setting, not only because there were no such institutions as prisons but also because the principle of such a practice would have been totally repugnant to the Akan mentality.

Perhaps I ought not to leave the topic of suicide without an Akan-oriented comment on the question of the right to die. This question is becoming increasingly urgent because of the technological facilities now available for prolonging life amid the terminal impairment of body and sometimes mind. It might be thought from the drastic treatment of suicide just noted and from the Akan belief that the life principle in man is divine that the Akan mind would recoil from the idea that human beings might have a right to terminate their own lives under the circumstances in question. But the contrary is true. Death, in the traditional Akan understanding of the matter, cannot adversely affect the life principle, which is immortal; death only means the separation of that principle from the rest of the human system. The whole point of life consists in the pursuit of human well-being both in one's own case and in concord with the well-being of others. When any such prospects are perma-nently eliminated by deleterious conditions, the artificial prolongation of painful life or, worse, of vegetative existence can make no sense to man, woman, ancestor, or God. In such circumstances respect for human beings would dictate the right to die in dignity. As for suicide, it was only those committed with known or presumed evil motives that elicited symbolic punishment. Such a thing as suicide committed from noble motives was not unknown in Akan society, and exculpatory maxims were not hard to find. According to one of the most characteristic of Akan sayings, "Disgrace does not befit an Akan-born" (*Animguase nfata okaniba*). More explicitly, the Akans often say, "Death is preferable to disgrace" (*Animguase de afanyinam owuo*). Defeated generals were known to take this to heart. Rather than return home in disgrace, they frequently elected to commit suicide in the field.

The Right to Land

As noted earlier, any human being was held, by virtue of his blood principle (*mogya*), to be entitled to some land. For the duration of his life any Akan had the right to the use of a piece of the lineage land. However, land was supposed to belong to the whole lineage, conceived as including the ancestors, the living members, and those as yet to be born. For this reason, in traditional times the sale of land was prohibited. And the prohibition was effective. But our ancestors reckoned without the conquering power of modern commercialism. Land sale is now a thriving racket in which chiefs yield no ground to commoners. As a foreseeable consequence, there are now many Akans and others who have no land to till or develop. Here then, sadly, is a human right, recognized of old, that seems to have been devoured by advancing time.

In traditional times land was regarded as so important an issue that matters relating to its ownership were not left to individual lineages alone. The chief, acting as usual on the advice of his council, had a certain right of redistribution. Normally, no lineage could be dispossessed of any of its land. But if large tracts of land in the possession of a given lineage remained untilled for a considerable time while another lineage by reason, say, of preeminent fertility was hard pressed for land to feed on, the chief could acquire a part of the unused land and allocate it to the group in need. The seeming inconsistency of this practice of land transfer with the notion that land ownership could not be changed because the land of the lineage belonged to past, present, and future members was resolved doctrinally as follows. The ancestors, indeed, retain prima facie entitlement to the land of their lineages. In general, lineage ancestors oversee the affairs of their living descendants. But just as in life the chief has the duty to see to the general welfare of the entire town or state, so also in the world of the dead the ancestors of the lineage of the chief, who remain chiefs even in their postmortem state, have town-wide or state-wide concerns. In particular, they have an interest in seeing to the equitable use of the available land. Hence in redistributing land as indicated, the living chief, who is supposed to be a link between the people and the ancestors, would be carrying out the wishes of the latter. Note that this does not empower a chief to acquire land belonging to a given lineage for his own personal purposes. No Akan doctrine countenances that. A chief always had a liberal allotment of land from the original landholdings of his lineage in the first place, and from extensive plots set aside especially for the office of the stool in the second place. The first he could use in his own name; the second in the name of the stool. Notwithstanding the re-distributive rider just outlined, therefore, the right to land was a very solid right. At all events, no justifiable redistribution could leave an originally well-endowed lineage short of land for its own livelihood. This right, then, conceived in Akan terms as a human right, was claimed within the lineage, but for the reasons indicated it could also be claimed against the state.

The right to land was one of the deepest bases of attachment to particular locations. However, in spite of all the culturally ingrained love of consensus, there were times in the past when dissensions, even within a lineage, proved irresolvable. In the face of this kind of situation some sections of the lineage preferred to move on in search of land and peace of mind. This was one of the ways in which some ethnic groups, the Akans in particular, became spread over great expanses of territory in the geographic area now called Ghana. Given this history, it is easy to understand that the right to remain in or leave a town or state would not be an issue for debate among the Akans. It was taken for granted.

Religious Freedom

My previous mention of the right to freedom of thought and expression referred to political issues. It is relevant, however, to ask whether the Akan system supported freedom of thought and expression in such areas as religion and metaphysics.

To consider religion first, there was no such thing as an institutionalized religion in Akanland. Religion consisted simply of belief and trust in, and reverence for, a Supreme Being regarded as the architect of the cosmos. The Akans took it to be obvious even to children that such a being existed— witness the saying: "No one shows God to a child" (*Obi nykyere akwadaa Nyame*). However, I know of no sentiment in the Akan corpus of proverbs, epigrams, tales, and explicit doctrines that lends the slightest support to any abridgement of the freedom of thought or expression. As a matter of fact, skeptics with respect to religious and other issues *(akyinyegyefo,* literally, debaters) were known in Akan society, but no harm seems to have befallen them.

The belief in the assortment of extra-human forces (including the ancestors) that is so often mentioned in connection with Akan, and in general African, religion does not seem to me to belong properly to the field of religion. Be that as it may, one must concede that any person in Akan traditional society disagreeing fundamentally with the Akan world view would have had a serious sense of isolation. Almost every custom or cultural practice presupposed beliefs of that sort. Yet if he was prepared to perform his civic duties without bothering about any underlying beliefs, he could live in harmony with his kinsmen in spite of his philosophical nonconformism. Here again, one may observe that persecution on grounds of belief is unheard of in Akan society.

The conflict between Christian missionaries and the chiefs of Ashanti in the early years of this century, when the campaign to convert the people of Ghana to the Christian faith was getting under way, provides an illuminating case study. In that conflict the Ashanti chiefs remained remarkably forbearing, merely insisting that all Ashantis, irrespective of their religious persuasion, should obey customary law. By contrast, the missionaries, without challenging the authority of the chiefs over the Ashanti people, objected to the participation of Ashanti Christians in any activities that seemed to be based on beliefs they regarded as incompatible with their faith, beliefs in what they called 'fetish'. Intellectually this issue has not been resolved even to this day. But the force of circumstances has seemed to give the upper hand, now to one party, and now to the other. By the 1930s and 1940s Christianity was in the ascendancy, and many of the chiefs themselves, including, a little later, the king of Ashanti himself, had become converts. Neither the psychology, nor the logic, nor the theology of such conversions was free from paradox. But it ensured the easing of the conflict by virtue of accommodations from the side of the Ashanti authorities. Then came political independence, and with it a certain reassertion of cultural identity on the part of the people, and, complementarily, greater tolerance for African ways on the part of the Christian dignitaries, both foreign and native. As a result, practices like traditional drumming and the pouring of libation to the ancestors, which a few decades ago were proscribed by the missionaries for being fetish-tinged, are now commonplace among Christians, sometimes even on occasions of Christian worship. In fact, one even hears of the Africanization of Christianity from some high-minded church circles. Evidently the wheel has turned 180 degrees, or nearly so.

In all this, two things stand out as indicative of the Ashanti (and, generally, Ghanaian) tolerance for different beliefs. First, there is the fact that a great many Ashantis, commoners and chiefs alike, found a way to embrace the new beliefs, while not erasing the older ones from their consciousness.[5] But second, and even more important, the Ashantis from the beginning were not much exercised about what actually went on in the minds of people in matters having to do with such things as their world view. Their main concern regarding the early Ashanti converts was simply with their actual civic conduct. You can get people to do or not do specific things, reasoned the Akans, but you cannot guarantee that they will think particular thoughts. Hence the futility, from their point of view, of trying to interfere with freedom of thought. Confronted with any such attempt, an Akan would typically say to himself or to a confidant: *Me kose kose wo mitirim*, meaning "My real thoughts are in my own head," which by interpretation means, "I carry in my own person proof of the futility of any attempt to control people's thinking." Not only, then, is it wrong from the Akan standpoint to try to curtail freedom of thought; it is, by and large, futile.

From their tolerant attitude toward other people's religious beliefs, it is sufficiently clear that the Akans made no exceptions of subject matter in the question of the freedom of thought. When they said "two heads are better than one" and "one head does not hold council" in extolling the virtues of consultation, they were not thinking of politics alone. They were aware that other minds always have the potential to bring to light new aspects of things familiar or recondite. In metaphysical matters they left little doubt of their sense of the presumptuousness of dogmatism, for their metaphysicians often spoke in paradoxes and riddles, purposely inviting individual speculative ingenuity. Witness, for example, the following poser from a metaphysical drum text:

> Who gave word to Hearing
> For Hearing to have told the Spider
> For the Spider to have told the maker of the world
> For the maker of the world to have made the world?

Conclusion

In summary, one finds a veritable harvest of human rights. Akan thought recognized the right of a newborn to be nursed and educated, the right of an adult to a plot of land from the ancestral holdings, the right of any well-defined unit of political organization to self-government, the right of all to have a say in the enstoolment or destoolment of their chiefs or their elders and to participate in the shaping of governmental policies, the right of all to freedom of thought and expression in all matters, political, religious, and metaphysical, the right of everybody to trial before punishment, the right of a person to remain at any locality or to leave, and so on. Although frequently people who talk of human rights have political rights uppermost in their minds, some human rights do not fall within the purview of any constituted authority. In the last analysis, a people's conception of human rights will reflect their fundamental values, and not all such values will ever acquire the backing of institutional authority. In any case, this discussion does not pretend to have disclosed all the human rights generated by Akan values.

Again, it is probably needless to point out that my outline of human rights is a portrayal of Akan principles rather than an assessment of Akan practice. One can assume, a priori, that in actual practice the reality must have been some sort of a mixture of both the pursuit and the perversion of precept. By way of empirical confirmation, let me mention, on the negative side, two examples—one a premeditated abrogation, the other a situational diminution of a human right. On the grounds that a deceased chief needed the services of attendants during his postmortem journey to the land of the dead, the Akans in former times would ritually kill some people on the death of an important chief for that function. Given the eschatology, the practice was logical. But the belief itself was an appalling contravention of the Akan precept that, as offspring of God, all human beings are entitled to equal respect and dignity. Not that the right to life, which is implicit in this idea of respect for persons, is absolute. In fact, only a little reflection suffices to show that every right is open to qualification in some circumstances. For instance, in certain easily imagined situations the right of self-defense will nullify an attacker's right to life. It is important to note, though, that a right can be overridden only by another right or some other kind of genuine moral principle. As for the specific question of human sacrifice, the principle of it is not unheard of in some other cultures that pride themselves on their belief in the sanctity of human life. Thus Christianity, for example, openly exults in the idea of an omniscient, omnibenevolent, and omnipotent deity ordaining his "only begotten son" to be killed so that his erring creatures might thereby have the chance of salvation.

What then is so objectionable about the Akan custom in question, which, happily, no one now openly defends? The answer is simple. It is drastically lacking in fairness, and it flies in the face of the golden rule, which is as explicit in indigenous Akan ethical thinking as it is in Christian ethics. Indeed, the principle that all human beings are entitled to equal respect is only a special case of the golden rule. Obviously, equal respect here does not require that a murderer or a swindler be accorded the same deference as, say, an upright benefactor of humankind. What it means, nevertheless, is that in our reactions to the one class of persons *just as much* as to the other we should always imaginatively put ourselves in their shoes. In essence, then, equal respect is a requirement of sympathetic impartiality. Now the fact is that, in spite of the profound respect that the Akans had for their chiefs, few cherished the notion of being killed in order to have the honor of serving their chiefs on their last journey. Accordingly, sympathetic impartiality should have destroyed that custom before birth. In general, no rights can be justifiably superseded in a manner oblivious to the principle of sympathetic impartiality. If there is any absolute principle of human conduct, this is it.

The second traditional Akan situation uncongenial to a human right is seen in the Akan attitude to the freedom of speech of nonadults. It is easy to understand that in a traditional society both knowledge and wisdom would tend to correspond with age. Hence the deliverances of the old would command virtually automatic respect. But an unhappy consequence of this was that the self-expression of minors was apt to be rigorously circumscribed. Dissent on the part of a minor in the face of adult pronouncements was almost equated with disrespect or obstinacy. It would perhaps be excessive to call this a positive invasion of a human right. Indeed, given the traditional ethos, minors usually came to internalize the imperative of acquiescence. But in the modern context such an ethos must take on an aspect distinctly inconsonant with the rights of nonadults in the matter of the freedom of expression.

Probably every culture can be viewed as a matrix of forces and tendencies of thought and practice not always mutually compatible. The characterization of cultural traits, therefore, frequently has to take cognizance of counter-vailing factors. Nevertheless, the bent of a culture will, if anything, stand out in heightened relief in the full view of such facts. On the question of human rights it can justly be said that, notwithstanding any contrary tendencies, the principles of human rights enumerated here did motivate predominantly favorable practices in traditional Akan society. Moreover, from the perspective of those principles one can check how faithful certain claims in contemporary African politics are to at least one African tradition. Regrettably, I must content myself here with only one, brief, illustration.

Many African governments today (June 1988) are based upon the one-party system. There are both critics and defenders of that system in Africa, and in the resulting controversy human rights have almost always been at issue. In some one-party apologetics the suggestion is made not only that the system is hospitable to all the desirable human rights but also that traditional African systems of government were of the one-party variety, in a full-blown or an embryonic form. As far at least as the Akan tradition is concerned, I hope that this discussion demonstrates that both claims are contrary to fact. Although the Akan system was not of a multiparty type, it was not a one-party type either. The decisive reason why the Akan system is antithetical to the one-party system is that no such system can survive the right of the populace, organized under their own spokesman, to question the decisions of the ruling body or to demand the dismissal of its leader. Since the traditional system featured this right, it was neither a one-party system nor even a simulacrum of it. For the same reason it is not true that the one-party system is compatible with all human rights. On this showing, our traditional systems require close analysis from the point of view of contemporary existential concerns. Human rights are certainly among the most urgent of these concerns. That Africa has suffered human rights deprivations from various causes in the past, including particularly the transatlantic slave trade and colonialism, is well-known history. It is surely an agonizing reflection that, aside from the vexatious case of apartheid, the encroachments on human rights in Africa in recent times have usually come from African governments themselves. To a certain extent the exigencies of post-independence reconstruction may account for this. But they cannot justify it. Nor, as just pointed out in the matter of the one-party system, can they be rationalized by appeal to any authentic aspect of African traditional politics, at least in the Akan instance. How to devise a system of politics that, while being responsive to the developments of the modern world, will reflect the best traditional thinking about human rights (and other values) is one of the profoundest challenges facing modern Africans. (I return to this problem in the next two chapters.) A good beginning is to become informed about traditional life and thought.

13

Philosophy and the Political Problem of Human Rights

Human rights are rights that are morally owed to human beings. There are philosophical problems in clarifying this notion, as in the case of all fundamental concepts of human life and thought. But the problem that has exercised the international community most severely arises from violations of human rights. Violations may come from individuals or from governments. In the former case they are private transgressions; in the latter they constitute political oppression. The latter is what principally engages contemporary concerns with human rights. This is a many-faceted problem, but it is quite clear that the greatest part of it comes from the ways of governments. However, while considerable blame may be ascribed to the moral degeneracy of some politicians, it may well be that the root of the problem lies in the form of democracy that is routinely recommended for all. That form might be called majoritarian democracy. In this chapter I propose to explore the hypothesis that a consensual form of democracy might be better able to forestall, if not all, then certainly many of the causes of the violations of human rights. This rethinking of democracy, especially in connection with human rights, well befits philosophy.

Human rights abuses are of many kinds and causes. For specificity and ease of analysis I shall focus on one kind. And because of the particular existential basis of my concerns in this discussion, I will choose my illustrations from Africa. The one general kind of human rights abuse to be considered is the denial by governments of political representation to citizens. In the last thirty years or so many African governments have been in the forefront of this program of abuse. Offenders have been both soldiers and civilians, and one may wonder whether the phenomenon has a cultural foundation. It does indeed, but in a rather indirect, or dialectical way; which makes it all the more instructive.

Naturally, our procedure of exposition will be indirect, coming to the question of human rights only later. We start with a certain traditional way of approaching governance in Africa. One must be cautious of indiscriminate generalizations about the whole of the African continent, but it seems from available accounts that statecraft in many parts of traditional Africa was based on the principle of consensus. Certainly, there are contrary cases,[1] but our purpose here is to see what can be learned from the positive ones, such as the traditional systems of government among the Zulu and the Swazi of southern Africa, and the Akans of West Africa.

I will give below a brief description of the Akan example, which I know by first-hand experience, of its survivals in our contemporary society and also through written accounts, such as that provided in Busia's *The Position of the Chief in the Modern Political System of Ashanti.*[2] The Akans have what you might call a culture of consensus. Consensus presupposes the possibility of difference. In fact, among any group of thinking persons this possibility will be frequently actualized. The Akans were sharply aware of this, but they traditionally maintained that any differences between human beings, theoretical or practical, can be reconciled. In practical matters, which will be our principal interest in this discussion, this view of human relations is encapsulated in a remarkable construct of fine art: Two heads of crocodiles are locked up in conflict over food, but they have one stomach. The lesson is that divergent interests arising out of individualized thought and feeling will lead to conflict in society; but ultimately all individuals share a common interest, and this constitutes the natural basis for the possibility of conflict resolution. Such resolutions will usually be achieved through the mutual pruning down of interests for the sake of harmony. This kind of deference to the common good was one of the hallmarks of the Akan ethos. It was this ethos that lay behind the quest for consensus in Akan social life, especially at the level of government.

Nevertheless, there is no pretense that consensus was always attained. Indeed, a striking universal of human culture is the gap between practice and precept. Yet, the contingencies of practice have a way of portraying the image of received precepts, and it is clear that traditional Akan practices of political decision-making did reflect an ideal of consensus which was conducive to the securing of an important human right. I am alluding to the citizen's right of representation with respect to every particular decision—a right which, as I shall explain below, is not consistently recognized in majoritarian democracy.

But first to the mechanics of representation: Akan traditional statecraft was based on kinship representation. Every lineage in a town or village had a head elected by consensus on grounds of seniority, reputation for wisdom, and rhetorical abilities. A lineage being all the individuals of a common ancestry (which in Akan society means descent from one woman), such a grouping could be somewhat large; much larger, certainly, than the unit named by the English word "family." All the lineage heads came together to form the local governing council which was presided over by the *ohene*, the natural ruler of the locality, called in English a "chief" by a not-altogether appropriate colonial translation which has gained orthodoxy by virtue of sheer termino-logical inertia. I propose to let sleeping terminologies lie.

Using, then, the terminology of "chieftaincy," let us note that the position of a chief was largely ceremonial and ritual, though he also had political responsibilities as chairman of the ruling council. Ritually, he was supposed to function as the mediating link between the living population and their departed ancestors. And ceremonially, he was regarded as the symbol of the unity of his domain. But politically he could act only on the advice of his council. Thus, although the office of a chief was basically hereditary, that fact did not compromise the representative character of the political decision procedure, since the power of decision lay with the council rather than the chief in his individual capacity. A local council, of course, had authority only over local affairs. But representatives of a number of councils constituted a regional council presided over by a "paramount" chief. In a domain as large as the Ashanti state there was a still higher council presided over by the king of the Ashantis.

So much for the structure of representation. What of the manner of deliberation? Here we meet what I think is the most important feature of the traditional system of decision-making: Deliberation in council was informed by two methodological aims; first, to elicit differences of opinion and, second, to iron them out in search of consensus. In pursuit of the first, the freest airing of opinions in council was encouraged. One relevant Akan saying is that even a fool is entitled to be heard. In pursuit of the second, no amount of discussion was thought to be too protracted. As Busia puts it, "So strong was the value of solidarity that the chief aim of the councilors was to reach unanimity, and they talked till this was achieved."[3]

Busia is right in the remark just quoted, but the use of the word "unanim-ity" calls for some comment. Unanimity is perhaps the perfection of consen-sus. But consensus does not always require unanimity, certainly not with respect to every aspect of every issue that may be under consideration. If discussion takes place in the spirit of mutual accommodation, it is possible to obtain unanimity with respect to what is to be done without necessarily getting unanimity as to its merits. One may accept that a given action may be taken, say, to build a town hall at a certain time and place, without thinking that this placing and timing are the best. The motivation for the acceptance might simply be the feeling on one's own part that, having had a fair hearing for one's arguments, it would be obstructive to oppose a proposal to the bitter end, if it had the support of the majority. This kind of thinking ensures a minimal kind of consensus, but it is consensus nonetheless, and it is essential for the operation of a system based on consensus. As a matter of fact, where there is a will to consensus there will, in the normal run of human affairs, usually be ways, such as persuasion and compromise, of gaining richer forms of consensus.

The reference to the majority in the last paragraph calls for some clarification. There is a subtle but crucial distinction between decision by majority vote and decision by consensus attained through a reasoned deference to the position of a majority. The first is decision in spite of the minority, the second is one inspired by the majority. In the first case, opposition survives decision; at the very least, on the psychological plane. In the second, decision incorporates at least the goodwill of opposition. Mark, I speak of opposition, not of *the* opposition. In the traditional Akan system the pattern of divergence in council did not ossify into the long-lasting polarity of government and opposition. Every member belonged to the basic mechanism of government. In the rare case in which a councilor might find it necessary to yield ground to a majority, he could reflect that the situation was *ad hoc* rather than systematic. Thus the circumstance did not engender alienation.

Nevertheless, decision by consensus (however minimalistic) is a much more difficult process than decision by majority vote. The latter subordinates the will of the minority to that of the majority, in the matter of the given decision, by a simple act of voting. That is what the former avoids by seeking the good will of all members through sincere dialogue. In fact, not only sincerity was needed but also patience. The councilors would continue discussion, as Busia notes, until "unanimity" was achieved. We may justly infer, then, that the quest for unanimity was a matter of deliberate principle with the traditional Akans. Theirs was a conscious transcending of the majority principle. For them, a mere majority is not an adequate basis for decision. Combined with this conviction was a stout belief in the possibility of consensus in human affairs. An oft-quoted Akan saying is that there is no disagreement that cannot be settled by dialogue. Whether this is over-optimistic or not, it was the basis of a distinct approach to democracy.

That approach involved two types of representation, first, the representation of each lineage in council and, second, the representation of each representative in the making of each decision. Both representations were secured through consensus, not always easily won. If such pains were taken in the pursuit of consensus, then, presumably, it was felt that people had a *right* of representation not only by way of having a representative in council but also by way of having their consent factored into every decision, indirectly through their representative. As we have seen, even in cases where a representative had unresolved reservations as to the merits of a proposal, his consent as to its adoption was a necessary factor; and it too had to be secured by means of persuasion.

There is a point of principle here that I would like to press. I take it that it is allowed on all hands that everyone has the right to be represented in any political council in which decisions are taken that affect her. This is a human right, if anything is. But the point of having a representative is to be represented with respect to all decisions, not just some of them. Ideally, this must mean not only that all representatives must have the opportunity to discuss all relevant issues, but also that their consent must be a condition for the adoption of any proposal. True, reality may not always be hospitable to an ideal, but at the very least it must mean that all representatives have an equal chance of influencing decisions. Any system that does not ensure this much cannot claim full sensitivity to the human right of representation. Arguably, this shortcoming is a systematic characteristic of majoritarian democracy.

By majoritarian democracy I mean a multi-party system of politics in which the party that wins the most seats at an election is normally entitled to form the government. In such a setup the losing party or parties become the opposition, singly or compositely. A political party, in this context, is an organization of people of like political and social opinions or attitudes or even habits which is dedicated to gaining power for the purpose of implementing their preferred policies. An opposition party is, of course, not part of the government in power, and its principal aim is to unseat it for the purpose also of implementing its own policies. But neither does the government party relent in its resolve to retain power by all the means accessible within the usually flexible rules of the game. The resulting struggle is hardly ever a model of human cooperation.

Consider now the situation of an opposition party with respect to the right of representation in decision-making. It is no secret that such a party will in general not have a significant imprint on the shape of national policy, if the government has a comfortable majority. However intensive the debating of issues, it will usually be a foregone conclusion that the government party will prevail by dint of numbers. Minority representatives will cast dissenting votes, but they will be overridden by the votes of the majority. This means, surely, that the right of the former and of their constituencies to be represented in the actual making of decisions is rendered nugatory. And this even in the best traditions of majoritarian democracy! Not unreasonably, the opposition will feel that their precious thoughts are paid scant attention by the government and will long for the time when roles can be constitutionally reversed; that is, if they are in a place where people are interested in playing the game according to the rules. They will not, of course, just wish for better days; they will organize both in and out of council or parliament (or whatever the relevant body may be called). In particular, they will settle down to truly oppose the policies of the government without excessive regard for such fine points as the merits of the matter in hand. Be that as it may, it should be clear that even at the best of times the politics of majoritarian democracy offers very little incentive to consensus; so little, indeed, that any system of democracy dictated by the requirement of consensus can be expected to exhibit a difference not of degree but of kind.

I anticipate some such rejoinder as the following. A democracy based on the majority principle (that is, on the principle that it is the right of the majority to rule) need not necessarily involve the trivialization of the ability of the minority to have an impact on political decision-making. In a sophisticated polity of this sort, such as is seen, for example in the United States, a complex system of committees and various mechanisms of checks and balances can ensure that the opposition or minority parties have a non-negligible influence on what is done or undone. Granted. But this is severely inadequate. It remains a fact that the underlying orientation is a philosophy and a psychology of winner-takes-all (or nearly all). In spite of any checks and balances, the electoral winners do actually accede to power and acquire an enriched sense of their importance, while the losers are dispossessed of power, if they previously had it, or, otherwise are eluded by it. As for the state of cheer that goes with the latter plight, the long faces usually visible during acknowledgements of electoral defeat should disabuse the mind of any misapprehensions. Since we have mentioned the United States, anyone who witnessed the contrasting pictures of joy and dejection that were printed on the faces, respectively, of the victors and the vanquished at the denouement of the 1992 general election will probably appreciate that they told stories far more profound than any inflation or deflation of personal egos. They were stories of empowerment and disempowerment, involving, in the latter case, the deprivation of what, from our previous indications, might be called the human right of decisional representation.

The poignancy of the last-mentioned predicament is multiplied many times in the modern African context. Because of the old tradition of consensual politics in many parts of Africa, which must still have at least an unconscious hold on the minds of many Africans, losing an election under a majoritarian dispensation (originally introduced via colonialism) causes a deep sense of exclusion, alienation, and hostility, in spite of any verbal adherence to the system. Moreover, those finely designed parliamentary palliatives, which in the United States or the United Kingdom, for instance, do mollify the opposition to some extent are in Africa often nonexistent, or, equivalently, existent only on paper. Meanwhile, the electoral victors, constitutionally exempted from the rigors of consensus-building, are known to easily succumb to the temptation to drink deep of the spring of power and become drunken thereof, to the drastic disadvantage of civil and human rights and sundry other dictates of morality and law. Before long a frustrated oppositionist, bereft of all sympathy for the system, makes contact with an independently disgruntled colonel or lesser military officer, who works his way to the radio station at the nation's capital in the small hours of the night and announces an abrupt interruption of the civilian orgy of power, thus ushering in an era of uniformed predators, unhampered by even paper regulations.

But has not all this sorry mess been brought to an end with the recent wave of multi-party democratic reform in Africa? Suppose it has. Even so, the best it might do for Africa is to transplant there the essentially adversarial system of government and opposition, such as is operated in the United States and the United Kingdom. But the results of the system in those places are not such as to cause any careful observer to swoon with admiration. It is, of course, better than military dictatorship. But, to say the least, it may not be conducive to rapid development among peoples whose conscious or unconscious memories are tinged with visions of the potentialities of government by consensus. In fact, even where the forms of majoritarian democracy have been established on the African ground its substance remains elusive. Opposition is still not infrequently seen on both sides as veritable war, with verifiable casualties. In any case, in quite a few parts of Africa now the multi-party democratic appearances cannot deceive anybody, unless it be some short-term foreign observers. In whatever way the matter is viewed, then, it seems clear that the notion that the recent trend toward multi-party politics in Africa is a permanent blessing may turn out to be one of the costliest fallacies ever entertained about the continent.

"But, what" you might ask, "is the alternative to democracy based on majority rule in the modern world? It may be conceded that consensus is a beautiful thing, but it cannot be achieved often enough to provide a basis for any practical system of democracy. Perhaps, in traditional times some African peoples were generally able to reach consensus in their political deliberations, but the conditions of life and economy in those circumstances most likely did not engender issues as acutely divisive as those that bedevil modern life. For example, the kinship basis of representation probably obviated the ideological polarities inherent in the modern party system. But there is, objectively, no returning to that uncomplicated approach to politics. Thus, while the majoritarian system may, in the abstract, be less than the ideal, all the realistic alternatives may be worse."

It must be admitted at once that any harkening back to the kinship politics of old would be an extremely reactionary move. But that is not the real issue. The root of the whole question of majoritarian democracy is to be found in the party system. Is that system essential to modern democracy? But first, what is the party system? It is the system in which political parties (as previously defined) are the basis of power. That is to say, parties are, as a matter of constitutional stipulation, the instrument for the acquisition of power and, when acquired, for its exercise. (This is the case even in coalition governments: The sharers of power are the parties, and individuals figure in the equation only as members of distinct parties.) A multi-party democracy is thus a system characterized by an organized and highly competitive struggle for power or in the interests of power. The divisiveness that this competition is apt to generate is proverbial and was the ground upon which the African advocates of the one-party system of government in the sixties and seventies principally rested their case against the multi-party system.[4] In this they had a sure intuition. But it was a true premiss from which they inferred a false conclusion by a bad argument.

The divisiveness of the multi-party system was very harmful to Africa in the period under discussion (and is likely to be so in the future), but the authoritarianism of the one-party system was more harmful still. Apart from the notorious civil rights abuses that it visited upon the African populations (through the political iniquities of their own leaders), the system was, *by definition*, a violation of a fundamental human right. "The Universal Declaration of Human Rights" of the UN declares explicitly in article 19 that "Everyone has the right of freedom of opinion and expression; this right includes freedom to hold opinions without interference and seek, receive and impart information and ideas through any media and regardless of frontiers," and in article 20 that "Everyone has the right of peaceful assembly and association." But a one-party state is one in which citizens are prevented, by law, from belonging to any political association but one, namely, the single, official party. Of the sophistries propounded by the advocates of the one-party state to disguise this infringement of a fundamental human right, the less said the better. Nor are any reasonable persons likely to shed any tears for the demise of that system in Africa and, for that matter, elsewhere.

A more important fact, however, is that the one-party system of politics is not the only possible alternative to the multi-party variety. There can be a non-party system. The Akan traditional system of old was exactly of this character, and it is from this rather than from its kinship orientation that we can derive a lesson for our contemporary purposes. (The proponents of the one-party system in Africa, by the way, regularly misperceived this non-party approach to governance in some African traditions as an authenticating precedent.) A non-party system is one in which parties are not the basis of power. People can form political associations to propagate their political ideas and help to elect representatives to parliament. But an association having the most elected members will not therefore be the governing group. Every representative will be *of* the government in his personal, rather than associational, capacity. In the matter of the filling of top legislative and executive positions various options are conceivable. For example, the elected representatives may elect a leader and charge her with the responsibility of forming an administration reflecting, as much as possible, all the tendencies of opinion identifiable within the representative body.

One thing can be noted at once. Political associations not being any longer instruments for seeking power, will be very unlike political parties, as we now know them. And this is why I have not started by calling them parties. But, of course, in a broad lexical sense, they will be parties. In this sense not all parties will be parties in the special sense defined early on. In that special sense, the power motivation, with its constitutional foundation, was one of the defining characteristics of a political party. In the absence of that motivation, a party, in the sense of a political association, would be more akin to a political discussion group than anything else. The moral bonus is likely to be incalculable. The dogmatism, intolerance, and inattention to the ethical refinement of means in relation to ends that parties, as power machines, are so apt to inspire, not to say instill, in devotees would, most likely, no longer be so rampant a feature of political life as they now are. As one consequence, the prospects of consensus in political decision-making can be expected to become infinitely improved. When representatives are not constrained by considerations regarding the fortunes of power-driven parties they will be more inclined in council to reason more objectively and listen more open-mindedly. And in any deliberative body in which sensitivity to the merits of ideas is a driving force, circumstances are unlikely to select any one group for consistent marginalization in the process of decision-making. Apart from anything else, such marginalization would be an affront to the fundamental human right of decisional representation.

It should be observed that although the system adumbrated is not a majoritarian one in that it does not operate with the notion of a majority party taking possession of power, the significance of majorities is not reduced to zero. If representatives are to be elected (on their own merits though not necessarily without the help of friendly associations), the candidate winning the highest number of votes must, subject to reasonable provisos, be the choice. Moreover, if a persistent stalemate in debate in council should threaten to bring the affairs of the state to a standstill, then it may, as a last resort, have to be broken with a majority vote. Such a pass of events can be expected to be rare in a non-party environment purposely designed to be congenial to persuasion, compromise, and accommodation. But its logical possibility cannot be overlooked. Even so, the commitment to consensus is palpable in this arrangement, as it is not in the majoritarian alternative. In those parts of Africa where there is a history of indigenous forms of consensual statecraft a non-party system of the type we have been hinting at could reactivate tendencies to consensus lying dormant in the communal unconscious, with happy consequences for political stability and the prospect of development. This is, however, by no means an exclusive concern of Africa; and, in fact, one excellent champion of the non-party system is the Yugoslav philosopher Mihailo Marković, who has worked out the idea in impressive detail. More pertinent still, the argument in favor of a non-party consensual system is quite general: decisional representation is a fundamental human right. But majoritarian democracy is incompatible with it because of its reliance on parties and its relatively exclusive empowerment of electorally victorious ones. Therefore, in the interests of the human right in question, some non-party system must be devised. Such a system must be committed to consensus as a way of ensuring, as far as possible, the decisional representation of citizens through their representatives. The Akan example is cited as proof, of which other cultural testimonies are not unknown outside Africa,[5] of the human possibility of government by consensus.

The connection with human rights prompts some final reflections. International declarations on human rights are usually lofty documents full of noble sentiments. But just because of this elevated tone they may sometimes carry ambiguities that minimize their intent. Thus the "Universal Declaration of Human Rights" asserts in article 21 that "Everyone has a right to take part in the government of his country directly or through freely chosen representatives." But since, as we have seen, it is possible for citizens to have "freely chosen representatives" who take part in parliamentary debates without real decisional representation, the declaration is not as instructive as might have been hoped. The "African Charter on Human and People's Rights"[6] gives even more cause for anguish. Certainly it does not yield ground to the UN proclamation in its affirmation of the citizen's right of representation and participation. Notice, in its 13th article, the high-minded interpolation (which I have italicized) in the almost word-for-word reproduction of article 21 of the previous document: "Every citizen shall have the right to participate *freely* in the government of his country either directly or through freely chosen representatives." But it adds the qualification "in accordance with the provisions of the law." In view of the fact that at the time of its adoption in 1981 and even of its entry into force in 1986, many African states had one-party provisions of the law which essentially nullified the purport of the article, any joy at the charter needed to be tempered with caution. The same lesson was even more clearly readable from the African edition of the UN declaration in favor of the right of association. "Every individual," it said in article 9, "shall have the right to free association *provided he abides by the law.*" (My italics.) Since obedience to the law often meant not venturing upon any political associating other than the state-prescribed one, any counting of blessings may have been premature.

The signatories to the African charter, by way of a "preamble," begin by, "*taking into consideration* the virtues of their historical tradition and the values of African civilization which should inspire and characterize their reflection on the concept of human and people's rights." My own contemplation of the virtues of my historical tradition inspires a conception of the human right of representation, which, as is apparent from this discussion, is more stringent than that which is evident in either the UN declaration or the African charter.

14

Democracy and Consensus

A Plea for a Non-Party Polity

It is often remarked that decision-making in traditional African life and governance was, as a rule, by consensus. Like all generalizations about complex subjects, it is perhaps legitimate to take this with a pinch of prudence. But there is considerable evidence that decision by consensus was often the order of the day in African deliberations, and on principle. So that it was not just an exercise in hyperbole when Kaunda, (democratically) displaced president of Zambia, said, "In our original societies we operated by consensus. An issue was talked out in solemn conclave until such time as agreement could be achieved" (Rohio and Mutiso, 476), or when Nyerere, retired president of Tanzania, also said, ". . . in African society the traditional method of conducting affairs is by free discussion" and quoted Guy Clutton-Brock with approval to the effect that "The elders sit under the big trees, and talk until they agree" (ibid., 478).[1]

Ironically, both pronouncements were made in the course of a defense of the one-party system. Of this I will have more to say below. But for now, let us note an important fact about the role of consensus in African life. It is that the reliance on consensus is not a peculiarly political phenomenon. Where consensus characterizes political decision-making in Africa it is a manifestation of an immanent approach to social interaction. Generally, in interpersonal relations between adults, consensus as a basis of joint action was taken as axiomatic. This is not to say that it was always attained. Nowhere was African society a realm of unbroken harmony. On the contrary, conflict (including mortal ones) among lineages and ethnic groups and within them were not infrequent. The remarkable thing, however, is that if and when a resolution of the issues was negotiated, the point of it was seen in the attainment of reconciliation rather than the mere abstention from further recriminations or collisions. It is important to note that disputes can be settled without the achievement of reconciliation.

Reconciliation is, in fact, a form of consensus. It is a restoration of goodwill through a reappraisal of the importance and significance of the initial bones of contention. It does not necessarily involve a complete identity of moral or cognitive opinions. It suffices that all parties are able to feel that adequate account has been taken of their points of view in any proposed scheme of future action or coexistence. Similarly, consensus does not in general entail total agreement. To begin with, consensus usually presupposes an original position of diversity. Because issues do not always polarize opinion on lines of strict contradictoriness, dialogue can function, by means, for example, of the smoothing of edges, to produce compromises that are agreeable to all or, at least, not obnoxious to any. Furthermore, where there is the will to consensus dialogue can lead to a willing suspension of disagreement, making possible agreed actions without necessarily agreed notions. This is important because certain situations do, indeed, precipitate exhaustive disjunctions which no dialogic accommodations can mediate. For example, either we are to go to war or we are not. The problem then is how a group without unanimity may settle on one option rather than the other without alienating anyone. This is the severest challenge of consensus, and it can only be met by the willing suspension of disbelief in the prevailing option on the part of the residual minority. The feasibility of this depends not only on the patience and persuasiveness of the right people but also on the fact that African traditional systems of the consensual type were not such as to place any one group of persons consistently in the position of a minority. Of this, more below.

But first, let us see how faith in consensus worked in one concrete example of an African traditional system of politics. It may be well to note, as a preliminary, that African political systems of the past displayed considerable variety. There is a basic distinction between those systems with a centralized authority exercised through the machinery of government and those without any such authority in which social life was not regulated at any level by the sort of machinery that might be called a government. Fortes and Evans-Pritchard (1940, 5), classify the Zulu (of South Africa), the Ngwato (also of South Africa), the Bemba (of Zambia), the Banyankole (of Uganda), and the Kede (of northern Nigeria) under the first category and the Logoli (of western Kenya), the Tallensi (of northern Ghana) and the Nuer (of southern Sudan) under the second. It is, or should be, a matter of substantial interest to political thinkers that societies of the second description, that is, anarchistic societies, existed and functioned in an orderly manner, or at least not with any less order than the more centralized ones. It is also, perhaps, easier in the context of the less centralized social orders to appreciate the necessity of consensus. Where the exercise of authority (as, for example, in the settlement of disputes) rested purely on moral and, perhaps, metaphysical prestige, it is obvious that decision by the preponderance of numbers would be likely to be dysfunctional. But it is more interesting to observe that the habit of decision by consensus in politics was studiously cultivated in some of the most

centralized and, if it comes to it, warlike, ethnic groups of Africa, such as the
Zulu and the Ashantis. By a somewhat paradoxical contrast, the authorities in
some of the comparatively less militaristic of the centralized societies, such as
the Bemba or the Banyankole, seem to have manifested less enthusiasm for
consensus in political decision-making than the Ashantis or the Zulu.[2] In what
immediately follows I propose to take advantage of the elaborate description
and analysis of the Ashanti traditional system of politics in K. A. Busia's *The
Position of the Chief in the Modern Political System of Ashanti*[3] and my own
personal experience to trace the course of consensus in the Ashanti political
example.

Lineage is the basic political unit among the Ashantis. Because they are a
matrilineal group this unit consists of all the people in a town or village having
a common female ancestor, which, as a rule, is quite a considerable body of
persons. Every such unit has a head, and every such head is automatically a
member of the council, which is the governing body of the town or village.
The qualifications for lineage headship are seniority in age, wisdom, a sense of
civic responsibility, and logical persuasiveness. All these qualities are often
united in the most senior, but non-senile, member of the lineage. In that case,
election is almost routine. But where these qualities do not seem to converge
in one person, election may entail prolonged and painstaking consultations
and discussions aimed at consensus. There is never an act of formal voting.
Indeed, there is no long-standing word for voting in the language of the
Ashantis. The expression which is currently used for that process (*aba to*) is an
obvious modern coinage for a modern cultural import or, shall we say,
imposition.

The point, then, at which the head of a lineage is elected is the point at
which consensus first makes itself felt in the Ashanti political process. This
office, when conferred on a person, is for life unless moral, intellectual, or
physical degeneration sets in. As the representative of the lineage in the
governing council of a town, he, or, in rare cases, she, is duty-bound to hold
consultations with the adult members of the lineage regarding municipal
matters. In any matter of particular significance consensus is always the
watchword. It is also the watchword at the level of the municipal council,
which, as indicated, consists of the lineage heads. That council is presided
over by the "natural ruler" of the town, called a *chief*. This word, though
tainted with colonial condescension, has remained in general use even in the
post-independence era by dint of terminological inertia. The 'natural' aspect
of this position lies in its basic hereditary status: normally, a chief can only
come from the royal lineage. But it is only basically hereditary, for a lineage
being a quite substantial kinship group, there is at any one time a non-
negligible number of qualified candidates. The choice, which is proposed by
the "queen mother" (the mother or aunt or maternal sister or cousin of the

chief), has to be approved by the council and endorsed by the populace through an organization called, in literal translation, "the young peoples' association" in order to become final.

Contrary to a deliberately fostered appearance, the personal word of the chief was not law. His official word, on the other hand, is the consensus of his council, and it is only in this capacity that it may be law; which is why the Akans have the saying that there are no bad kings, only bad councilors. Of course, an especially opinionated chief, if he also had the temerity, might try, sometimes with success, to impose his will upon a council. But a chief of such habits was as likely as not to be eventually deposed. In truth, as W. E. Abraham, also speaking of the Akans, points out in *The Mind of Africa*, "kingship was more a sacred office than a political one"[4] (77). The office was "sacred" because a chief was supposed to be the link between the living population and their departed ancestors, who were supposed to supervise human interests from their postmortem vantage point. Insofar as it was political, it bore substantial analogies to the status of a constitutional monarch. The chief was the symbol of the unity of his kingdom and, in the normal course of his duties, fulfilled a variety of ceremonial functions. But he was unlike a constitutional monarch in being a member (at least as a lineage personage) of the ruling council and in being in a position to exercise legitimate influence on its deliberations by virtue, not of any supposed divine inspiration but rather of whatever intrinsic persuasiveness his ideas may have.

If these facts are borne in mind it becomes apparent that the council was strongly representative with respect to both the nature of its composition and the content of its decisions. This representativeness was duplicated at all levels of authority in the Ashanti state. The town or city councils were the most basic theater of political authority. Representatives from these councils constituted divisional councils presided over by "paramount" chiefs. These latter units also sent representatives to the national council presided over by the "Asantehene," the king of the Ashantis, at the highest level of traditional government. Decision was by consensus at all these levels.

Now, this adherence to the principle of consensus was a premeditated option. It was based on the belief that *ultimately* the interests of all members of society are the same, although their immediate perceptions of those interests may be different. This thought is given expression in an art motif depicting a crocodile with one stomach and two heads locked in struggle over food. If they could but see that the food was, in any case, destined for the same stomach, the irrationality of the conflict would be manifest to them. But is there a chance of it? The Ashanti answer is "Yes, human beings have the ability eventually to cut through their differences to the rock bottom identity of interests." And, on this view, the means to that objective is simply rational discussion. Of the capabilities of this means the Ashantis are explicit. "There is," they say, "no problem of human relations that cannot be resolved by dialogue." Dialogue, of course, presupposes not just two parties (at least), but also two conflicting positions: "One head does not hold council." Nor was any suggestion that one voice might be entitled to be heard to the exclusion of others countenanced for one moment: "Two heads are better than one," says another maxim. Indeed, so much did the Ashantis (and the Akans in general) prize rational discussion as an avenue to consensus among adults that the capacity for elegant and persuasive discourse was made one of the most crucial qualifications for high office.

I would like to emphasize that the pursuit of consensus was a deliberate effort to go beyond decision by majority opinion. It is easier to secure majority agreement than to achieve consensus. And the fact was not lost on the Ashantis. But they spurned that line of least resistance. To them, majority opinion in itself is not a good enough basis for decision making, for it deprives the minority of the right to have their will reflected in the given decision. Or to put it in terms of the concept of representation, it deprives the minority of the right of representation in the decision in question. Two concepts of representation are involved in these considerations. There is the representation of a given constituency in council, and there is the representation of the will of a representative in the making of a given decision. Let us call the first formal and the second substantive representation. It is obvious, then, that you can have formal representation without its substantive correlate. Yet, the formal is desired for the sake of the substantive. On the Ashanti view, substantive representation is a matter of a fundamental human right. Each human being has the right to be represented not only in council but also in counsel in any matter relevant to his or her interests or those of their groups. This is why consensus is so important.

Nor are pragmatic reasons lacking to the same purpose. Formal representation without substance is apt to induce disaffection. If the system in use is such as to cause some groups to periodically be in substantively unrepresented minorities, then seasonal disaffection becomes institutionalized. The results are the well-known inclemencies of adversarial politics. From the Ashanti standpoint consensus is the antidote. But, again, can consensus always be had? As already noted, the Ashantis seem to have thought that it could, at least in principle. But suppose this is not the case. Even so, it can always be aimed at, and the point is that any system of politics that is seriously dedicated to this aim must be institutionally different from a system based on the sway of the majority, however hedged around with "checks and balances."

What is the bearing of these considerations on democracy? Current forms of democracy are generally systems based on the majority principle. The party that wins the majority of seats or the greatest proportion of the votes, if the system in force is one of proportional representation, is invested with governmental power. Parties under this scheme of politics are organizations of people of similar tendencies and aspirations with the sole aim of gaining power for the implementation of their policies. Systems of this kind may be called majoritarian, and those based on consensus consensual, democracies. The Ashanti system was a consensual democracy. It was a democracy because government was by the consent, and subject to the control, of the people as expressed through their representatives. It was consensual because, as a rule, that consent was negotiated on the principle of consensus. (By contrast, the majoritarian system might be said to be, in principle, based on "consent" without consensus.)

The Ashanti system, furthermore, was not a *party* system in the sense of the word "party" noted in the last paragraph, which is basic to majoritarian democracy. But in a broad lexical sense there were parties. The lineages were parties to the project of good government. Moreover, in every Ashanti town the youth constituted themselves into an organized party under a recognized leader who was entitled to make representations directly (though not as a member) to the relevant council on all matters of public interest. The sense in which the system in question did not feature parties is that none of the groups mentioned organized themselves for the purpose of gaining power in a way which entailed others not being in power, or worse, being out of it. For all concerned, the system was set up for participation in power, not its appropriation, and the underlying philosophy was one of cooperation, not confrontation.

This is the aspect of the traditional system to which the advocates of the one-party system appealed in their attempts to prove its African ancestry and authenticity. The illusory analogy was that in a one-party system there is no conflict of parties. No party loses because *the* party wins. The comparison is faulty because in the traditional setup, no party lost because all the parties were natural partners in power or, more strictly, because there were no parties. In the one-party situation the reason why no party loses is because murdered parties don't compete. (If these last remarks should occasion any sense of inconsistency, a careful disambiguation of the term "party" in this context should dissipate it.)

The disappearance of the one-party system from the African scene is, and should remain, unlamented. But my reason for mentioning this is not to flog a dead horse; it is, in fact, to point out the good parts of a bad case. One valid point which was made again and again by the one-party persuaders is that there is no necessary connection between democracy and the multi-party system. An associated insight was that indigenous African systems of politics, at least in some well-known instances, offered examples of democracy without a multi-party mechanism. But although the traditional systems in question avoided this mechanism, it should be constantly borne in mind that, as already noted, it had room for parties in the broad sense. This is important because these parties provided the centers of independent thought presupposed by the very idea of meaningful dialogue in the process of political decision-making—those conditions of rational interaction that the one-party system was so efficient in destroying.

In the drive toward democracy in Africa in the past half-decade or so, African dictators, civilian and military, were under sustained Western pressure to adopt the multi-party way of life. This proved politically fatal to some of them, though others eventually discovered tricks for surviving multi-party elections. There is no denying, of course, that some gains in freedom have accrued to Africa. But how substantial have these been and to what extent have these developments built on the strengths of the indigenous institutions of politics in Africa? It is hard to be convinced that this question has as yet attracted enough attention.

The cause of this relative neglect of the question may conceivably be connected with its difficulty. The conditions of traditional political life were surely less complicated than those of the present. The kinship networks that provided the mainstay of the consensual politics of traditional times are simply incapable of serving the same purpose in modern Africa. This is especially so in the urban areas, where industrialization, albeit paltry in many parts of Africa, has created conditions, such as sharp socio-economic cleavages, which carry all or many of the ingredients of ideological politics. In these circumstances it may well seem a trifle too utopian to envisage the possibility of a non-party approach to politics.

It might seem, furthermore, that the account of traditional politics given above essentially involves exaggerations of harmony in traditional life. In fact, even if consensus prevailed in the politics of certain ethnic groups in Africa, historically inter-ethnic relations involving those same groups have, *by nature*, been marked, or more strictly, marred, by frequent wars, the most extreme negations of consensus. The point is not just that there have been ethnic wars from time to time, as was conceded early on, but more seriously that the ethnic orientation of the various groups, by their own inward fixations, has tended to generate conflict in their external relations. Of this the contemporary world has unspeakably tragic illustrations. It might seem, therefore, that neither in the past nor in the present nor in any foreseeable future can consensus be seen to have been, or to promise, a realistic basis for politics in any African state that is a composite of distinct ethnic units. On the contrary, so it might appear, the more pluralistic approach of a multi-party system, provided it incorporates reasonable safeguards against the tyranny of the majority, offers the more practical option.

The premises of both objections may be granted, quite readily in the first case and with a qualification in the second. But the conclusions in favor of the multi-party system in both cases are nonsequiturs. As regards the premisses, it is true that any suggestion that the kinship basis of traditional politics could be a model for contemporary African politics can be dismissed as an anachronistic nostalgia. But, in the matter of conflict between the ethnic groups, it should be noted that African history furnishes examples not only of conflict but also of cooperation between them. Still, the history of inter-ethnic conflict and the problem of its contemporary reverberations ought not to be minimized. Interestingly, exactly this is one of the reasons why the idea of a consensual non-party system ought to be taken especially seriously in Africa.

One of the most persistent causes of political instability in Africa derives from the fact that in ever so many contemporary African states certain ethnic groups have found themselves in the minority both numerically and politically. Under a system of majoritarian democracy this means that, even with all the safeguards, they will consistently find themselves outside the corridors of power. The frustrations and disaffections, with their disruptive consequences for the polity, should not have caught anybody by surprise.

Consider the non-party alternative. Imagine a dispensation under which governments are not formed by parties but by the consensus of elected representatives. Government, in other words, becomes a kind of coalition— a coalition not, as in the common acceptation, of parties, but of citizens. There is no impediment whatsoever to the formation of political associations to propagate preferred ideologies. But in councils of state, affiliation with any such association does not necessarily determine the chances of selection for a position of responsibility. Two things can be expected. First, political associations will be avenues for channeling all desirable pluralisms, but they will be without the Hobbesian proclivities of political parties, as they are known under majoritarian politics. And second, without the constraints of membership in parties relentlessly dedicated to wresting power or retaining it, representatives will be more likely to be actuated by the objective merits of given proposals than by ulterior considerations. In such an environment a willingness to compromise, and with it the prospects of consensus, will be enhanced.

Consensus is not just an optional bonus. As can be inferred from my earlier remarks, it is essential for securing substantive, or what might also be called decisional, representation for representatives and through them for citizens at large. This is nothing short of a matter of fundamental human rights. Consensus as a political decision procedure requires, in principle, that each representative should be persuaded, if not of the optimality of each decision, at least of its practical necessity, all things considered. If discussion has been even moderately rational and the spirit has been one of respectful accommodation on all sides, surviving reservations on the part of a momentary minority will not prevent the recognition that, if the community is to go forward, a particular line of action must be taken. This should not be confused with decision-making on the principle of the supreme right of the majority. In the case under discussion the majority prevails not over, but upon, the minority—they prevail upon them to accept the proposal in question, not just to live with it, which is the basic plight of minorities under majoritarian democracy. In a consensus system the voluntary acquiescence of the minority with respect to a given issue would normally be necessary for the adoption of a decision. In the rare case of an intractable division a majority vote might be used to break the impasse. But the success of the system must be judged by the rarity of such predicaments in the workings of the decision-making bodies of the state. A less unwelcome use of majorities might occur in the election of representatives. Here choice may have to be determined by superior numbers in terms of votes. But even here the representatives will be under an obligation to consult with all the tendencies of opinion in their constituencies and work out, as much as possible, a consensual basis of representation.

Further points of detail and even of principle remain to be spelled out, but these indications must make it plausible to suppose that in the consensual non-party system no one group, ethnic or ideological, will be afflicted with the sense of being permanent outsiders to state power. That alone should suffice to forestall some, at least, of the unhappy conflicts that have bedeviled African life into our own times. Thus, far from the complexities of contemporary African life making the consensual, non-party precedents of traditional African politics now unusable, they make them indispensable. For this reason, if for none other, the exploration of that alternative to multi-party politics should commend itself to the urgent attention of contemporary African philosophers and political scientists. But there is nothing peculiarly African about the idea itself. If it is valid, especially with respect to its human-rights dimension, it ought to be a concern for our whole species.

15

Postscript

Reflections on Some Reactions

One universal well-entrenched in the philosophical psyche is the penchant for disagreement. This tendency manifests itself not only in communication across cultures but also within them. If cultural relativism is correct, incidentally, philosophical disagreements should not arise in the first theater of human relations. Nor, indeed, is that doctrine well-adapted to accounting for the same phenomenon in the second.[1] Yet historically, such disagreements, sometimes of quite a fundamental character, have occurred more frequently and more intensely within cultures than between them. One reason for this may lie in the fact that there has been precious little philosophical dialogue between the various cultures of the world.

Cultures do not, of course, literally communicate: only individuals do. A substantial step was taken in intercultural dialogue when the two American scholars Parker English and Nancy Steele Hamme directed their critical attention in their article, "Morality, Art and African Philosophy,"[2] to my comparative discussions of morality in Akan and certain forms of Western thought in "Custom and Morality,"[3] and other places. The question of custom and morality is so important in intercultural dialogue that I propose, in responding to them, to take the opportunity to provide further clarifications of the issues at some length. As noted in the Introduction, one of my concerns in the paper just mentioned was to establish a clear criterion for distinguishing between morality in the strict sense and custom. Morality is universal but custom need not be. Hence, departures from morality in any culture are a just cause of criticism, and, *if appropriate*, of efforts in rational dissuasion. The same is not necessarily true of custom. I maintained that the Christian missionaries who worked among our people in some important instances confused the customs of their culture with morality and tried, with a fair measure of success, to impose the former in the guise of the latter on the Africans whom they sought to lead from "darkness." I was also keen to show that Akan traditional morality was humanistic in the sense that it based morality, in the strict sense, that is, on the quest for the harmonization of human interests on the principle of sympathetic impartiality. By contrast, the form of Christianity carried to Akanland by the evangelists construed morality in a supernaturalistic sense, thus, in effect, reducing morality to taboo.

In their critique, which is obviously based on considerable research and reflection, English and Hamme argue that, contrary to my claims, Akan moral thought was supernaturalistic and authoritarian. They insist, moreover, that it was more authoritarian in both a supernaturalistic and a secular way than contemporary Akan thought. As regards the missionaries, the authors say that although they displayed an authoritarianism which "obviously did involve supernaturalistic thought" in that they demanded "that traditional beliefs about spiritual entities and the moral principles they endorsed be assimilated to Christian ones more than vice versa," in fact, "few traditional Akans viewed the missionaries as being self-serving in ways that were significant and malignant"[4] (Mosley, 1995, 416). It is unfortunately clear that English and Parker are arguing with me at cross-purposes. This is principally because they are not adequately attentive to my distinction between morality and custom. A large part of the evidence upon which they draw in trying to show the supernaturalistic basis of Akan morality, in fact, falls within the category of custom in the broad sense defined by me in "Custom and Morality," to which I shall return below. In part also, their case is based on allusions to laws specifying crimes and punishments, which, far from being the basis of Akan morality, as the authors suggest, are, at best, derivations from it and, at worst, contingent accretions.

By far, the most striking misdirection in their discussion is their effort to demonstrate that traditional Akan moral thought was *more* supernaturalistic than its contemporary form, in the belief that I had been arguing the contrary of this thesis. A related thesis of theirs is that I make the "surprising" claim that "Western moral thought is more 'supernaturalistic' and less 'humanistic' than is that of traditional Akans"[5] (ibid., 408). First of all, this quotation suggests that I made a more blanket attribution of a philosophical persuasion to the Western world than I actually did. In the article in question I was explicitly aware of the need for caution in this kind of thing: "The Western intellectual situation is characterized by a great diversity of philosophic persuasions, and prudence dictates abstention from unqualified generalizations" (see chapter 6). Accordingly, regarding ethical supernaturalism, what I said was only that "there is a highly influential tradition of ethical supernaturalism" in the West. I then indicated in the same paragraph that "this view of ethics is particularly popular, *though not universal* among Christians" (see chapter 6, italics added). The relatively more encompassing generalization I made was about nonhumanistic, not supernaturalistic, ethics. Even here I was guarded. What I said was that "if you take account of popular as well as technical thought, it may justly be said that the dominant bent of Western ethics is nonhumanistic" in a certain clearly delimited sense (see chapter 6). That this is a quite circumscribed claim would be appreciated by noting, for example, that it does not follow that the dominant bent of technical moral thought in the West is nonhumanistic. Also, that it does not even follow that Western moral thought is supernaturalistic will be realized if it is understood that, although all supernaturalistic thought is nonhumanistic, not all nonhumanistic thought is supernaturalistic. I illustrated the last part of this claim with Kant's moral philosophy, which was nonhumanistic but also nonsupernaturalistic.

An even more radical difficulty with my being credited or, more strictly, debited with the comparative claim under examination is this: I could not have held that Western thought or contemporary (Western-influenced) Akan moral thought was more supernaturalistic than traditional Akan thought unless I also thought that the latter was supernaturalistic in some measure, however diminutive. My position, however, is that the natural/supernatural distinction does not even make sense in the Akan world view, and I have argued this in some of the articles cited by the authors themselves—in, for example "African Philosophical Tradition: A Case Study of the Akan" (chapter 9). Even if they do not accept my argument, it is still misleading to represent my position in a way that presupposes the intelligibility of that dualism within the Akan conceptual framework.

They do not, indeed, accept my claim that within Akan thinking there is no demarcation of one realm of being as natural from another, over and above it, as supernatural and that, for the Akans, reality is one comprehensive cosmic order in which everything goes according to law. In a longer, as yet unpublished, version of their paper they reject my suggestion on the grounds that it is inconsistent with another part of my account of the world view of the Akans according to which they believe (in the words of the authors) that "spiritual entities which are not constrained by physical laws can interfere with what would otherwise be the law-like behavior of people and other physical objects." Since what is in question is the Akan view of things, this is a peculiar reason for disagreement, for that view may conceivably harbor an inconsistency. In fact, however, there is no inconsistency here; at least, not the one charged. And the reason why English and Hamme seem to see an inconsistency is significant as illustrating one of the more intractable causes of incomprehension in discourse between divergent conceptual schemes. What seems to be happening is this. The authors have the conception of a category of laws, called physical, which defines a realm of operation conceptually exclusive of other possible realms such as the 'spiritual'. Any suggestion of phenomena from the 'spiritual' realm having an impact on elements of the 'physical' realm then automatically invokes notions of interference and disturbance (another concept the authors use in the present context) damaging to law-likeness. This manner of conceptualization is widely received among some historically important schools of Western thought, and it seems difficult for devotees to imagine its absence from any system of thought. Hence, by some process of conceptual transference, it is taken to be operative in Akan thought, too, with the consequence that the inconsistency alleged by the authors becomes plausible. I might add that in this matter they do not stand alone racially, for many African scholars too have assimilated the underlying model of conceptualization, and would happily cooperate in the critique under study.

But consider for a moment a mode of thought in which the spiritual/physical dichotomy does not arise at all. There is one *spatio-temporal* universe in which there are indeed various orders of existence. However, phenomena within these spheres and interactions between them are all according to cosmic laws, some familiar, others more out-of-the-ordinary, but none contradicting any other. Some phenomena will be governed by laws resembling those which, in another world view, are called physical, but they will be viewed without the postulate of exclusivity; so that an event occurring in the human domain in consequence of recondite, extra-human, causes will not be seen as an interference in that order of existence but as just one of the ways of this world. No one set of orders will be taken to define a sphere corresponding to the 'natural' and others to define a sphere corresponding to the 'supernatural.' Such, in barest outline, is the basic character of the Akan worldview, by my understanding.

Let us therefore illustrate with an Akan example. An illness—say, a fever—may be brought on by mosquito bite. This is familiar causation, and familiar medicines are known to combat it in the indigenous herbal pharmacology. But an illness may seem to defy all the best herbal treatments. In that case, the hypothesis that it is, say, an affliction visited on the person concerned by an ancestor for a behavioral lapse will begin to be considered. Within indigenous methodology there are ways of confirming or disconfirming such a hypothesis. Without reviewing the merits or demerits of that methodology, we only need to point out that, if it is concluded that the illness has an ancestral origin, the situation will not be felt to be an ontological interference or anything like that. Such punishment is as culturally recognizable within this world view as the punishment of a child by a parent in this world, even if it is not as frequent. The ancestors are human-like in imagery and even more human-like in their functions. They are conceived to differ from human mortals only in their superior rectitude, reduced susceptibility to the laws of motion applying to the interactions of familiar objects, and in their super-human (but note: not supernatural) ability to affect the lives and fortunes of the living without visible contact. The conception of the ancestors and their world is so charged with this-worldly analogies that the persistent habit, in the literature, of calling them spiritual and supernatural can only be thanks to a terminological inertia of a colonial provenance. English and Hamme are somewhat close to appreciating the premiss of this remark when they note that "traditional Asantes conceived the afterlife as an extension or mirror of the prevailing hierarchies of lived existence. Thus a deceased *Asantehene* [King of the Asantes] was still an *Asantehene*. In afterlife he had the same status and role, together with the same needs and requirements—wives, servants, clothes, gold, food—as he had in his biological existence."[6]

There are, then, good reasons for discounting any attributions of supernaturalism to the Akans. But the question still remains as to what the basis of Akan morality is. In regard to this, there is a maximum need for clarity about what we mean by 'morality' and 'basis'. I have argued in "Custom and Morality"[7] (chapter 6 above) that morality has to do with the empathetic harmonization of human interests. But there are countless issues of human relations and others surrounding such defining moments as birth, marriage, and death, to mention but a few, that go beyond this basic ideal. All these belong to the province of custom. Frequently, however, people treat normative rules of custom as moral topics. This is unobjectionable so long as it is borne in mind that morality is being broadly construed. Since I had formulated my claim about the humanistic basis of Akan morality in explicit reference to morality in the strict sense, it would have been a boon to fruitful dialogue if English and Hamme had taken account of this fact in disputing my position. As it turns out, however, in exploring Akan art objects in order to elicit the normative significance of their symbolism, the authors seem to think it a discovery about the 'supernaturalistic' basis of Akan morality if they can point to an art object, say the Golden Stool of the Asantes, which gives rise to a rule of conduct connected with some extra-human consideration. They cite, for example, the rule never to speak ill of the Golden Stool, since it was supposed to be an object conjured from the heavens embodying the *Sunsum* (something like the 'spirit') of the Asante nation. But this is a matter of custom, not of morality, strictly so called.

Meanwhile, English and Hamme somehow do not notice what is arguably the most ethically significant art motif of the Akans. This is an image depicting two crocodiles with one stomach and two heads locked up in conflict over food. I have commented on this symbolism in the paper last mentioned.[8] Here I would like to emphasize an embedded message which is hard to miss; namely, that the ultimate cause of trouble in the moral domain is shortsightedness. Clearly, the recommended remedy for shortsightedness is rational reflection. And the one stomach implies that rational reflection will reveal that, by and large, we all have common interests. There is another implication, even more germane to ethics: If there is only one stomach, then the motivation for the harmonization of interests (as perceived by the individual heads) will be not just rational calculation but also sympathetic identification.

That the basis of morality in the strict sense is sympathetic impartiality follows immediately. In chapter 6 I have indicated that my own ethical thinking is in the most complete harmony with this philosophy of morals.

But let us take up the question of what is meant by the basis of morality. It is apparent from even the brief remarks in the last paragraph (not to mention the explanations in chapter 6) that by this concept we mean the criterion of moral rightness or wrongness. It is therefore difficult to believe that English and Hamme are talking of the same thing that I was talking about when they say things like "Komfo Anokye [the legendary advisor to a legendary Asante king] . . . presented a formal constitution that outlined a code of seventy-seven laws to be observed by all. These laws are regarded as the basis for traditional Akan moral thought"[9] (in Mosley, 1995, 413). They do not indicate by whom those laws are so regarded. But whoever they are, they cannot be the people who thought up the crocodile metaphor or recognized it as an epitome of ethical wisdom. This last reference is not, of course, to every traditional Akan. Whole peoples do not excogitate a philosophy, nor even occupy themselves with its interpretation. The communal philosophy of Akan morals was created by individual Akan thinkers. Nevertheless, the flow of thought and information on matters of basic good and evil is so pervasive in a communalist society such as Akanland that the ordinary canons of good upbringing are everywhere impregnated with this rational outlook on morals. Ask any group of average Akans why people should not, for example, develop designs on their neighbors' spouses and the answer will not be because Okomfo Anokye or the ancestors said it should not be done. That would strike people as an infantile thing to say. The reply would be rather that it is because you should not do unto others what you would not that they do unto you. The vaguely biblical phraseology should not deceive anybody into thinking that these Akans would be indebted to the Son of Man for this answer. The Akans have various ways of framing the thought in their own language, some literalistic, others highly epigrammatic. And, by the way, although it is obviously true that some of their most important philosophical conceptions about morality (and other things) are expressed in art motifs,[10] it is not true, as English and Hamme[11] seem to hint, that these are the main records of that thinking. There is, in fact, a large repertoire of ethical maxims, proverbs, tales, allegories, etc., in the Akan oral tradition not engraved on wood or other media of art.[12]

The point about the stratification of intellectual interest among the Akan population (or any population, for that matter) is of direct relevance to the question of the role of custom in Akan society and the attitude of people to it. Akan traditional sages, philosophic or not, do have a cognitive interest in the rationale for Akan customs and, in many cases, can explain and clarify them. But there is a large mass of the Akan populace who seem content, for the most part, to accept the authority of their customs simply because they were laid down by our ancestors. This is significantly different from their attitude to strict morality, which is, as a rule, founded on rational reflection. The explanation, in all probability, is the following. Customs are contingent rules of behavior which may, and often do, vary from place to place and time to time. Frequently they are based on no other reasons than circumstantial convenience; sometimes they are based on no reasons at all, but on idiosyncratic preference. There are, indeed, cases in which customs are based on reasons of utility or prudence or on cosmological beliefs. But in such cases those reasons are often tied up with empirical explanations hard to come by, unlike the situation in pure morality where the essential reasons are purely a priori. Not surprisingly, therefore, not too many people are conversant with the reasons or eager to research them. Why, for example, do the Akan inherit matrilineally? Why are Akans not supposed to work on Thursdays? Why, if one has the occasion to greet a group of people, ought one to greet from right to left and not the other way round or *ad lib*? And why is sex in the bush so absolutely proscribed by the Akans?

The reasons for these customs are well known in some cases and less so in others. The inheritance system is based on the Akan conception of the constituents of the human person according to which people get their blood, which is made the ground of lineage membership, from their mother. As for the Thursday no-work rule, it derives, apparently, from the belief that Thursday is the day of the earth "goddess." Connected with the same "goddess" is the rule against sex in the bush. She simply dislikes that form of recreation and will cause the soil to become infertile in reprisal if it is indulged in, according to a well-known account. In regard to the rule of greeting, we note that the left is generally associated with negativity and other inglorious significations among the Akans. In this heterogeneous assortment of reasons, those involving the earth "goddess" are worthy of special note. A piece of conduct is, on the face of it, held to be wrong solely and simply because of the dislikes of an extra-human being. There is no indication that she is thought to dislike it because it is wrong on some independent grounds. A prohibition of this sort is properly called a taboo. It is, in its essence, as far removed from morality as can be.[13] However, I have suggested elsewhere[14] that, contrary to official teaching, the real reason why our ancestors laid down this rule must have been to secure to unaccompanied women in the bush freedom from unapproved embraces and any forcible sequels, which, surely, is an excellent practical reason. In an age of skepticism it should take no special powers of imagination to guess this. But then, it follows that, from the perspective of the ingenious ancestors who put out the extra-human story, the rule in question is not a taboo, but one of precautionary common sense. On this showing, it is not at all outlandish to speculate that perhaps all the apparent taboos may have been pedagogic expedients and were taboos in anything like a serious sense only for the unknowing. Since the philosophy of a culture is the production of the philosophers of the group rather than the populace, a further implication is that the role of taboo in the traditional Akan theory of values may be nil. In "Custom and Morality" (chapter 6) it seemed to me worth pointing out that, in contrast to this, insofar as orthodox Christian doctrine—though, not every form of Christian doctrine—defines moral goodness in terms of the will of God, it reduces morality to taboo. If this sounds surprising it may, perhaps, serve as an intellectual wake-up call.

Consider now, in light of the immediately preceding discussion, the claim by English and Hamme that "Traditional Akans used beliefs about the authority and action of spiritual entities to an overwhelming extent in teaching and enforcing their moral principles."[15] If the word 'moral' is taken in the strict sense, this remark contains a serious error, as is clear from the explanations given above. I have explained, furthermore, that there are good reasons why the use of the word 'spiritual' should be discouraged in this context. Beings such as the ancestors, as they are postulated in the Akan world view, are at best quasi-material entities, to use an unavoidably artificial term. It should also, at this stage, be easy to understand that questions of the teaching and enforcing of any rules of conduct, whether they be of morality or custom, are importantly different from questions of their basis. Thus, although the ancestors are supposed to have a part in the enforcement of the rules of good behavior, their wishes are certainly not taken to constitute the definition or justification of any of those rules. The ancestors are, of course, regarded as the authors of the customs of the society. But they are supposed to have established them while they lived and on criteria deriving from mortal experience. Moreover, in their post-mortem state, their assumed part in the enforcement of rules is a reinforcement of the efforts of mortal authorities, not a substitute for them.

It is only when we consider the category of taboo that it might be said, as the authors imply, that the normative pedagogy of the Akan sages included the use of stories about the wishes of quasi-material beings designed to concentrate the minds of the not-so-sophisticated on the path of conventional virtue. But it is an overwhelming exaggeration to suggest that this method was used to "an overwhelming extent" in the teaching of even the customs of Akan society; for, apart from anything else, the apparent taboos constituted only a subset of the customs. I might point out that in traditional Akan society morality is taught not to adults but to children by parents or other people *in loco parentis,* of whom there are always large numbers in the kinship setup. In fact, any such teaching for an adult would be in the nature of remedial education. The routine teaching of morality to adults from the pulpit on Sundays that is so characteristic of Christianity is totally foreign to Akan culture.[16]

To return to custom, there are, indeed, important customs that are based on beliefs about quasi-material entities. (Here we are talking of genuine beliefs, not, as in the case of the taboos, of ancestral make-belief.) The pouring of libation to the ancestors on various occasions is one such custom. Another is the whole array of funeral observances that are such a constant factor of Akan life.[17] But here a somewhat subtle distinction has to be grasped. The quasi-material aspect of the customs in question does not determine their normative force but only their application. What this means will emerge more clearly with an illustration. Take one of the funeral customs of the Asantes, a subdivision of the Akans. As English and Hamme note,[18] on the grounds that a king in life remains a king in death and has analogous privileges in the afterlife, the Asantes in the past, on the death of an Asante king, used to kill people to accompany him as servants. The implied principle of this gloomiest of gloomy customs is that a king ought to be provided with servants. Given that a king remains a king in the afterlife, it follows that the principle applies there too. In this reasoning the normative principle is a premiss not a conclusion, and it is independent of the other premiss, which is the eschatological claim. Therefore, the fact that a custom is connected with extra-human beliefs does not necessarily show that its normative force derives from that context. Anyone who takes this clarification to heart should be able to resist any temptation to exaggerate the role of extra-human beings in the normative thinking of the traditional Akans.

With reference specifically to the dreadful custom under discussion, English and Hamme address the following challenge to me: "If this does not count as overriding the welfare of individuals for spiritualistic purposes, then Wiredu needs to explain what would count as such."[19] Well, nothing would count as such, since, as I have explained, there are no such things as *spiritualistic* purposes in the Akan scheme of things. In fact, however, the custom is as terrible an overriding of the welfare of individuals, for any purpose, as can be imagined. As it happens, before the authors wrote I had agonized in print on the matter. In "An Akan Perspective on Human Rights," chapter 12 (written in 1988 and published in 1990),[20] I commented as follows: "Given the eschatology, the practice was logical. But the belief was an appalling contravention of the Akan precept that, as offsprings of God, all human beings are entitled to equal respect and dignity." In any case, "It is drastically lacking in fairness, and it flies in the face of the golden rule." On this matter, then, the authors and I are in agreement. But the reason they introduce this subject is that they want to show, as we have already noted, that "traditional Akan thought was much more supernaturalistic than is contemporary Akan thought" and that "the bulk of the available evidence" shows that "traditional Akan thought was also more authoritarian in more secular terms."[21] And this because they somehow had the impression that I was maintaining the contrary. I was not. As far as concerns supernaturalism, the reader by now knows how to disentangle the conceptual superimposition. In the second case, however, the comparison is so imponderable that I do not care to venture an opinion.

English and Hamme seem to think also that it was part of my concerns to show that the moral thought of the Christian evangelists was more authoritarian than traditional Akan thought. The comparison may be correct, but it was not in my program to even suggest it. I did, however, assert that the evangelical type of outlook could lead to "authoritarian moralism." My reason was not, as the authors suggest, because the missionaries "often claimed universalism and superiority for their own moral principles." If those principles were strictly moral, there would have been nothing wrong in claiming that they were universal, for that is exactly what they would be. The trouble, I thought, was that they sometimes sought to impose their own customs on the Akans (as they did on other Africans) in the aggressive conviction that they were moral principles. I conjecture that part of the reason for this deplorable project was that the missionaries may not have been philosophically clear about the distinction between custom and morality. In general, I think that intercultural relations have, historically, often been marred, sometimes with tragic consequences, by this intellectual error.

The question of authoritarianism demands a little more attention. In my discussions of the traditional Akan social system I have never tried to hide my opinion that it harbored a significant element of authoritarianism. I remarked in "An Akan Perspective on Human Rights" (chapter 12) that this "is seen in the Akan attitude to the freedom of speech of nonadults. . . . the self-expression of minors was apt to be rigorously circumscribed."[22] In light of this and my decrying of the 'ritual' killing of people on the death of an Ashanti king, I might have hoped for a possible communion with the angels on the question of human rights. But Rhoda E. Howard in her essay on "Group and Individual Identity in the African Debate on Human Rights" included in the same volume in which my last-mentioned article was published, complains, speaking of me, that "he does not note the indigenous age and gender stratification of Akan society. Nor does he discuss the system of indigenous slavery among the Ashanti, one Akan group, a system that by the late nineteenth century was quite brutally exploitative." She comments further that discussions like mine "actually confirm the view that traditional Africa protected a system of obligations and privileges based on ascribed statuses, not a system of human rights to which one was entitled merely by virtue of being human." I believe, on the contrary, that, barring some inconsistencies, whose seriousness I have had no wish to minimize, the traditional Akan outlook was predominantly consonant with the rights in support of which she writes so forcefully, though I cannot argue this here.

I agree with Rhoda Howard that human rights are rights that human beings have simply in virtue of being human. This, in fact, was my starting point. (See chapter 12.) But it cannot be taken for granted that all cultures have the same understanding of what it is to be human, and what I sought to expound in my contribution (chapter 12) was the Akan understanding and how it grounds the rights in question. The reflective propagation of such information from the standpoint of the different cultures of the world seems to me to be the beginning of intercultural wisdom. Some disparities can be anticipated, but that should not be taken to carry any relativistic consequences. Because morality, in the strict sense, is universal, and because, in the last analysis, human cognition has the same foundation everywhere, the resolution of any such intellectual or ideological differences is, in principle, possible. The essays in the first two parts of this volume are, each in their own way, arguments for this thesis. I find, in fact, that there is not much in Rhoda Howard's article that I disagree with, and this is, most likely, not unconnected with the basic universalism which she and I have in common.

As for the sins of omission, I plead "guilty with an explanation" (except in the case of age 'stratification', regarding which I plead innocent, since I deplored it in the article). The explanation is that I understood my task in the article to be one of providing "a portrayal of Akan principles rather than an assessment of Akan practice" (chapter 12). Matters such as the 'ritual' killings and the raw deal for minors I regarded as illustrations not of principles but of their perversion. Had I treated of slavery and gender injustice in Akan society, I would have placed them in the same light. But these last two evils of traditional Akan society present special problems of conceptual delineation; they are so different from their approximate analogues in Western society as to require elaborate explanations, on pain of automatic misapprehensions. Such explanations (not to be confused with justifications) demand their own time and place. I am now inclined, however, to regard those abuses as deformities not just of practice but also of principle.

I come now to the intracultural theater of philosophical dialogue. African philosophers are not less industrious in debate among themselves than other members of the speculative species. Personally, I count it as a blessing that some of my most persistent critics have been good friends of mine. Goodwill being taken for granted on all sides, the genuine issues can be pursued wherever they lead in a spirit of give-and-take free from petty cavilling. It is a pleasure, therefore, to respond (briefly) to the comments of Henry Odera Oruka[23] on my "Are There Cultural Universals?" (chapter 3) in his article entitled "Cultural Fundamentals in Philosophy: Obstacles in Philosophical Dialogues."[24] I had argued, to summarize somewhat drastically, that morality and basic rationality, though not in this order, were cultural universals. As to this, Oruka suggests, noting correctly that I "did not shut the door to the admission of other possible cultural universals" that 'intuition' also should be recognized as a cultural universal.[25] By 'intuition' he means "a form of mental skill which helps the mind to extrapolate from experience and come to establish extrastatistical inductive truths . . . or to make a correct/plausible logical inference without any established or known rules of procedure."[26] I am not absolutely sure that this is an attribute of the mind distinct from those already taken note of in my discussion, but I can find no ground of objection to according it the status claimed by Oruka.

Even more interesting is Oruka's remarks on my view of morality as a universal. My argument is that morality is a universal because it is necessary for the existence of a human community. As already indicated, morality, on my view, is the quest for the harmonization of human interests on the principle of sympathetic impartiality. On the other hand, Oruka, in effect, argues, citing "Rawls' principle of rational egoism," that sympathetic impartiality may not, in fact, be necessary. Rational egoism alone, that is, a calculating impartiality *sans* sympathy, may well do the trick. "In Rawls' state of nature," he comments, "individuals lack 'sympathetic impartiality' and they do not even acquire it in a civil state, otherwise there would be little need for police, prisons and class wars. They remain egoists and many of them are still rational, otherwise the society would have melted away."[27] If the individuals were, indeed, fully rational, they surely would have no need for the "police and prisons and class wars." What I fear they might need, if they were rational *humans* without an iota of the feeling of sympathy, would be a great number of psychiatrists of a superhuman breed. It seems to me a highly plausible psychological hypothesis, not at all recondite, that a human being without a trace of sympathy in his or her own breast, or hope of the same from any other, will inevitably suffer the gravest type of breakdown. In truth, the problem of morality is not that human beings don't have sympathy, but rather that they don't always have enough of it. And that is why, or part of why, people need the police, etc. Morality is an ideal, and a special one. We cannot do without a modicum of it, but we must do without its maximum. Perhaps some beings can get by with impartiality without sympathy. But we *humans* need both.

In the article in question Oruka[28] argues also that the various cultures of the world have their own peculiarities which are apt to impede dialogue. This is true and important. It is especially important in the area of language, and in all the chapters of part II, though not in them alone, I have sought to illustrate the difficulties of intercultural understanding in philosophy emanating from this cause. In the specific case of the theory of truth my suggestion that, owing to some linguistic disparities, certain forms of the correspondence theory of truth, which in English can give the appearance of shedding light on the nature of truth, reduce in Akan to a trivializing tautology (see chapter 8) elicits vigorous criticisms from A. G. F. Bello in his paper "Philosophy and an African Language."[29] In its clarity and balance, Bello's article is a model of philosophical criticism, and I am glad to take the opportunity afforded by his objections to offer some clarifications of my position. Dr. Bello's principal concern is to warn against the incautious use, by African philosophers, of considerations about their various vernaculars in their philosophical argumentation. Although he begins with an approving recall of my own earlier remarks that in philosophy "language can only incline, not necessitate" and that it would be premature to insist that philosophy should be taught in the vernacular everywhere in Africa, he maintains that in two of my articles, "The Akan Concept of Mind" and "The Concept of Truth in the Akan Language" (chapter 8), I seem to "abandon the caution" thus recommended[30] (p. 5). In my discussion below I will restrict myself mainly to the second of these articles since it is the one he concentrates on.

To start with some misunderstandings simple to correct, Bello refers to the following statement of mine, "The other main theories of truth traditional in Western philosophy, namely, the pragmatic and coherence theories, do not suffer any trivialization on being translated into Akan, but they take on a new look if they are measured against the task of elucidating the notion of something being so, which reflection on the concept of truth in the Akan language presses on our mind" (p. 112), and immediately comments, "Though Wiredu does not substantiate these two [latter] claims, the net result of his analysis is to recommend to his readers the pragmatic and coherence theories, which, according to him, are at bottom one." Bello supposes also that I recommend these theories simply because I find their rival, the correspondence theory, unsatisfactory on the grounds that it reduces to an unenlightening tautology when translated into my vernacular. There are two mistakes in these comments. First, I do not argue in my paper that *simply* because the correspondence theory cannot be translated into Akan without tautology it is defective in some way. On the contrary, the point I was trying to clarify was that it could happen that truth is correctly definable in terms of fact without this teaching any wisdom interculturally about the nature of truth. And my reason was that in addition to the translational anticlimax, everything that can be expressed using the concepts of truth and fact can be expressed in Akan by means of the notion of *nea ete saa* (what is so). This last claim will loom large in this rejoinder, but for now let us attend to the second mistake, which is this. When I say that a theory does not suffer trivialization on being translated into Akan I do not mean—and I cannot be rightly interpreted to mean—that it is therefore any better than one which suffers trivialization. It may not suffer that fate and yet be egregiously absurd in Akan discourse, and outside it too.

Furthermore, to see a theory in a new light is not necessarily to see it in a better light. My conjecture is, to speculate a little, that Bello perceives the statement of mine which is the subject of debate here as an advocacy of the pragmatic theory, because he knows from another piece of mine that I (basically) favor that theory of truth.[31] In that piece I argued also that if the notion of coherence is interpreted in what I take to be the right way, then the coherence and pragmatic theories of truth can be seen to be at bottom one. I might mention, however, that I remain unpersuaded by either the idealistic or positivistic or post-positivistic formulations of the coherence theory of truth, on account of their inappropriate conceptions of coherence. Even in the case of the pragmatic theory, it might be prudent to point out that my sympathy extends only to the version due to John Dewey according to which truth is warranted assertibility, subject to a rider explained in the piece concerned.[32] In all this what is specially to be emphasized is that when I have taken it into my head to argue in favor of the pragmatic or against the correspondence theory, I have done so on independent grounds, that is, on the basis of considerations that do not depend on the peculiarities of Akan or any other language, as can be verified from my discussion of the theory of truth lastly referred to.

The misapprehension that in "The Concept of Truth in the Akan Language" I am using untranslatability into Akan without tautology to knock down the correspondence theory and promote its pragmatic and coherence rivals unfortunately colors Bello's entire understanding of my position. This must be the explanation for his warning "that we must be wary of using purely linguistic facts (for example translatability or non-translatability) as knock-down arguments for philosophical beliefs or doctrines."[33] The same problem afflicts his characterization of my general method in the two articles mentioned earlier on, which, in his words, is to reason as follows: "This theory does not translate into my language without tautology or repetition . . . therefore its rivals are preferable." Anybody with a modicum of logical sense must be anguished at having such a form of argument imputed to him or her; for, apart from anything else, it is plainly oblivious to the fact that contrary propositions may all be false together. "But this," says Bello, "seems to be roughly what Wiredu does in his analysis. Witness what he does with the correspondence theory of truth. He says, in effect: 'There is no one word in Akan which translates the cognitive meaning of truth; neither is there any one word which translates "fact." Both translate into "is so" or "what is so." Moreover, whatever can be said with fact can be said using the notion of *nea ete saa*. To define truth as correspondence to fact in Akan is, therefore, to say "what is so is what is so," an unenlightening repetition. Therefore, the correspondence theory is unstatable without tautology, and thus cannot be proffered as a solution to the problem of truth. Moreover, the problem of the relation of truth to fact is not fundamental'."[34]

Although the summary just quoted can easily be improved, what is interesting is that it does not fit Bello's general characterization of my procedure, owing, among other things, to the fact that it contains the contention that "[Moreover], whatever can be said with fact can be said using the notion of *nea ete saa*." In spite of having included this component of my argument in his summary, it is obvious that Bello does not at all reckon with its significance. Otherwise, it would not have seemed to him apposite to react in the following manner:

> My reaction to this argument is that if the correspondence theory is unstatable in the Akan language, so much the worse for that language. That, in itself, says nothing about the correspondence theory; nothing about its plausibility or its being fundamental or not. However, it does say a lot about the Akan language. It means that the language is not suitable for discussing certain theories. It also means that the Akan-speaking peoples have to brace up to the fact that their language or conceptual apparatus needs development in this small area in which it does not facilitate clarity and exactness of thought, since it promotes the constant conflation of the meanings of 'truth' and 'fact', by rendering both as *nea ete saa* (literally, what is so).[35]

The puzzle is: If the Akans, using the one notion of *nea ete saa*, can express whatever can be expressed in English with both 'truth' and 'fact', then why should they lose sleep over not employing separate expressions for the purpose after the manner of English-speaking peoples? Compare the case of equivalence and the 'If and only if' locution. As I explain in the paper under discussion, the Akan language has a phrase for equivalence, namely, 'kosi faako' and it has, of course, a way of expressing 'if-then', namely, 'se-ende'. Thus equivalence can be defined in Akan as follows:

(**P** ne **Q** kosi faako) kyere se [(Se **P** a ende **Q**) na (Se **Q** a ende **P**)].
This corresponds in English to:
(**P** and **Q** are equivalent) means [If **P** then **Q**) and (If **Q** then **P**)].

The phrase 'kyere se' means 'means' and 'ne' and 'na' in their respective positions both mean 'and'. Nevertheless, there is no verbal counterpart to 'If and only if' in Akan. So that what is expressed in English by means of both '**P** is equivalent to **Q**' and '**Q** if and only if **P**' can be expressed in Akan using just '(**P** ne **Q** kosi faako).' Why should the Akans be exercised on account of this economy? They need not, because the situation does not reveal any expressive incompleteness in their language. Given negation ('enye **P**', i.e., 'not **P**') and disjunction ('**P** anaase **Q**', i.e., '**P** or **Q**'), conjunction ('**P** na **Q**', i.e., '**P** and **Q**') and conditionality and equivalence (as exhibited already), the Akans have very much more than is needed for constructing a propositional logic that is both semantically and deductively complete. Moreover, there do not exist even reasons of convenience for wanting to introduce a separate expression for 'If and only if' in Akan. And, actually, even in English-speaking formalizations of propositional logic, both equivalence and the bi-conditional are represented by one symbol. Here again, Bello recalls my use of this logical illustration, but its significance somehow passes him by.

What now emerges is that from a supposition such as that the Akans express both 'truth' and 'fact' by one phrase, namely, *nea ete saa*, it does not follow that they are conflating anything and are, consequently, in need of any verbal or conceptual development in this area of discourse, unless it can be shown that there is something that can be expressed with the two notions in English which cannot be expressed with that one notion in Akan (excepting, of course, the disputed non-equivalence of the two notions). Suppose, on the contrary, that everything that can be expressed in English using 'fact' and 'truth' can be expressed by means of the notion of 'nea ete saa', then, surely the problem of the relationship of truth with fact will not exist in Akan, although, of course, it may be, and in fact it is, an important problem in English. We can go further. The Akan who reflects on this inter-linguistic state of affairs will be justified to conclude that 'truth' and 'fact' are essentially equivalent concepts. This does not mean that some type of a correspondence theory might not be propounded. For example, one might propose a proto-Tarskian definition of truth as follows:

(1) 'P' is true =df. 'P' states a fact
                                              and
(2) 'P' states a fact =df. P

In terms of a time-honored illustration,

(1') 'Snow is white' is true =df. 'Snow is white' states a fact
                                              and
(2') 'Snow is white' states a fact =df. Snow is white.

If one uses 'if and only if' and applies Hypothetical Syllogism, one obtains Tarski's material adequacy condition: "'P' is true if and only if P." Tarski, of course, goes on to refine the right hand side of the equivalence in the manner already hinted at above. In my opinion, even that refinement only brings us to the beginning of a fruitful philosophical explanation of the concept of truth. Be that as it may, as far as logic is concerned, we can turn any of the available equivalences the other way round, *salva veritate*, obtaining, for example:

Snow is white if and only if 'Snow is white' is true.

Moreover, as far as intuitive definability is concerned, there is no reason why one might not define fact in terms of truth, starting[36] with

'P' states a fact if and only if 'P' is true
        which quickly brings us to
'P' states a fact if and only if P.

Intuitively, a definition of **A** in terms of **B** normally suggests that **B** is more easily understood than **A**. In the case of truth and fact, the one concept—if truth be told—is no more nor less enigmatic than the other; which suggests that one can have, within certain limits, a Ramseyan redundancy theory not only of truth but also of fact. English-speaking philosophers fret a lot over the problem of truth but not as much over the problem of fact. Indeed, one hardly hears of the latter problem. Yet, as I try to show in "The Concept of Truth in the Akan Language," the real problem of any philosophically substantive correspondence theory of truth is, *in fact*, a problem about facts, a problem of the ontological elucidation of the notion of fact.

One thing that should be clear from the foregoing is that the essential equivalence of the notions of truth and fact—'essential' in view of grammatical and idiomatic disparities—is arguable too inside English discourse and is implicit in some well-known accounts of truth.[37] I think that this equivalence thesis can be justified, but it is not part of my project here to do it. I bring this whole matter up here only because it illustrates an important principle of intercultural discourse. It is the principle of what I have called independent considerations (see Introduction). In the present context it may be stated in the following form: If a philosophical suggestion emanating from considerations relating to a natural language has any cross-cultural validity, it ought to be demonstrable or supportable with arguments not depending on the peculiarities of the original language. This principle has a crucial bearing on the next principal point Bello makes in his article regarding the use of African vernaculars in philosophy, which will be taken up below. But before then, perhaps, the general point ought to be emphasized that whenever everything that is expressible in one language by means of two or more concepts can be expressed in another using a single concept, that is a good reason for supposing the equivalence, in one way or another, of the multiples. In the specific case of truth and fact in English, on the one hand, and 'nea ete saa' in Akan, on the other, Bello (a Nigerian philosopher who is knowledgeable in Akan) need not accept the claim of equivalence. But he must brace himself to the realization that if it is true, then, because of an inter-linguistic consideration, if for no other, the correspondence theory, which he holds dear,[38] might be due for some rethinking.

Bello does not, in fact, prohibit all uses of African vernaculars in African philosophical discourse. He observes, for example, that "African languages can [also] be employed in the task of supporting or refuting 'popular' (or 'unpopular') conceptions about African thought and culture, for example, that Africans are in all things religious, that African morality is based on religion, that African traditional beliefs are either irrational or 'non-rational', etc. A close look at African languages will [also] be necessary if we want to elucidate some of the concepts that 'traditional' Africans lived by, for example, predestination, sacrifice, divination, kinship, etc."[39] But he advises balance: "Now, all Africans do not speak or understand the Akan language. . . . The cacophonous chorus that will result from employing vernaculars for all philosophical activities will mar philosophical communication not only between Africans and the rest of the world, but also among Africans themselves."[40] Cacophony is, perhaps, in the ear of the listener, but since I agree in principle with the sentiments so lucidly expressed by Bello, I would like to assure him and all concerned that I do not advocate the use of the vernacular "for all philosophical activities." But I do recommend that wherever possible African philosophers should take cognizance, in their philosophical meditations, of the intimations of their own languages. I elaborate on this in many of the chapters in this volume, especially, "Formulating Modern Thought in African Languages" and "The Need for Conceptual Decolonization in African Philosophy" (chapters 7 and 10, respectively).

However, meditation is not publication, and when it comes to the latter, I endorse the call for caution. I myself look forward to the time when African philosophers will not need to be culturally particularistic in the manner under discussion. But, for the time being, it may be necessary to hold forth in international print on the Yoruba conception of this or the Akan conception of that or the Luo conception of the other mainly because of the historical fact of colonialism, which led not only to the relative neglect of our indigenous philosophies in our own thinking but also to the distortions of our conceptual frameworks through their articulation in the medium of foreign categories of thought (see, for example, chapter 7). There is no way in which the necessary corrections and elucidations can be made without the closest attention to the vernaculars concerned. Since this also involves conceptual self-exorcism on the part of African philosophers themselves, they can learn from each other by testing interpretations of other African languages in their own vernaculars. Besides, many of the important linguistic and conceptual points that arise in debates about their vernaculars between African philosophers speaking the same language need not be mysteries to their African colleagues speaking different languages or even to non-Africans, because they can often be evaluated using only logic and first principles. A case in point is Bedu-Addo's critique of my "The Concept of Truth in the Akan Language" (chapter 8), to which Bello refers in illustrating the point that unrestrained use of African vernaculars could be a bar to even inter-African communication. Bello comments that "only an Akan-speaking philosopher could meaningfully have contributed to, or arbitrated in, the debate between Wiredu and Bedu-Addo." This is, however, not uniformly the case with all the main issues in the exchange.

Bedu-Addo is an excellent classicist and philosopher of the Akan stock. In the theory of truth his sympathies are with the correspondence theory, and he believes that the theory loses none of its attractions when cast in the Akan language. His criticisms of my position, which are detailed, vigorous, and clear, raise many interesting issues.[41] My point-by-point rebuttal will appear elsewhere. Here, I will merely call attention to one point in illustration of the fact that non-Akans too can sometimes 'arbitrate' such controversies. I had maintained in my discussion of the concept of truth in the Akan language (chapter 7) that the version of the correspondence theory of truth which says that a statement is true if and only if it corresponds to fact reduces to an unenlightening tautology in the Akan language because in Akan both the concepts of truth (in the cognitive sense) and fact are expressed by the same notion, namely, the notion of *nea ete saa* (what is so). Far from being trivialized in this way, he maintains that the correspondence theory is supported by the conceptual situation in the Akan language. In particular, he denies that 'fact' can be expressed at all in Akan in terms of the notion of *nea ete saa*. So, how does he consider that 'fact' may be translated into Akan? As it happens, he himself bids us consider this question in connection with the task of translating a sentence like "It is a fact that it is raining" into Akan. And his verdict is: "The correct Akan translation of the English sentence is: *Eye nokware se nsu reto*. (Literally, 'it is true that it is raining')."[42] Consider now what translation of the correspondence theory just mentioned this secures for us in the specific case of the meteorological sentence: nothing, obviously, other than something like *Se woka se asem se nsu reto ye nokware a nea ekyere nese eye nokware se nsu reto*. This translates back into English, as even a non-Akan should expect, as "If you say that the sentence 'It is raining' is true what it means is that it is true that it is raining." Again, one does not have to speak Akan to notice the triviality of this message.[43] I do not myself agree that 'fact' is best translated into Akan by means of *nokware* (in its cognitive sense, i.e., truth), but it strikes me that in this translation Bedu-Addo is indirectly manifesting the effects of that economy of the Akan language by which it expresses both 'truth' and 'fact' by the same notion.

Issues such as this are worthy of the closest attention among contemporary Africans, for there is always the danger that they might unwittingly assimilate some of the conceptually parochial intimations of the metropolitan languages that, for historical reasons, they find themselves philosophizing in. This is the theme discussed in some detail in "Formulating Modern Thought in African Languages: Some Theoretical Considerations" (chapter 7). The very title of the discussion, however, evoked some reservations from a reviewer of the volume in which it originally appeared.[44] In a basically friendly comment on the article, Owomoyela[45] objects that the title seems to imply that Africans have not been doing any modern thinking. In strict logic, however, what it implies is that, if there is modern African thought, it is not expressed in African languages. I do not doubt that we do have modern African thought in various disciplines. But the problem is that, with few exceptions, these are written in one metropolitan language or another. In philosophy this has created real conceptual tangles requiring a lot of thought to disentangle. (This problem also engages my attention in chapter 10: "The Need for Conceptual Decolonization in African Philosophy"). It is high time we settled down to that task in African philosophy, along with all the multifarious others.

Notes

3. Are There Cultural Universals?

1. Ruth Benedict, "Psychology and the Abnormal," *Journal of General Psychology*, vol. 10, 1934.

2. Benjamin Lee Whorf, *Language, Thought and Culture: Selected Writings of Benjamin Lee Whorf*, ed. J. B. Carroll (New York: Wiley, 1956).

3. Willard Van Orman Quine, *Word and Object* (Cambridge, Mass: M. I. T. Press, 1960), p. 47.

4. I understand part of what Alasdair MacIntyre is saying in his 1984 Presidential Address to the Eastern Division Meeting of the American Philosophical Association to be of this tenor. (See *Proceedings and Addresses of the American Philosophical Association*, vol. 59, no. 1, Sept. 1985.)

5. This too is the reason why the contingent variety of phonetic articulation in different languages noted by Ruth Benedict (see note 1 above) do not have any relativistic implications.

6. Thomas Kuhn's own position in regard to relativism in his *The Structure of Scientific Revolutions* (2nd ed. Chicago: University of Chicago Press, 1970) is not the easiest thing to pinpoint.

7. On the argument of this paragraph and its first rider, see further Kwasi Wiredu, "Canons of Conceptualization," *The Monist*, vol. 76, no. 4, Oct. 1993.

8. There are pitfalls in the full formulation of the Golden Rule, some of them well known. A most rigorous analysis, formulation, formalization, and proof of the rule is provided by Harry G. Gensler, in "The Golden Rule Calculus" in chapter 9 of *Symbolic Logic: Classical and Advanced Systems*, (Englewood Cliffs, N. J.: Prentice-Hall, 1990). On this ground the book may be accounted one of the best texts on ethics.

9. See, for example, Kwasi Wiredu, "The Moral Foundations of an African Culture," in Kwasi Wiredu and Kwame Gyekye, *Person and Community: Ghanaian Philosophical Studies, I* (Washington D.C.: The Council for Research in Values and Philosophy), 1992. Also in Harley E. Flack and Edmund D. Pellegrino, *African-American Perspectives on Biomedical Ethics* (Washington D.C.:Georgetown University Press), 1992.

10. I have discussed the matters touched on in this paragraph in some detail in chapter 6, "Custom and Morality: A Comparative Analysis of Some African and Western Conceptions of Morality." Paper presented at Gustavus Adolphus College, Minnesota, March 1991, and at Baruch College, New York, May 1991.

5. Universalism and Particularism in Religion from an African Perspective

1. See, for example, John S. Mbiti, *African Religions and Philosophy* (London: Heinemann, 1969), p. 2.

2. On this see further Kwasi Wiredu, "Morality and Religion in Akan Thought" in H. Odera Oruka and D. A. Masolo, eds., *Philosophy and Cultures* (Nairobi: Bookwise, 1983).

3. For convenience, I am using the word "God" here. But this is subject to a rider to be entered subsequently.

4. W. E. Abraham asserts, correctly, I think, that "if a distinction can be drawn between worship and serving, then the Akans never had a word for worship. Worship is a concept that had no place in Akan thought." *The Mind of Africa* (Chicago: University of Chicago Press, 1962), p. 52.

5. I have commented, in "Morality and Religion in Akan Thought," on this quote from Danquah's "Obligation in Akan Society," *West African Affairs* 8 (1952): 6 along with that from Busia's "The Ashanti," in Darly Forde, ed., *African Worlds* (Oxford: Oxford University Press, 1954).

6. Kwame Gyekye insists very spiritedly on the locative connotation of the Akan concept of existence, but he does not draw the empirical implications.

7. My own explication of the concepts of existence and object-hood is essentially in conformity with the Akan conception of existence. In this connection, see my "Logic and Ontology" series (Wiredu, 1973–75). The definition of an object which emerged from those discussions was that an object is what can be the non-conceptual referent of a symbol. It should not strain human resources to show that any such referent will have to be in space.

8. As will become clear, my own conceptual orientation is decidedly Akan in this respect.

9. K. A. Busia, for example, speaks of "the belief held among African communities that the supernatural powers and deities operate in every sphere and activity of life" in *Africa in Search of Democracy* (London: Routledge and Kegan Paul), p. 9. This in spite of the fact that in his earlier work, *The Challenge of Africa* (New York: Praeger, 1962), p. 36, he had remarked on "the apparent absence of any conceptual cleavage between the natural and the supernatural" in Akan thought. Gyekye in *An Essay on African Philosophical Thought*, p. 69, also says that "the Akan universe is a spiritual universe, one in which supernatural beings play significant roles in the thought and action of the people."

10. I argue against relativism in "Are There Cultural Universals?" (chapter 3). See also Kwasi Wiredu, "Canons of Conceptualization," *Monist*, vol. 76, no. 4 (October 1993), and Wiredu, "Knowledge, Truth, and Fallibility," in I. Kucuradi and R. S. Cohen, eds., *The Concept of Knowledge* (Boston: Kluwer Academic, 1995).

11. For a longer answer see Kwasi Wiredu, "The Akan Concept of Mind" in *The Ibadan Journal of Humanistic Studies*, October 1983. Also in Guttorm Floistad, ed., *Contemporary Philosophy: A New Survey* (Boston: Kluwer, 1987).

12. Gyekye, in attributing spiritual beliefs to the Akans uses a definition of this sort, "The Supreme Being, the deities, and the ancestors are spiritual entities. They are considered invisible and unperceivable to the naked eye: This is in fact the definition of the word 'spiritual' . . ." in *An Essay on African Philosophical Thought*, p. 69.

13. The species-wide dimensions of the Akan sense of solidarity are explicit in a number of traditional maxims. When the Akans say, for example, that *onipa hia moa*, which literally means "a human being needs help" but is more strictly to be rendered in some such wise as "a human being, simply in virtue of being human, is deserving of help"—when the Akans say this, they mean absolutely and explicitly *any* human being. If you add to this sense of human fellowship the acute sense of the vulnerability of an individual in a strange place—the Akans say *okwantufo ye mmobo*, meaning the plight of a traveler is pitiable—then you begin to understand the ideology behind the hospitality to strangers, black or white, for which the Akans, and actually, Ghanaians generally, are famous.

14. Akan culture may not be unique in this regard. It is, for example, an open question how appropriate it is to describe the early Greek beliefs about their motley collection of gods and goddesses as a religion. It is no less an open question whether Theraveda Buddhism is a religion or a non-religious philosophy of life translated into a way of life.

15. This does not mean, however, that the concept of religion corresponds to anything in the Akans' conceptualizations of their own experience or external existence. As one might expect from the fact, noted earlier on, that they do not, rightly, as I think, make a sharp distinction between the material and the spiritual, they do not operate with anything like the distinction between the secular and the religious. Many students of African "religion" have noted this but have strangely drawn from it, or deduced it from, the inverted impression that in African life everything is religious. Thus Mbiti, speaking of African ways of thought, remarks that "there is no formal distinction between the sacred and the secular, between the religious and the non-religious, between the spiritual and the material areas of life," *African Religions and Philosophy*, p. 2. But he supposes that this is because "traditional religions permeate all the departments of life" (loc. cit.). And he goes on to say things like "religion is their whole system of being," p. 3. See also K. A. Busia, *Africa in Search of Democracy*, chapter 1: "The Religious Heritage"; Kofi Asare Opoku, *West African Traditional Religion* (London: F.E.P. International, 1978), chapter 1: "African Traditional Religion: A General Introduction"; Kwesi A. Dickson, *A Theology in Africa* (New York: Orbis, 1984), chapter 2: "The African Religio-Cultural Reality." Since all these writers are Africans—actually they are all Ghanaians, except Mbiti, who is Ugandan—it might have been hoped that they would have stopped to ponder how the blanket attributions of religiosity to their peoples might be expressed within the indigenous languages. The difficulty of the experiment might well have bred caution. In any case, logic alone should have inspired doubt as to the conceptual significance of the idea of being religious in the thought of a people who, by general admission, do not have the distinction between the secular and the religious in their framework of categories.

6. Custom and Morality

1. Morality in the strict sense thus has its focus on human beings. But morality in the broad sense, that is, our general system of values, need not be thus restricted; it can have an ecological sweep.

2. *Journal of General Psychology*, X, 1934.

3. This is the burden of Ifeanyi Menkiti's "Person and Community in African Traditional Thought," in Richard A. Wright, *African Philosophy: An Introduction*, 3rd ed., University Press of America, 1984.

7. Formulating Modern Thought in African Languages

1. Okot p'Bitek, *African Religions in Western Scholarship* (Nairobi: East African Literature Bureau, c. 1970).

2. John S. Mbiti, *African Religions and Philosophy* (London: Heinemann, 1970), chap. 3, esp. 17–18. The suggestion can, of course, be faulted on other grounds. It should be remarked, however, that this chapter of the book is of considerable philosophical interest.

3. Dr. George P. Hagan of the Institute of African Studies, University of Ghana, has called attention to an alternative Akan traditional formulation of this principle in an unpublished manuscript. He gives it as *Nokware mu nni abra* which means "There is no conflict in truth."

4. See, for example, Gordon Hunnings, "Logic, Language and Culture," *Second Order: An African Journal of Philosophy* 4, no. 1 (January 1975).

5. See J. E. Wiredu, "Truth as a Logical Constant, with an Application to the Principle of Excluded Middle," *Philosophical Quarterly* (October 1975).

6. In some many-valued systems of logic there is an appearance of the rejection of the principle of Noncontradiction [-(p & -p)]. Thus, in one of Bochvar's systems, -(p & -p) is not a thesis, not being a tautology. The point, however, is that, because the logical constants have different matrices from those of classical logic, the formula -(p & -p) in this context is not identical with the classical principle of Noncontradiction. Moreover, the principle is presupposed at a metalogical level. Note also, in any case, that although -(p & -p) is not a tautology in the system in question, ⅂(p∧⅂p) is. See Nicholas Rescher, *Many Valued Logic*, New York, McGraw-Hill, 1969, chap. 2, esp. 33. There is a grosser trifling with the principle of Noncontradiction in the "paraconsistent logic" or "dialectical logic" recently canvassed by some otherwise solid logicians. See, for example, R. Routley and R. K. Meyer, "Dialectical Logic, Classical Logic and the Consistency of the World," *Studies in Soviet Thought* 16 (1976); or R. Routley, "Dialectical Logic, Semantics and Metamathematics," *Erkentnis* 14 (1979). (For a critique see Joseph Wayne Smith "Logic and the Consistency of the World," *Erkentnis* 24 [1986].) In my opinion any difference between paraconsistentism and paralogism lies in the possibility of an unequivocally consistent interpretation of the proffered symbolisms.

7. J. B. Danquah, *The Akan Doctrine of God*, 2d ed. (London: Frank Cass,1968), with a new introduction by K. A. Dickson. Dr. Danquah, however, does not appear at all times to have abided by the full implications of this wording. George P. Hagan in "Black Civilization and Philosophy: Akan Tradition of Philosophy" (paper delivered at FESTAC [Festival of African Culture], Lagos, Nigeria, 1977) argues very plausibly from an Akan drum text and a number of sayings, in effect, that the Akan conception of creation is not creation out of nothing.

8. Though this is not the point immediately at issue here, it might be useful to note that it is not quite correct to say that a people like the traditional Akans worship God. It is a questionable assumption that, if a people believe in a Supreme Being, then they must have institutions or procedures describable as worship directed to that Supreme Being. If Christian Europe has such procedures, that is little reason for supposing that all peoples must have them. The Akans conceive of God as a supremely good, powerful, and wise being. It is not clear why such a being has to be worshipped.

9. In the Twi Bible (that is, the Bible as translated into the Akan language), St. John's sentence reads as "Mfiase no na Asem no wo ho, na Asem no ne Nyankopon na ewo ho, na Asem no ye Onyame." The best one can do in rendering Asem into English in this context is to say "a piece of discourse," so, even if we suppress our qualms about translating "Onyame" as "God," a strict retranslation yields: "In the beginning the Piece of Discourse was there, the Piece of Discourse was there with God and the Piece of Discourse was God," which, though not as hilarious as the Luo version, is no more intelligible.

10. They have illustrious historical antecedents in men like St. Cyprian, Tertullian, and St. Augustine.

11. The only alternative translation permitted by Akan idiom would be quite alarming. The sentence would read "The trouble was God."

12. The reference here is to the African who speaks no language in which the relevant concepts are already received.

13. Any dictionary that translates "God" as "Nyame," "Onyankopon," or vice versa glosses over this necessity to the disadvantage of genuine Akan thinking. Christaller, the German author of the first Twi-English Dictionary, did this, but so have Akrofi and Botchey, themselves Ghanaians. See J. G. Christaller, *Dictionary of the Asante and Fante Language Called Tshi (Twi)* (Basel, [1881] 1933); C. A. Akrofi and G. L. Botchey, *English-Twi-Ga Dictionary* (Accra: Waterville Publishing House, 1968; Rev. ed. 1980).

14. The reader might like to be reminded that when concepts and forms of thought are said to be African or Western there is no implication that they are intrinsically ethnic.

15. See A. Adu Boahen, *Clio and Nation Building*, Inaugural Lecture, Accra, Ghana: Ghana Universities Press, 1975: 20ff.

16. See Kwasi Wiredu, *Philosophy and an African Culture* (Cambridge University Press, 1980), 21–22, 29, 30.

17. Note that this would have been arrived at by a different route from that of the Western advocate of reformation. The Western "reformationist" thinks of reformation as the justification of a comprehensive practice called punishment; the Akan "reformationist" would start with a critique of the institution of retribution he encounters in his society, and his reflection would take the form of examining the morality of retribution and, along with it, deterrence, reformation, and any other possible approach to misconduct.

18. See Tsu-Lin Mei, "Chinese Grammar and the Linguistic Movement in Philosophy," *Review of Metaphysics* 14 (1961).

19. For a critique of this see J. E. Wiredu, "Predication and Abstract Entities," *Legion Journal of the Humanities* 2 (1976).

20. See, for instance, Alonzo Church, "The Need for Abstract Entities in Semantic Analysis," *American Academy of Arts and Sciences Proceedings* 80 (1951). Reprinted in I. M. Copi and J. A. Gould, *Contemporary Readings in Logical Theory* (New York: Macmillan, 1967). I have criticized this kind of theory at length in J. E. Wiredu, "Logic and Ontology," *Second Order: An African Journal of Philosophy* (January 1973, July 1973, July 1974, and January 1975).

21. Kwasi Wiredu, "Philosophical Research and Teaching in Africa: Some Suggestions [toward Conceptual Decolonization]" (paper delivered at UNESCO conference on Philosophical Teaching and Research in Africa, Nairobi, Kenya, June 1980). Published in *Teaching and Research in Philosophy* (Paris: UNESCO, 1984). See also Kwasi Wiredu, "The Akan Concept of Mind," *Ibadan Journal of Humanistic Studies*, no. 3 (October 1983; G. Floistad, ed., *Contemporary Philosophy: A New Survey*, vol. 5: *African Philosophy* (Boston: Kluwer Academic, 1987).

22. Kwame Gyekye: "The Akan Concept of a Person," *International Philosophical Quarterly* (September 1978): 278. Gyekye has an updated account of the Akan concept of a person in *An Essay on African Philosophical Thought* (Philadelphia: Temple University Press, 1995), chapter 6.

23. K. S. Busia, "The Ashanti," in *African Worlds*, ed. Daryll Ford (Oxford, 1954), 197.

24. I have tried to sort these things out in K. Wiredu, "The Akan Concept of Mind."

25. This is not to say that the Akans are empiricists. Of course, not all Akans are philosophers. Nor need an Akan philosopher be an empiricist. Indeed, if he or she pays due attention to the Akan language, the basic thesis of classical empiricism will

be found incoherent. Empiricism is not necessarily truly empirical in orientation. See John Dewey, "An Empirical Survey of Empiricisms," in *Dewey on Experience, Nature and Freedom*, ed. Richard J. Bernstein (New York: Arts Press, 1960). Moreover, we are here directly concerned with Akan traditional categories of thought, not with Akan traditional thought about Akan categories of thought.

26. K. A. Busia, *The Challenge of Africa* (New York: Praeger, 1962), 36. Busia, unfortunately, in this same work as in others (for example, *Africa in Search of Democracy* [London: Routledge and Kegan Paul, 1967]), wrote as if the Akans had a place for the concept of the supernatural in their thought.

27. Mbiti, *African Religions and Philosophy*, 5. This insight, however, as in the case of Busia, is inconstant in Mbiti's pages.

28. For example, in the paper on "The Akan Concept of Mind" referred to earlier, I have distinguished four problems of mind: (1) the metaphysical problem of how mind conceived as a nonmaterial entity is related to the body, a material entity; (2) the question of how the concept of mind is related to that of thought; (3) the problem of the basis of the possibility of thought; and (4) the issue of how the category of brain process is related to that of thought. Only the first is declared to be a pseudoproblem not arising within Akan thought.

29. In the case of the metaphysics of substance and quality, we have already noted the opposition of David Hume. In contemporary English-speaking philosophy, Bertrand Russell was one of the most unremitting critics of the metaphysical notion of substance: "'Substance' . . . is a metaphysical mistake, due to transference to the world-structure of the structure of sentences composed of a subject and a predicate" (*History of Western Philosophy* [London: George Allen and Unwin, 1946], 225). In an earlier book Russell had called for the expurgation of the metaphysical notion of substance from philosophy and commented, "A great book might be written showing the influence of syntax on philosophy; in such a book, the author could trace in detail the influence of the subject-predicate structure of sentences upon European thought, more particularly in this matter of 'substance'" (*An Outline of Philosophy* [New York: Meridian Books, 1927], 1960). Ayer's discussion of substance in his *Language, Truth and Logic*, 2nd ed. (London: Victor Gollancz, 1946) was scarcely more accommodating. He actually said that philosophers who advocated the doctrine of substance had been "duped by grammar" (p. 45; see also p. 42).

30. Kwasi Wiredu, *Philosophy and African Culture*, 35.

31. Formulating modern logic in African languages is going to be an important part of the general program of formulating modern knowledge therein. Victor Ocaya made an interesting attempt in this direction in his Master's thesis, "Logic within the Acholi Language" (Makerere University, Kampale, Uganda, 1978).

32. See also chapter 8 and "Postscript."

33. David Mitchell, *Introduction to Logic*, 2d. ed., Hutchinson University Library (London, [1962], 1064).

34. Recall also our reference to the Chinese critic of the subject and predicate distinction in linguistic philosophy; see n. 17 above.

35. I first introduced the notion of tongue-dependency in "The Concept of Truth in the Akan Language" (chapter 8; see also my paper on "Philosophical Research," cited in n. 19). For comments on some criticisms of the present point and other theses in chapter 8, see the "Postscript."

36. On this claim see Kwasi Wiredu, (chapters 2, 3, and 4 above).

37. The equally well-known speculations of Quine on the indeterminacy of translation have no necessary relativistic forebodings for us. To say that "manuals for translating one language into another can be set up in divergent ways, all compatible

with the totality of speech dispositions, yet incompatible with one another" (W. V. O. Quine, *Word and Object* [Cambridge, Mass.: MIT Press, 1960], 27), is to say something, which, if true, will affect all translations, not just "radical" translations, for it follows from the point we have just made that all "radical" translations, "that is, translation of the language of an untouched people(!)," can be "de-radicalized" through sustained cultural intercourse. More radically, the thesis must affect translation inside one and the same language.

8. The Concept of Truth in The Akan Language

1. A different etymology is sometimes suggested for 'nokware'. Some say that the word consists of 'ano' which, as we have seen, literally means 'mouth', and 'kwa' which means 'to polish' or, somewhat metaphorically, 'to make good', 'to protect'. Adopting this etymology would not make any essential difference to our main thesis, since the 'polishing' or 'protecting' would have to be construed morally.

2. There is a close relation between 'nyansa' (wisdom) and 'nimdee' (knowledge). ('Nim' means know, 'ade' means thing; so that 'nimdee' means the knowing of things.) One can, of course, know many things without being wise (Heraclitus), but one cannot be wise without knowing quite some things. When the things at issue are principles and philosophical notions, 'nyansa' (wisdom) coincides with 'nimdee' (knowledge) in Akan thought. Thus for many purposes the 'anyansafo' will be the same as the people who are said to have 'nimdee'.

3. I shall henceforward normally use 'truth' to render the cognitive concept of truth.

4. See further my *Philosophy and an African Culture* (Cambridge, 1980) p. 155, where this passage is quoted and commented upon.

5. The great elaborateness of Tarski's theory arises from his supposition that the schema "'p' is true if and only if p" cannot be universally quantified into a general definition of the form "(p) 'p' is true if and only if p" because the 'p' in quotes in the first component is only a name and one cannot quantify over a mere name. But I do not believe this account of quotation.

9. African Philosophical Tradition

1. As to the identity of the Akans, let me quote a previous description of mine. "The word *Akan* refers both to a group of intimately related languages found in West Africa and to the people who speak them. This ethnic group lives predominantly in Ghana and in parts of adjoining Ivory Coast. In Ghana they inhabit most of the southern and middle belts and account for about half the national population of 14 million. Best known among the Akan subgroups are the Ashanti. Closely cognate are the Denkyiras, Akims, Akwapims, Fantes, Kwahus, Wassas, Brongs, and Nzimas, among others" ("An Akan Perspective on Human Rights," in Abdullahi Ahmed An-Na'im and Francis M. Deng, eds., *Human Rights in Africa* (Washington, D.C.: The Brookings Institute, 1990, p. 243). The Akans have been the subject of some famous anthropological, linguistic, and philosophical studies. See notes 45–50.

2. Professor Claude Sumner of Addis Ababa University, Ethiopia, has brought out five volumes of historic writings in Ethiopian philosophy in a continuing program of publication under the general title *Ethiopian Philosophy* (Addis Ababa: Central

Printing Press, vol. I, 1974; Addis Ababa: Commercial Printing Press, II, 1974, III, 1978, IV, 1981, V, 1982). See also Sumner's "Assessment of Philosophical Research in Africa: Major Themes and Undercurrents of Thought," in *Teaching and Research in Philosophy: Africa* (Paris: UNESCO, 1984), esp. pp.159–67, and his "An Ethical Study of Ethiopian Philosophy," in H. Odera Oruka and D. A. Masolo, *Philosophy and Culture* (Nairobi, Kenya: Bookwise, 1983). Of interest also is the appendix on "Ethiopian Sources of Knowledge" in V. Y. Mudimbe's *The Invention of Africa* (Bloomington: Indiana University Press, 1988).

3. Practically the entirety of a recent anthology on African philosophy is devoted to this controversy. I refer to Tsenay Serequeberhan, ed., *African Philosophy: The Essential Readings* (New York: Paragon House, 1991). An earlier anthology edited by Richard A. Wright (*African Philosophy: An Introduction* [New York: University Press of America, third edition 1984, first published 1977]) contained quite a number of articles dealing with the controversy. A powerful catalyst was Paulin J. Hountondji's *African Philosophy: Myth and Reality* (Bloomington: Indiana University Press, 1983), first published (in French) in 1976. My own *Philosophy and an African Culture* (New York: Cambridge University Press, 1980), among other things, gave considerable attention to the issues involved, and Kwame Gyekye's *An Essay on African Philosophical Thought* (New York: Cambridge University Press, 1987) contains a good balance of discussions of this methodological question and of substantive issues. Two recent books by H. Odera Oruka are also very relevant here. Much of his *Trends in Contemporary African Philosophy* (Nairobi, Kenya: Shirikon Publishers, 1990) is occupied with the debate in question. The same is true of his *Sage Philosophy: Indigenous Thinkers and Modern Debate on African Philosophy* (Nairobi, Kenya: African Center for Technology Studies [ACTS] Press, 1991). This is the local version of the work of the same title published in 1990 by E. J. Brill, Leiden. The book's section on the 'indigenous thinkers' has an importance which will be commented on below. A great part of the earlier phase of the controversy was taken up with the critique of the conceptions of African philosophy represented by Placide Tempel's *Bantu Philosophy* (Paris: Presence Africaine, 1959, first published in French translation from the original Dutch in 1945), and John S. Mbiti's *African Religions and Philosophy* (London: Heinemann, first edition, 1969, second edition, 1990).

4. The potential importance to the modern African tradition of philosophy of work which exploits the literary and scientific resources of the modern world, but which is not rooted in African culture beyond the fact that Africa also exists in the modern world is sometimes questioned by foreign (as well, *mirabile dictu*, as African) scholars. Thus, commenting on my "Classes and Sets" (*Logique et Analyse*, Jan. 1974), an article in which I discussed some issues in the conceptual foundations of set theory, Prof. Ruch, a European teacher of philosophy in Africa, declares, ". . . when such an eminent African philosopher as, for example, J. E. Wiredu ["J. E." being my former initials] writes a scholarly article on the logic of classes and sets his philosophical article contains nothing specifically African." Such work, therefore, according to him, could never become part of African philosophy. See E. A. Ruch and A. K. Anyanwu, *African Philosophy: An Introduction to the Main Philosophical Trends in Contemporary Africa* (Rome: Catholic Book Agency--Officium Libri Catholici, 1981), p. 16 (in a chapter written by Ruch). I appreciate Prof. Ruch's gracious address, but I cannot embrace the abridged prospects he holds up for African philosophy in the modern world. When an African expresses sentiments akin to Ruch's that can only be attributed to a backward-looking tendency, which though understandable in view of what Africa has historically suffered at the hands of Western imperialism, etc., will not help Africa in her existence in the modern world. True, there is absolutely no question

but that contemporary African philosophers, as a breed, ought to investigate the philosophical thought in their culture and build upon its insights, of which I believe there are plenty, as will be apparent from this paper. But not to appropriate for their own tradition any resource necessary for the philosophical understanding of the modern world on the grounds that it is not rooted in their culture would be nothing but pointless self-abnegation.

5. On this see further, Kwasi Wiredu, "On Defining African Philosophy," in Serequeberhan, *African Philosophy*, especially 92ff.

6. To have some conception of the wonders of memorization that some human beings in an oral tradition are capable of, consider how many *Odu* (groups of versified recitations with addenda) a would-be master of the Ifa divination system of the Yorubas must memorize. According to Professor E. Bolaji Idowu, "We cannot tell exactly how many of the recitals there are within the corpus. However, we know that they are well grouped under headings to which are given the generic name of *Odu*. There are two hundred and fifty six of these *Odu*; and to each of them . . . are attached one thousand six hundred and eighty stories or myths called pathways, roads or courses." *Olodumare: God in Yoruba Belief* (London: Longman, 1962), pp. 7–8.

7. Leiden: E. J. Brill, 1990.

8. Oxford: Oxford University Press, 1965, original French version, 1948.

9. H. Odera Oruka, *Sage Philosophy*, p. 119. This quotation and the others to follow are translations into English by Professor Oruka of taped remarks made to him or his colleagues in the vernacular by the Kenyan sages.

10. New Haven: Yale University Press, 1934.

11. Oruka, pp. 115–16.

12. Ibid., p. 134.

13. Ibid., p. 37. See also p. 137.

14. Ibid., p. 38.

15. London: Ethnographica, 1986.

16. New York: Cambridge University Press, 1987.

17. See the citations below.

18. The late Okot p'Bitek, Ugandan poet, man of letters, and conceptual analyst of no mean standing, argued with vigor and sophistication that his ethnic group, the Central Luo, do not even have a place in their conceptual scheme for any concept of creation or of a supreme being. This he did in two books, *Religion of the Central Luo* (Nairobi, Kenya: East African Literature Bureau, 1971), and *African Religions in Western Scholarship* (Nairobi: East African Literature Bureau, 1970). In the case of the Akans, although there is a widespread belief in the existence of some kind of a supreme being, skeptics are not unknown in Akan society.

19. J. B. Danquah, in his *The Akan Doctrine of God: A Fragment of Gold Coast Ethics and Religion*, the most famous book on Akan philosophy, suggests an even more drastic Akan qualification on omnipotence. "The Akan idea is of an ancestral creator and head of the very real and near community. . . . The omnipotence of the high-father cannot be greater than the reality of this community" (p. 24). See also pp. 55–56 and 87–89. The book was first published in 1944 and reissued in 1968 with a new introduction by Prof. Kwesi Dickson (London: Frank Cass).

20. *The Challenge of Africa* (New York: Frederick A. Praeger, 1962), pp. 11–13. The first three chapters of this book are especially relevant to Akan philosophy. The first two chapters of another book of his are similarly relevant. The book is *Africa in Search of Democracy* (New York: Frederick A Praeger, 1967). Busia also contributed a celebrated chapter on "The Ashanti" to the volume on *African Worlds: Studies in the Cosmological Ideas and the Social Values of African Peoples*, ed. Daryll Forde (Oxford:

Oxford University Press, 1954). There is a briefer piece on "The African World-view" in Jacob Drachler, ed., *African Heritage* (New York: Macmillan, 1963). Both articles are extremely useful for the investigation of Akan philosophy. Worthy of mention, finally, is *The Position of the Chief in the Modern Political System of Ashanti* (London: Frank Cass, 1968), which, though not a philosophical text, contains valuable sources for the study of Akan political philosophy.

21. "Black Civilization and Philosophy: Akan Tradition of Philosophy," paper presented at the festival of African culture (FESTAC) held in Lagos, 1976.

22. Ibid.

23. I discussed this locative conception of existence and its implications for the concept of nature in "An African Conception of Nature," presented at the Boston Colloquium in the Philosophy of Science, Boston University, Massachusetts, February 1986. Gyekye also insists on the locative character of the Akan conception of existence; see his *Essay*, p. 179.

24. This seems to be a widespread characteristic of African languages. Thus Alexis Kagame, the late well-known Bantu metaphysician and linguist says, "Throughout the Bantu belt, the verb 'to be' can never express the idea of existence, nor, therefore, can the word 'being' express the notion of existing. The celebrated axiom 'I think, therefore, I am' is unintelligible, as the verb 'to be' is always followed by an attribute or by an adjunct of place: I am good, big etc., I am in such and such a place, etc. Thus the utterance '. . . therefore I am' would prompt the question: 'You are . . . what? . . . where?'" ("Empirical Apperception of Time and the Concept of History in Bantu Thought," in *Cultures and Time*, ed. Paul Ricoeur (Paris: UNESCO, 1976), p. 95.

25. See chapter 3.

26. See my four-part series on "Logic and Ontology" in *Second Order: An African Journal of Philosophy* (Ile-Ife, Nigeria: University of Ife Press [now Obafemi Awolowo University Press], Part I, Jan. 1973; II, July 1973; III, July 1974; IV, Jan. 1975, especially the last two). See also chapter 2.

27. For more discussion of the notions of the spiritual and the supernatural, see chapter 5.

28. Such premeditated attributions of mysticism to Africans may be observed in, for example, E. G. Parrinder's "Mysticism in African Religion," in J. S. Pobee, ed., *Religion in a Pluralistic Society* (Leiden: E. J. Brill, 1976).

29. See chapter 7: "Philosophy, Mysticism and Rationality" in my *Philosophy and an African Culture*.

30. I have discussed this and related issues in "Death and the Afterlife in African Culture," originally presented at a colloquium at the Woodrow Wilson International Center for Scholars, Washington, D.C., 1988 and published in *Perspectives on Death and Dying: Cross-Cultural and Multi-Disciplinary Views*, ed. Arthür Berger et al. (Philadelphia: The Charles Press, 1989).

31. See, for example, the article cited in note 27.

32. For details see my "The Concept of Mind with Particular Reference to the Language and Thought of the Akans" in G. Floistad, ed., *Contemporary Philosophy, Volume 5: African Philosophy* (Boston: Kluwer Academic, 1987).

33. For example, J. J. C. Smart, "Sensations and Brain Processes," *Philosophical Review*, 1959; reprinted in Paul Edwards and Arthur Pap, eds., *A Modern Introduction to Philosophy* (New York: Collier Macmillan, third edition, 1973) and in several other anthologies.

34. *Leibniz: Basic Writings*, translated by Dr. George R. Montgomery (La Salle: Open Court Publishing, 1962), p. 19.

35. The Yorubas have an even more picturesquely dramatic and elaborate formulation of essentially the same doctrine. See, for example, Idowu's *Olodumare*, p. 174.

36. *The Mind of Africa* (Chicago: University of Chicago Press, 1962), p. 60. With an epigrammatic economy of words and a dense richness of information and reflection, Abraham manages to cover all the main aspects of Akan philosophy in chapter 2 (pp. 44–115).

37. This point and various others in regard to the Akan concept of a person are discussed in my "The African Concept of Personhood," in Harley E. Flack and Edmund D. Pellegrino, eds., *African-American Perspectives on Biomedical Ethics* (Washington, D.C.: Georgetown University Press, 1992).

On the normative aspects of African conceptions of human personality, see also Ifeanyi A. Menkiti, "Person and Community in African Traditional Thought," in Richard A. Wright, ed., *African Philosophy: An Introduction* (New York: University Press of America, third edition, 1984) and Meyer Fortes's "On the Concept of the Person among the Tallensi" in Meyer Fortes, *Religion, Morality and the Person: Essays on Tallensi Religion*, edited and with an introduction by Jack Goody (New York: Cambridge University Press, 1987). For a critique of the attribution of a normative conception of personhood to Africans by Menkiti, see Kwame Gyekye, "Person and Community in Akan Thought," in Kwasi Wiredu and Kwame Gyekye, eds., *Person and Community: Ghanaian Philosophical Studies, I* (Washington, D.C.: Council for Research in Values and Philosophy, 1992). My own exposition is in basic agreement with Menkiti's.

38. See Kwame Gyekye's *Essay*, chapters 8–10. Also Kwasi Wiredu, "The Moral Foundations of African Culture" in Flack and Pellegrino, *African-American Perspectives on Biomedical Ethics.*

39. Busia's *The Position of The Chief*, cited in note 23, is the most accessible source of the raw materials of the Akan philosophy of politics. Abraham's discussion of Akan philosophy includes accounts of the Akan theory of government and of its legal system (see *The Mind of Africa*, pp. 75–88). G. P. Hagan has an extremely interesting paper entitled "Is There an Akan Political Philosophy?" (paper presented at seminar on Ghana Culture at the University of Ghana, Legon, April 1975). B. E. Oguah, in his "African and Western Philosophy: A Comparative Study," a generally thought-provoking essay, has some useful comments on Akan political philosophy. The paper is included in Richard A. Wright's anthology *African Philosophy*. See chapters 12–14.

40. See J .B. Danquah, "Obligation in Akan Society," *West African Affairs*, No. 8, 1952, London: Bureau of Current Affairs (for the Department of Extra-Mural Studies, University College of the Gold Coast); J. N. Kudadjie, "Does Religion Determine Morality in African Societies?: A Viewpoint" in J. S. Pobee, ed., *Religion in a Pluralistic Society* (Leiden: E. J. Brill, 1976); Kwasi Wiredu, "Morality and Religion in Akan Thought" in H. Odera Oruka and S. A. Masolo, eds., *Philosophy and Culture* (Nairobi, Kenya: Bookwise, 1983); Kwame Gyekye, *Essay*, chap. 8; Kwasi Wiredu, "The Moral Foundations of African Culture" (paper mentioned in note 38).

41. See my *Philosophy and an African Culture*, p. 19.

42. John Hospers, a soft determinist at bottom, but a hard determinist in rhetoric, suggests a basically similar criterion as far as (the English-speaking concept of) responsibility is concerned in "What Means this Freedom?" in Sidney Hook, ed., *Determinism and Freedom in the Age of Modern Science* (New York: Collier Books, 1958), p. 131. His "Free Will and Psychoanalysis" (*Philosophy and Phenomenological Research*, 1950, reprinted in Edwards and Pap, *op. cit.*) also, on the whole, makes a lot of sense from an Akan standpoint.

43. Moritz Schlick, in chapter 7 of his *Problems of Ethics* (reprinted in Edwards and Pap, *op. cit.*, chapter 6: "When Is a Man Responsible?") almost arrives at this result.

44. See my *Philosophy and an African Culture*, p. 17.

45. Christaller was responsible for the first full-length dictionary of the Akan language: J. G. Christaller, *A Dictionary of the Asante and Fante Language Called Tshi (Twi)* (Basel: Evangelical Missionary Society, 1881, 2nd. ed. 1933). He also wrote a grammar of Akan: *A Grammar of the Asante and Fante Language called Tshi* (Basel: 1875). The verbal formation 'Tshi' is an outcome of European struggles to pronounce 'Twi' which is the name of the version of Akan spoken by the Ashanti, the Akims, the Kwahus, and the Akwapims, these being subgroups of the Akan people. The Fante are another subgroup, speaking another, thinly varied version of Akan. An extremely interesting discussion of Akan philosophy through its Fante wing is B. E. Oguah's "African and Western Philosophy: A Comparative Study," in Richard A. Wright, *African Philosophy*.

46. R. S. Rattray wrote a great deal about the Akans. Of particular interest are the following books: *Ashanti Proverbs* (Oxford: Oxford University Press, 1916) (this is a translation and exegetical annotation of a selection from J. C. Christaller's *A Collection of 3600 Tshi Proverbs* [Basel: Evangelical Missionary Society, 1879] which was published in the vernacular); *Ashanti* (Oxford: Oxford University Press, 1923); *Religion and Art in Ashanti* (Oxford: Oxford University Press, 1927); and *Ashanti Law and Constitution* (Oxford: Oxford University Press, 1929).

47. Diedrich Westermann, *Africa and Christianity* (Oxford: Oxford University Press, 1937).

48. See, for example, J. B. Danquah's critique of Rattray and Westermann in chapter 2 of his *The Akan Doctrine of God* (London: Frank Cass, [1944] 1968). K. A. Busia enters a gentle demurer with respect to Rattray on page xi of his *The Position of a Chief*.

49. Of interest here, in addition to his *The Akan Doctrine of God*, is his *Akan Laws and Customs* (London, 1920) and his article on "Obligation in Akan Society" in *West African Affairs*, no. 8, 1952 (London: Bureau of Current Affairs).

50. London, 1911. One might mention also his *Gold Coast Native Institutions* (London, 1903).

51. Nkrumah was just about getting ready for the oral defense of his thesis when the call went to him from his country to return home to participate in the leadership of the independence struggle. He left at once.

52. The first edition (1964) of Kwame Nkrumah's *Consciencism* was published by Heinemann Educational Books, London. The second edition was brought out by Panaf Books, London, in 1970. The second edition of *Towards Colonial Freedom* came out in 1962 from Heinemann.

53. London: Frank Cass, 1968. (See also note 20.)

54. However, Akan workers in other fields, especially religion, have produced works relevant to Akan philosophy. We may note the following: Peter Sarpong, *Ghana in Retrospect* (Accra-Tema, Ghana: Ghana Publishing, 1974); Kofi Asare Opoku, *West African Traditional Religion* (London: FEP International, 1978); John S. Pobee, *Towards an African Theology* (Nashville, Tennessee: Abingdon, 1979); Kwesi A. Dickson, *Aspects of Religion and Life in Africa* (Accra, Ghana: Ghana Academy of Arts and Sciences, 1977); and *Theology in Africa* (New York: Orbis Books, 1984). A remarkable book by one of Ghana's most famous artists, the late Kofi Antubam, on *Ghana's Heritage of Culture* (Leipzig: Koehler & Amelang, 1963), had considerable materials of a philosophical significance in the study of the Akans. As in the beginning, some of the recent philosophical studies of the Akans have been done

by foreign scholars. A perceptive treatment of Akan philosophy in its Akwapim version is contained in "Causal Theory in Akwapim Akan Philosophy" by Helaine Minkus in the anthology by Richard A. Wright on *African Philosophy*, previously cited. This material is a spin-off from the author's doctoral dissertation (Northwestern University, 1975) on *The Philosophy of the Akwapim Akan of Southern Ghana*. Earlier ventures into Akan philosophy by another foreigner were much more controversial and, in part, somewhat obscure. We are referring to the writings of Eva L. R. Meyerowitz: *The Sacred State of the Akans* (London: Faber and Faber, 1951); "Concepts of the Soul among the Akans of the Gold Coast," *Africa*, vol. XXI, no. I, Jan. 1951; *The Akan of Ghana: Their Ancient Beliefs* (London: Faber and Faber, 1958).

55. Chicago: University of Chicago Press, 1962. In 1964 Abraham wrote an article on "The Life and Times of Wilhelm Anton Amo" in *The Transactions of the Historical Society of Ghana*. This was about a Ghanaian who taught philosophy in Germany in the eighteenth century. An interesting question that arises is: He was an African and a philosopher, but did his work constitute an African Philosophy? The answer is that his work was in the German tradition of his time and place, but if a significant number of Africans should take up his work and build on it, it would become an integral part of African philosophy and thus come to belong to the two traditions, which is not at all a rare species of philosophical interconnection. The first part of this answer might occur to Ruch (see note 4) but not the second.

56. New York: Cambridge University Press, 1987.

57. See my "On Defining African Philosophy" in Tsenay Serequeberhan, ed., *African Philosophy* (New York: Paragon House, 1991), pp. 104–105 for a list of a small sample of the varied publications of contemporary African philosophers.

58. For example, the reader of Gyekye's *Essay* will note that there are some very substantial differences in the way he and I interpret and use the tradition we share.

10. The Need for Conceptual Decolonization in African Philosophy

1. See Kwasi Wiredu, "Philosophical Research and Teaching in Africa: Some Suggestions [Toward Conceptual Decolonization]" in *Teaching and Research in Philosophy: Africa* (Paris: UNESCO, 1984).

2. See, for example, *Philosophy and an African Culture* (London: Cambridge University Press, 1980), pp. 216–32; "Canons of Conceptualizations," *The Monist*, vol. 76, no. 4 (October 1993); and "Knowledge, Truth and Fallibility," in I. Kucuradi and R. S. Cohen, eds., *The Concept of Knowledge* (Boston: Kluwer Academic, 1995). See also chapter 3.

3. *The Philosophical Writings of Descartes, Volume II*, translated by John Cottingham, Robert Stoothoff, and Dugald Murdoch (New York: Cambridge University Press, 1984), p. 14.

4. See Norman Malcolm's critique of Lewis and others on this issue in "The Verification Argument," in Max Black, ed., *Philosophical Analysis*, 1950.

5. Of the great Western philosophers none, perhaps, was more scathing of this quest for certainty than John Dewey, witness his *The Quest for Certainty* (New York: Minton, Balch, 1930; Capricorn Books, 1960). Yet, in the apparent resurgence of pragmatism in recent times it is not clear how well and truly the allurements of that ideal have been resisted, all the fulminations against 'foundationalism' notwithstanding.

6. See *The Republic of Plato*, for example V, 478. In the translation by Francis MacDonald Cornford (New York: Oxford University Press, 1945), see p. 185.

7. Infallibility has marched on with other disguises too, such as Indubitability, Incorrigibility, Absolute Validity, etc. For example, some of the logical positivists, such as Schlick (but unlike Neurath), insisted that an 'observation sentence' (as also an analytic one) is indubitable or absolutely certain in the sense that it makes "little sense to ask whether I might be deceived in regard to its truth" (Moritz Schlick, "The Foundation of Knowledge," in A. J. Ayer, ed., *Logical Positivism*, Free Press of Glencoe, 1959, p. 225. Compare Otto Neurath, "Protocol Sentences," in the same volume.)

8. An entry in a dictionary written long ago by German scholars is quite useful: Rev. J. G. Christaller, Rev. C. W. Locher and Rev. J. Zimmermann, *A Dictionary, English, Tshi (Asanti), Akra* (Basel: Basel Evangelical Missionary Society, 1874), p. 46: **Certain**, *it is* ——— , ewom ampa; **Certainly**, *adv.*, ampa, nokware, potee.

9. John S. Mbiti, *African Religions and Philosophy* (London: Heinemann, second edition, 1991), p. 108.

10. Leopold Sedar Senghor, "The African Road to Socialism" (1960) in *On African Socialism*, translated and with an Introduction by Mercer Cook (New York: Frederick A. Praeger, 1964).

11. Alexis Kagame, "Empirical Apperception of Time and the Conception of History in Bantu Thought," in Paul Ricoeur, ed., *Cultures and Time* (Paris: UNESCO, 1976) p. 95.

12. In *An Essay on African Philosophical Thought*, Kwame Gyekye very correctly insists on the locative character of the Akan concept of existence (see pp. 179 and 181).

13. See further chapters 5 and 9.

14. I am aware of the objection that a locative conception of existence will have to be dumb in respect of the existence of abstract objects, like, say, numbers. My reply is that abstract objects are objects only in a figurative sense, and figurative locations are not hard to come by.

15. The extremely useful anthology of *Readings in African Political Thought* (London: Heinemann, 1975), ed. Gideon-Cyrus M. Mutiso and S. W. Rohio, included in part VII some of the best arguments for and against the one-party system.

16. See, for example, M. Fortes and E. E. Evans-Pritchard, eds., *African Political Systems* (Oxford: Oxford University Press, 1940).

11. Post-Colonial African Philosophy

1. This reference to professionals is not intended to indicate a school of thought among contemporary African philosophers. All who are paid to teach philosophy are professional philosophers, irrespective of their doctrinal or methodological persuasion. This remark is necessary because some people seem to think (quite mistakenly) that I did at some point, or even now, consider myself as belonging to a school of thought in contemporary African philosophy "self-designated" as "professional philosophers." See, for example, Tsenay Serequeberhan, *The Hermeneutics of African Philosophy* (New York: Routledge, 1994), Introduction, p. 5 and n. 8.

2. See Kwame Nkrumah, *Consciencism: Philosophy and Ideology for De-Colonization* (London: Panaf, second edition, 1970, first edition, London: Heinemann,1964); Leopold Sedar Senghor, *On African Socialism*, translated and with an introduction by Mercer Cook (New York: Praeger, 1964); Ahmed Seku Ture, *Strategy and Tactics of the Revolution* (Conakry, Republic of Guinea: National Printing Press, 1977); Julius

K. Nyerere, *Ujamaa: Essays on Socialism* (New York: Oxford University Press, 1968); Kenneth Kaunda, *A Humanist in Africa* (London: Longman, 1966). An extremely useful anthology on contemporary African political thought is *Readings in African Political Thought*, ed. Gideon-Cyrus M. Mutiso and S. W. Rohio (London: Heinemann, 1975). This collection contains substantial extracts from many more relevant sources than are listed above.

3. Tsenay Serequeberhan, "Philosophy in the Present Context of Africa," symposium paper at APA meeting, Central Division, Louisville, Kentucky, April 1992, or *The Hermeneutics of African Philosophy*, Introduction and chapter 1.

4. See Serequeberhan, *The Hermeneutics of African Philosophy*, Introduction and chapter 1.

5. Cf. title of Anthony Appiah's book *Necessary Questions* (Englewood Cliffs, NJ: Prentice-Hall, 1989).

6. New York: Paragon House, 1991.

7. New York: Cambridge University Press, 1987.

8. New York: Peter Lang, 1991.

9. Let us take a little time to scotch a common error. If something is not *specially* linked to African life or experience, that does not mean either that it is not linked with it at all or that it may not be profitably linked with it. Suppose that debates about the universal applicability of the Law of Excluded Middle in mathematics have not hitherto been an African concern. So what? Is the question any less germane to mathematics as used in Africa than mathematics as used elsewhere? Of course not. Moreover, no one is entitled to rule out the possibility of Africans eventually taking their place in the forefront of world contributions to modern mathematics and its philosophical elucidation. And if such researches have a cultural component, why not bring the African cultural bent to bear upon them?

10. For more details see Kwasi Wiredu, "On Defining African Philosophy" (written and first presented in 1981), reprinted in Tsenay Serequeberhan, ed., *African Philosophy: The Essential Readings* (New York: Paragon House, 1991). Today, anyone attempting the same kind of listing would have his or her hands somewhat heavy with the contributions of Anthony Kwame Appiah alone. Note, for example, his *Assertion and Conditionals* (London: Cambridge University Press, 1985), *For Truth in Semantics* (Oxford: Basil Blackwell, 1986), and *Necessary Questions* (1989). This is not to overlook his work dealing with Africa, such as his recent *In My Father's House: Africa in the Philosophy of Culture* (New York: Oxford University Press, 1992).

11. See chapter 3.

12. The full title of the work is *Sage Philosophy: Indigenous Thinkers and Modern Debate on African Philosophy*. It was published in 1991 in Nairobi, Kenya, by the Acts Press of the African Center for Technology Studies, and in Leiden in the same year by E. J. Brill.

13. The allusion is to Serequeberhan's comment (in the paper previously mentioned) on a comment by Ernest Wamba-Dia-Wamba in the latter's article "Philosophy in Africa: Challenges of the African Philosopher," reprinted in Serequeberhan's anthology *African Philosophy: The Essential Readings*.

14. These conditions constitute criteria of due reflection for anyone, whatever her culture, contemplating the appropriation of intellectual materials from another culture. But in a place like Africa they also amount to a prescription for what I have elsewhere called conceptual decolonization. See Kwasi Wiredu, "Philosophical Research and Teaching in Africa: Some Suggestions," in *Teaching and Research in Philosophy: Africa, Studies on Teaching and Research in Philosophy Throughout the World*, vol. 1 (Paris: UNESCO, 1984).

15. It would, of course, be a kind of genetic fallacy to suppose that simply because a given doctrine is encouraged by the characteristics of a foreign language it is false. And an African would be guilty of a fallacy hardly less egregious if she were to think that the philosophical preconceptions inspired by her own vernacular are sound simply on account of that provenance. Any such truth value assignments will have to be established on independent grounds. Moreover, in the present case, which involves cross-cultural comparisons, the grounds must be cross-culturally intelligible and warrantable. In the particular case of mind-body dualism I have attempted a critique of this sort in "The Concept of Mind with Particular Reference to the Language and Thought of the Akans," in Guttorm Floistad, ed., *Contemporary Philosophy, A New Survey: Volume V, African Philosophy* (Dordrecht, Holland: Martinus Nijhoff, 1987).

12. An Akan Perspective on Human Rights

1. The Akans have, historically, been the subject of some famous anthropological, linguistic, and philosophical studies by foreign scholars, such as R. S. Rattray, *Ashanti* (Oxford University Press, 1923), and *Religion and Art in Ashanti* (Oxford University Press, 1927); J. G. Christaller, *Dictionary of the Asante and Fante Language Called Tshi (Twi)*, 2nd ed. (Basel, 1933); and E. L. Mayerowitz, *The Sacred State of the Akan* (London: Faber and Faber, 1951); and native scholars such as Casely Hayford, *Gold Coast Native Institutions* (London: Sweet and Maxwell, 1903); J. B. Danquah, *The Akan Doctrine of God* (London, 1946); and K. A. Busia, *The Position of the Chief in the Modern Political System of Ashanti* (London: Frank Cass, 1951). Two important recent philosophical studies are W. E. Abraham, *The Mind of Africa* (University of Chicago Press, 1962); and Kwame Gyekye, *An Essay on African Philosophical Thought: The Akan Conceptual Scheme* (Cambridge University Press, 1987).

2. W. E. Abraham has a memorable description of the Ashanti army in battle deployment in *Mind of Africa,* pp. 83–84. K. A. Busia gives an illustrated description in *Position of the Chief,* p. 14.

3. Abraham, *Mind of Africa,* p. 77.

4. See, for example, Busia, *Position of the Chief,* pp. 66, 70–71.

5. Other Ashantis extended the same courtesy to Islam.

13. Philosophy and the Political Problem of Human Rights

1. See, for example, Audrey I. Richards, "The Political System of the Bemba Tribe—North-Eastern Rhodesia" and K. Oberg, "The Kingdom of Ankole in Uganda," both in M. Fortes and E. E. Evans-Pritchard, eds., *African Political Systems* (Oxford: Oxford University Press, 1940).

2. London: Frank Cass, 1968. See also, the same author's *Africa in Search of Democracy* (London: Routledge and Kegan Paul, 1967), chapter 2: "The Political Heritage," for a briefer account.

3. K. A. Busia, *Africa in Search of Democracy,* p. 28.

4. See, for example, Gideon-Cyrus M. Mutiso and S. W. Rohio, eds., *Readings in African Political Thought* (London: Heinemann, 1975), Part VII.

5. For example, among the Quakers decision-making was historically by consensus. Community action had to be based on consensus. Accordingly, discussions among the Friends at meetings would go on till that kind of meeting of minds was reached. Some

American Indian peoples, too, notably the Iroquois, are known to have required consensus as a basis of community decision and action.

6. See, for example, H. Hamalengwa, C. Flinterman, and E. V. O. Dankwa, eds., *International Law of Human Rights in Africa* (Boston: Martinus Nijhoff, 1988), pp. 5–19. See also pp. 163–66 for the "Universal Declaration of Human Rights."

14. Democracy and Consensus

1. K. A. Busia also comments on the same single-minded pursuit of consensus as it obtained among the traditional Akans of Ghana in his *Africa in Search of Democracy* (London: Routledge and Kegan Paul, 1967). The passage will bear extended quotation:

> When a council, each member of which was the representative of a lineage, met to discuss matters affecting the whole community, it had always to grapple with the problem of reconciling sectional and common interests. In order to do this, the members had to talk things over: they had to listen to all the different points of view. So strong was the value of solidarity that the chief aim of the councilors was to reach unanimity, and they talked till this was achieved. (p. 28)

2. See, for example, Max Gluckman, "The Kingdom of the Zulu of South Africa"; I. Schapera, "The Political Organization of the Ngwato of Bechuanaland Protectorate" (present-day Botswana); and Audrey I. Richards, "The Political System of the Bemba Tribe—North-Eastern Rhodesia," (in present-day Zambia), all in Fortes and Evans-Pritchard, eds., *African Political Systems*, (Oxford: Oxford University Press, 1940).

3. The Ashantis are a subgroup of the Akans. Other subgroups are the Akims, Akuapims, Denkyiras, Fantes, Kwahus, Brongs, Wassas, and Nzimas. The Akans, as a whole, constitute nearly half the population of Ghana, occupying parts of the middle and southern parts of the country. The Ivory Coast is also home to some Akan groups. The account given of the Ashanti system is true, in all essentials, of the Akans in general.

4. W. E. Abraham in *The Mind of Africa* (Chicago: University of Chicago Press, 1962), p. 77, explains,

> . . . because the king was surrounded by councilors whose offices were political, and was himself only a representation of the spiritual unity of the people, it was quite possible to remove him from office; the catalogue of the possible grounds of removal was already held in advance.

15. Postscript

1. In addition to the negative thoughts on relativism in chapter 3 I have given more detailed criticisms in Kwasi Wiredu, "Canons of Conceptualization," *The Monist*, vol. 76, no. 4 (Oct. 1993), and Kwasi Wiredu, "Knowledge, Truth and Fallibility," in I. Kucuradi and R. S. Cohen, eds., *The Concept of Knowledge* (Boston: Kluwer Academic, 1995).

2. Published in Albert G. Mosley, *African Philosophy: Selected Readings* (Englewood Cliffs, NJ: Prentice Hall, 1995).

3. In Albert G. Mosley, ed., *African Philosophy: Selected Readings*. See chapter 6.

4. Mosley, p. 416.

5. Mosley, p. 408.

6. Mosley, p. 414.

7. This book was still in the press when the unbearable news of Oruka's death on December 9, 1995 came. He was reported to have been fatally hit by a car in Nairobi while trying to cross a street to go and visit a friend at a nearby hospital. The damage to African philosophy is irreparable.

8. See also Kwasi Wiredu, "Moral Foundations of an African Culture," in Wiredu and Gyekye, eds., *Person and Community: Ghanaian Philosophical Studies* (Washington D.C.: Council for Research in Values and Philosophy, 1992), p. 197.

9. Mosley, p. 413.

10. See also Kwame Gyekye, *An Essay on African Philosophical Thought* (New York: Cambridge University Press, 1987), pp. 159–61.

11. Ibid., p. 409.

12. See, for example, Kofi Antubam, *Ghana's Heritage of Culture* (Leipzig: Koehler and Amelang, 1963), a text cited also by English and Hamme.

13. See, for example, J. B. Danquah, *The Akan Doctrine of God: A Fragment of Gold Coast Ethics and Religion* (London: Frank Cass, 1944), second edition with introduction by Kwesi Dickson, 1968; W. E. Abraham, *The Mind of Africa* (Chicago: University of Chicago Press, 1962), chapter 2; Kwame Gyekye, *An Essay on African Philosophical Thought*; N. K. Dzobo, "Knowledge and Truth: Ewe and Akan Conceptions," and "African Symbols as Sources of Knowledge and Truth," in Wiredu and Gyekye, *Person and Community*.

14. On taboos in Akan life see Peter Sarpong, *Ghana in Retrospect: Some Aspects of Ghanaian Culture* (Tema, Ghana: Ghana Publishing, 1974), ch. 7, and Gyekye, *An Essay on African Philosophical Thought*, pp. 134–35.

15. Mosley, p. 414.

16. Kwasi Wiredu, "Morality and Religion in Akan Thought," in H. Odera Oruka and D. A. Masolo, eds., *Philosophy and Cultures* (Nairobi, Kenya: Bookwise, 1983). Reprinted in Norm R. Allen, Jr., *African-American Humanism: An Anthology* (New York: Prometheus Books, 1991).

17. On this see further Kwasi Wiredu, "Morality and Religion in Akan Thought," in Allen, 1991, p. 221.

18. Mosley, p. 415.

19. Mosley, p. 415.

20. That the custom of pouring libation to our ancestors is a traditionally important custom does not necessarily imply that it is an appropriate custom in contemporary life. My own lack of enthusiasm for this custom can be observed in *Philosophy and an African Culture* (London: Cambridge University Press, 1980), ch. 3: "How Not to Compare African Traditional Thought with Western Thought," esp. pp. 41–42. It is possible that the pouring of libation will evolve into a symbolic remembrance or celebration of our ancestors. In that case, my reservations would evaporate. That I am not enthused about our contemporary funeral habits is also in evidence on pp. 44–45 of the same work. In some ways, however, contemporary funeral practices are a perversion of historical custom.

21. Mosley, p. 415.

22. Originally published in Abdullahi Ahmed An-Na'im and Francis M. Deng, eds., *Human Rights in Africa: Cross-Cultural Perspectives* (Washington D.C.: Brookings Institute, 1990).

23. See also Kwasi Wiredu, *Philosophy and an African Culture*, pp. 2–5.

24. In *Quest: An International African Journal of Philosophy*, vol. IV, no. 2 (December 1990).

25. Ibid., p. 28.

26. Ibid., p. 29.

27. Ibid., p. 27.

28. Ibid., pp. 31–35.

29. Published in *Quest: An African Journal of Philosophy*, vol. 1, no. 1 (June 1987).

30. Ibid., p. 5.

31. See Kwasi Wiredu, *Philosophy and an African Culture* (Cambridge: Cambridge University Press, 1980), ch. 10, section III: "The Theory of Truth."

32. Ibid., pp. 201–203 and 211.

33. Bello (1987), p. 7.

34. Ibid., p. 8.

35. Ibid., p. 8.

36. Strawson says, "Facts are what statements (when true) state." P. F. Strawson, "Truth," *Proceedings of the Aristotelian Society*, supplementary vol. XXIV (1950). Reprinted in Joseph Margolis, ed., *An Introduction to Philosophical Inquiry* (New York: Alfred A. Knopf, 2nd edition, 1978), p. 293. Herbst also has defined fact in terms of truth by saying that a fact is what is stated by a true statement. See Peter Herbst in Anthony Flew, ed., *Essays in Conceptual Analysis* (London: Macmillan, 1956).

37. Such as Strawson's, see ibid.

38. See A. G. A. Bello's unpublished Ph.D. thesis: "Truth and Fact: An Objectivist Reply to Wiredu's Anti-Objectivism," Department of Philosophy, University of Ibadan, Nigeria, 1985.

39. Bello (1987), p. 9.

40. Ibid., pp. 9–10.

41. See Bedu-Addo, "The Concept of Truth in Akan" in P. O. Bodunrin, ed., *Philosophy in Africa: Trends and Perspectives* (Ile-Ife, Nigeria: University of Ife Press, 1985).

42. Ibid., p.76.

43. See also Kwasi Wiredu, "The Correspondence Theory of Judgment," *African Philosophical Inquiry*, vol. 1, no. 1 (1987). Partially reprinted in Safro Kwame, *Readings in African Philosophy: An Akan Collection* (Lanham: University Press of America, 1995), pp. 189–90.

44. V. Y. Mudimbe, ed., *The Surreptitious Speech* (Chicago: University of Chicago Press, 1992).

45. Oyekan Owomoyela: Review of V. Y. Mudimbe, ed., *The Surreptitious Speech*, in *African Studies Review*, 1992. For a less friendly and more uncomprehending discussion of my views by the same author, see "Africa and the Imperative of Philosophy: A Skeptical Consideration," *African Studies Review*, vol. 30, no. 1 (1987). Reprinted in Tsenay Serequeberhan, ed., *African Philosophy: The Essential Readings* (New York: Paragon House, 1991) and Albert Mosley, *African Philosophy: Selected Readings* (Englewood Cliffs, NJ: Prentice-Hall, 1995). The analysis of Owomoyela's misunderstandings, however, does not belong here.

Index

Abraham, W. E., 134, 223*n*55, 226*n*2(1); on Akan philosophy, 221*n*36, 221*n*39; on chiefs, 185, 212*n*4; on *sunsum,* 128
Abstraction, 22, 23, 25
Accident, category of, 96–97
Acholi people, 81
Action, 22–23
Adwene (mind), 16–17, 98, 126, 129
African languages: ontological concepts in, 97–98; use of in African philosophy, 3–4, 93, 118, 207–8
—translating modern concepts into: Christian theology concepts, 81–82, 85, 88–93, 214*n*8, 214*n*9, 214*n*11, 215*n*13; conceptual misunderstandings from, 82–83; logical concepts, 84–85; metaphysical concepts, 86–93, 214*n*7; scientific terms, 85–86
African philosophy: and foreign language , 4, 152–53, 226*n*15; and indigenous language, 3–4, 93, 118, 207–8; post-colonial role of, 146–53; professionalism in, 134, 145, 147–48, 151, 224*n*1; scope of, 148–49; statesmen-philosophers, 133–34, 145–46, 148, 150–51; and the utilization of traditional thought, 113–14, 147–51, 218*n*3, 218*n*4; Western conceptual domination of, 151–53, 225*n*14
—African traditional philosophy: communal aspects of, 115; indigenous thinkers in, 115–17, 218*n*3; as oral tradition, 113–14, 217*n*2, 218*n*3, 219*n*6; sources of, 114–19
—decolonization, 4–5; of language, 136–42; of politics, 143–44; of religion, 142–43
Akans, 157, 217*n*1, 227*n*3(1); conditional religious devotion by, 48–49; consensus among, 173–76, 227*n*1(1); customs of, 62–63, 66–74, 197; drum language of, 119–20; foreign studies of, 226*n*1(1); funeral traditions of, 169–70, 195, 199, 228*n*20; government structures of, 162,

173, 221*n*39; humanist ethics of, 29–30, 65, 71, 74–75, 129, 191–92, 195, 202; justice system of, 164–65; land rights of, 159, 165–67; marriage concepts of, 72–74; military organization of, 161–62; political participation by, 163–64; political representation of, 7–8, 173–76; polygamy among, 69–71; reaction of to human error, 94–96, 100, 215*n*17; religious freedom among, 167–69; respect for elders among, 67–68, 170; spiritual concepts of, 52–55, 199, 212*n*12; taboos of, 75–76, 197, 228*n*14; urbanization of, 71–72
—language: abstract concepts in, 24, 123; certainty concepts in, 139–40; equivalence concepts in, 109; kinship terms in, 93–94; linguistic comparisons to English, 24–25; mind concept in, 16–17, 98–99, 125–26, 216*n*28; non-existence concept in, 15–16; religious terms in, 45–46; subject-predicate distinction in, 97–98; substance and quality terms in, 97–98, 100; transcendental metaphysics translated into, 88–89, 214*n*8, 214*n*9; truth concepts in, 5, 105–8, 110–12, 139–40, 203–9; vocabulary development in, 86, 87–89
—traditional philosophy: and contemporary written philosophy, 133–35, 222*n*45, 222*n*54; cosmology of, 119–25, 150, 219*n*19 (*see also* Supreme Being); and destiny, 127, 131–33, 221*n*35; empirical orientation of, 99, 125, 215*n*25; extrahuman forces in, 47–49, 53–54, 56, 76–77, 99, 167; and free will, 6, 130–33, 221*n*42; locative concept of existence in, 49–50, 55, 121–22, 141–42, 212*n*6, 212*n*7, 220*n*23, 220*n*24, 224*n*14; misconceptions about, 118–19, 124; nature-supernature distinction in, 35–36, 50–52, 99–100, 123–25, 193–95, 212*n*9; personhood concept in,

KWASI WIREDU is Professor of Philosophy at the University of South Florida, Tampa. His publications include *Philosophy and an African Culture* and (with Kwame Gyekye) *Person and Community: Ghanaian Philosophical Studies.*